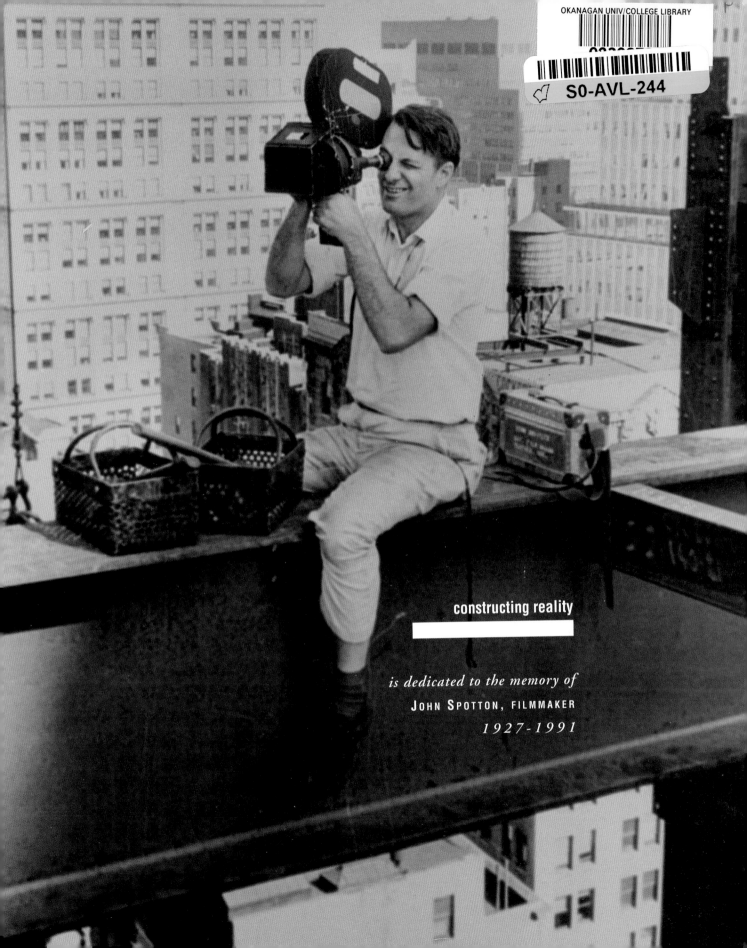

constructing reality

is dedicated to the memory of
JOHN SPOTTON, FILMMAKER
1927-1991

constructing reality

EXPLORING MEDIA ISSUES IN DOCUMENTARY

BY ARLENE MOSCOVITCH

THE NATIONAL FILM BOARD OF CANADA

The *Constructing Reality Resource Book* is part of the *Constructing Reality* package which includes nine hours of video programming on six videocassettes. For extra copies of the book, write to:

Education Office, Marketing, D-5
National Film of Board of Canada
P.O. Box 6100, Station A
Montreal, Quebec
H3C 3H5

Canadian Cataloguing in Publication Data
Moscovitch, Arlene
    Constructing reality: exploring media issues in
    documentary
ISBN 0-7722-0500-0

1. Documentary films — Production and direction
I. National Film Board of Canada. II. Title
PN1995.9.D6M68 1993   070.1'8   C93-094057-1

Every reasonable attempt has been made to attribute copyright material used in this publication. Information regarding inadvertent errors or omissions of copyright information is welcomed by the publisher, and efforts will be made to correct same in future editions.

Printed in Canada

Constructing Reality: Exploring Media Issues in Documentary was produced by the National Film Board, Ontario Centre, with the financial support of the Canadian Studies Directorate, Department of the Secretary of State of Canada.

PROJECT DIRECTORS *David Adkin & Arlene Moscovitch*
DIRECTOR, VIDEO PRODUCTION *David Adkin*
AUTHOR, RESOURCE BOOK *Arlene Moscovitch*
PRODUCERS *John Spotton, Michael Allder*
EXECUTIVE PRODUCERS *John Taylor, Dennis Murphy*
PROJECT CO-ORDINATOR *JoAnn Harrison*
ORIGINATOR, PROJECT CONCEPT *Anne Taylor*
EDITOR *Charis Wahl/Ex Libris*
COPY EDITOR *Merrill Fearon*
DESIGN *Alex Hass, Hodgson & Hass*
COVER PHOTOGRAPHY *Ali Kazimi*

Constructing Reality: Exploring Media Issues in Documentary was developed with the participation of the following people: Ferne Cristall, media educator, Peterborough Collegiate Vocational School; Richard Fung, independent video producer and writer; Tove Fynbo, English teacher, Northview Heights Secondary School; Bob Pritchard, media and art educator, Inglenook Community High School; Trish Skrzypczyk, English teacher, Emery Collegiate Institute; Peter Steven, film critic and writer; and George Ventura, media educator, West Toronto Collegiate. For offering us their classrooms and their comments, we would also like to thank teachers Desiree Francis of Clarkson Secondary School, David Reid of Jarvis Collegiate, and Nick Rogers, formerly of Streetsville Secondary School. Thanks are also due to staff and students at West Toronto Collegiate for allowing us to interview them and photograph students at work.

Contents: *Resource Book and Video*

about this resource

Constructing Reality: Exploring Media Issues in Documentary is a collection of stimulating, stirring documentaries that suggests, we hope, something of the richness, variety and power of which this genre is capable. The package is not a course on documentary nor a selection of all-time "greats"; rather, it provides an opportunity to consider some critical concepts that an encounter with a passionate, playful or provocative exploration of "real life" can engender. Such concepts include: the relationship between fact and fiction; objectivity; truth; point of view; voice; and the construction of reality. The urge to document social injustice as a way of working towards social change, and the re-telling of history, are also part of the tapestry.

This wide-ranging video resource including extensive print material has been produced, primarily, for those interested in media education. However many of the selected films and videos are equally applicable in subject areas as diverse as history, social studies, politics, English, art, Native studies, women's studies, and critical literacy at the high school, college, and university level.

The package was initially conceived with senior high-school students and educators in mind; however, whenever we do educators' conference workshops on topics such as "fact, truth and objectivity", or "voice and authority in the media", there are almost always members of the general public at our sessions. This resource is for these people, too.

Like its predecessor, *Media & Society, Constructing Reality* was conceived as an image bank or anthology, rather than a lock-step course of study. This approach allows for maximum flexibility in the use and combination of selections and themes, and stimulates teachers' confidence in their own ability to tailor a media curriculum to meet the particular needs, abilities and interests of their students.

One of the challenges of this project was to choose material that would stir and intrigue young people, thereby undermining any preconceptions about the documentary genre (developed, no doubt, after too many instructional films on the domestic habits of the bee or the secret life of prairie wheat fields.) We also wanted students to develop means of looking at documentary critically, so they could examine crucial concepts such as "truth", point of view and voice or authority, which have such impact on the ways in which they see their own lives. Finally, we felt that, whenever possible, students should have some hands-on experience of what it's like to recreate actuality, whether with still cameras or camcorders.

Constructing Reality was developed with the input of two groups. Our media consultants told us what was happening in the independent-documentary sector in Canada. They also brainstormed with us the crucial points and productions to consider in this compilation. Our education consultants, enthusiastic and knowledgable about the viewing and teaching of media, screened all the videos and films, tested them with their students, and advised us on concept development and classroom applicability. These educators were drawn from schools with very different student bodies — some homogeneous, others highly diverse in their racial, socio-economic, and ethnic mix.

It was important to us that *Constructing Reality* be rooted in what students and teachers like and respond to, as opposed to what we thought they should like and respond to. To discover their reactions to the films we had chosen, we carried out extensive testing. As a result of this process, we feel that we have compiled a selection of films and videos that "works" for senior high-school students.

This is not to say that every film will work for every group. We did discard titles that bored most viewers, but did not include productions solely on the grounds of mass popularity. Certain films are part of the collection because some students will appreciate them greatly, although they may leave other students baffled or indifferent. It is precisely this divergence in reactions and tastes that we tried to consider when structuring this resource.

about the video selections

The video compilation consists of 34 film and video selections. It includes complete productions; excerpts; interviews with two filmmakers; and two original productions — *What is a Documentary?* and *Techno-babies: The Making of a Television Documentary* — shot specifically for this package.

Most of the documentaries chosen were produced by the National Film Board or independent Canadian filmmakers. One was produced by the Canadian Broadcasting Corporation, another by the British Broadcasting Corporation. We screened hundreds of films and videos and made our final choices based on the following criteria: 1) that the film/video make effective use of the medium — i.e., that it have an artistic integrity and vitality that make it successful on its own terms;

2) that the film/video stimulate, interest, and
challenge audiences, especially older teenagers;

3) that the film/video raise critical questions and
issues about documentary form or content;

4) that the film/video be Canadian, whenever
possible.

In addition, we wanted to include in our collection
works by women and men, by filmmakers from a
variety of racial and cultural backgrounds, and by
filmmakers from various regions of the country.

The material in this collection has been grouped into
six sections: WAYS OF STORYTELLING; SHAPING
REALITY; THE POLITICS OF TRUTH; THE CANDID
EYE?; VOICES OF EXPERIENCE, VOICES FOR CHANGE;
and THE POETRY OF MOTION. An introductory
piece, WHAT IS A DOCUMENTARY?, precedes WAYS OF
STORYTELLING. Six Study Extracts are included as
part of SHAPING REALITY. As the "INDEX OF FILMS
AND TOPICS," in this book suggests, one can find
many other ways of grouping these same films.

Video location codes for each particular selection
appear at the lower right of the screen. (See pp. vi
and vii for a complete listing of these codes.) In
addition, in two of the Study Extracts, individual
shots have been numbered to give viewers a sense of
how the sequences are constructed. These numbers
appear at the lower left of the screen.

about the resource book

For each selection, the Resource Book provides a
description of the film, ideas for discussion,
suggested activities, and an annotated listing of
further resources. In addition, the book includes
relevant articles, background information on
various aspects of filmmaking, and interviews with
directors, editors, cinematographers, sound
recordists and, in one case, the subject of the film.

The interviews have been included for a number of
reasons: to provide background material; to
emphasize that documentary filmmaking is a *process*
in which both serendipity and planning play a part;
and to suggest that a documentary is the product of
countless decisions made by all-too-fallible people
striving to do their best, rather than being an
unmediated, transparent window onto reality. As
well, given our desire to have people critically
examine the notion of a single authoritative and
(usually) authoritarian voice, we wanted to offer an
array of voices. (All the interviews, with the
exception of Gil Cardinal's and Tom Daly's, were
conducted and edited by the author.)

We strongly suggest that students read the interviews only after they have thoroughly discussed their own reactions to and ideas about a film.

A section at the end of the book— "Film and Video Terms: An Introduction"— explains some basic terms in order to provide a common vocabulary with which to discuss and analyze the media and the processes involved in media construction.

An "Index of Themes" presents alternatives for organizing and combining the material in the collection; it is intended to spur users to find their own connections and contradictions. Also included at the end of the book, for handy reference, is an "Index of Films and Topics."

working with film and video

When dealing with film and video in a classroom setting, it may be helpful to keep the following points in mind:

- If, as McLuhan suggests, the media are our environments — the waters in which we swim — then all of us are co-learners when it comes to examining that which surrounds and affects us. There are few experts teaching media; an exploratory, non-hierarchical approach can lead to productive and exhilarating learning experiences for teachers and students alike.

- Dealing with the issues raised by some of these films will likely lead into areas of controversy. Don't be afraid to enter.

- To initiate discussion after a screening, it is often effective to begin with the viewers' personal responses. If these are slow in coming, you might want to consider questions such as: Are there any images, sounds, or incidents in the film/video that stand out in your mind? Is there anyone with whom you strongly identify? Any place? Is there anyone with whom you particularly agree or disagree?

- Meaning resides not in the "text" of the film/video image but in the complex interactions between films/videos and the people who view them. What viewers — teachers as well as students — bring to the film or video depends not only on their individual experience but also on the values, ideas and beliefs current in their society. So there is no one single, "correct" interpretation of a "text" to be discovered, but rather individual interpretations to be put forth as a starting point for creative and critical work.

John Grierson

Neighbours

the National Film Board: a Canadian alternative

The National Film Board of Canada is the oldest active government film-production agency in the world. Now past its fiftieth anniversary, it remains committed to the principles established under its first Film Commissioner, John Grierson: to make films that reflect the Canadian identity, to reinforce a sense of social purpose, and to foster artistic and technical innovations in filmmaking. In doing so, it has completed more than 8000 productions, has won almost 3000 international awards, and has, at present, 7600 titles in active distribution through film and video.

The NFB is renowned for its documentaries, a form defined by Grierson as "the creative treatment of actuality", and for its pioneering work in animation, which began with Norman McLaren in the early 1940s. McLaren's 1952 Oscar-winning film *Neighbours* has been described as the most eloquent argument for peace ever made. It has been

CRY OF THE WILD

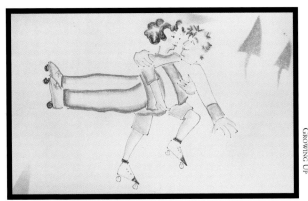

GROWING UP

The French Production unit, created in the late 1950s, played a leading role in the flowering of québécois cinema during the next three decades in both documentary and feature film production. During the 1960s, the NFB started making feature films, began its innovative program of social awareness Challenge for Change/Société Nouvelle, and produced Labyrinth, a revolutionary new style of film projection that would lead to the creation of Imax. The 1970s saw the creation of many films focussed on Quebec, as well as the establishment of Studio D, the first publicly funded women's production unit in the world.

borrowed more than 100,000 times from NFB libraries; more than 2500 prints have been sold world-wide.

Well before the advent of television, a unique distribution system — which included projectionists travelling on rural circuits, film councils, regional film libraries, and film clubs — made it possible for NFB productions to be screened in all parts of Canada. In addition, many shorts were shown regularly in cinemas across the country.

Today, NFB productions are created in six regional centres that make extensive use of freelance filmmaking talent. Classroom and home videos have become, along with television and 16mm film rental, important distribution channels. In addition to the documentaries and animated films for which

Speak It! From the Heart of Black Nova Scotia

Hunters and Bombers

the Board is world-famous, innovative film styles and approaches have been introduced in low-budget alternative dramas, in docudramas that meld elements of both drama and documentary, in computer animation, and in films by and for women which have nourished the Canadian women's movement for two decades.

From an international perspective, the NFB is unique. A government institution accountable to Treasury Board, it nonetheless has considerable freedom to challenge the status quo. The NFB is also in the fortunate position of being able to foster creativity, Canadian content, and social values over making a profit.

Some see the NFB as one alternative to the mass-media mills that are rapidly becoming a major industry in the global village. It is in the spirit of providing such an alternative that this selection of documentary material has been made.

what is a documentary?

Video location 00 in *What is a Documentary?*

20 minutes

1993

Director: *David Adkin*

Producer: *Michael Allder, NFB*

[A documentary is] the creative treatment of actuality.
JOHN GRIERSON, PRODUCER AND FILM CRITIC

Documentary is telling a story with elements from life.
DAVID SOBELMAN, FILMMAKER

A documentary is a film in which the actors don't get paid.
PATRICK MACFADDEN, JOURNALIST AND FILM CRITIC

I don't have the last word on what documentary means. But for me, documentary is an opportunity to observe and to document important moments that have great meaning in terms of how we experience our lives together.
LAURA SKY, FILMMAKER

Documentary program means an information program that is not designed to be purely entertainment and which may include drama or variety techniques in achieving its information goal.
INDEPENDENT PRODUCTION AGREEMENT, ALLIANCE OF CANADIAN RADIO AND TELEVISION ARTISTS (ACTRA)

The best documentary films are provocative challenges to the status quo, films that have an edge, a point of view, films which incite controversy and public debate, contributing to a healthy democracy . . .
CANADIAN INDEPENDENT FILM CAUCUS

What Is a Documentary? provides viewers with a quick preview of the films and issues contained in this nine-hour collection. It begins by exploring definitions and perceptions of the genre by students, teachers, and filmmakers. The piece then considers some of the differences between drama and documentary, and the ways in which each form often incorporates elements of the other. Using segments of interviews and clips from the films in this package, the introduction also examines the notions of "truth" and "objectivity", so closely linked in people's minds with the documentary genre.

There is no one single, all-encompassing definition of the term **documentary,** as the comments to the left suggest. However John Grierson's commonly-cited phrase "the creative treatment of actuality" is perhaps the most useful, for at least two reasons. First, it emphasizes the documentary form's concentration on the actual, its basis in real-life events, issues and people. As well, it suggests that far from being transparent windows onto reality, documentaries — like all other forms of filmmaking — are mediated *constructions*, the result of countless decisions made by individuals struggling to produce coherent, thoughtful, and passionate (or so one hopes) *interpretations* of reality.

Documentaries use a variety of picture and sound elements, most of which are listed at the right. The choice and use of these elements are shaped by the *point of view*, that is, the vantage point from which the story is told. The point of view can be omniscient (*Memorandum, The Spaghetti Story*); that of a character in the film (*New Shoes, Richard Cardinal: Cry from a Diary of a Métis Child*); that of several characters (*Of Lives Uprooted, Children of War*); or personal to the filmmaker (*The Journey, Foster Child*). For discussion of the ways in which ideology affects point of view, see THE POLITICS OF TRUTH, p. 113.

These elements can be combined in any number of documentary forms — in a film centred on a specific event (*Flamenco at 5:15*); in a film that documents a process (*The Spaghetti Story, Techno–babies: The Making of a Television Documentary*); in a film about a journey (*City of Gold*); or about historical circumstances (*The Ballad of Crowfoot*), to name but a few.

Documentary is but one genre of non-fiction film, a category which also includes industrial, nature, travel, news, and educational productions.

picture elements* *may include:*

- *original live-action footage*
- *stock footage: archival material or footage from other films*
- *interviews*
- *re-enactments*
- *still photos*
- *documents, titles, headlines, cartoons and other graphics*
- *black screen*

sound elements* *may include:*

- *synchronous sound, i.e., sound recorded simultaneously with corresponding visuals*
- *wild sound, i.e., sound recorded on its own, without any corresponding visuals*
- *voice-over: voices or commentary used with separately filmed   visuals*
- *narration: scripted voice-over, spoken by a narrator, filmmaker or participant in the film*
- *sound effects*
- *music*
- *silence*

* *Adapted from Michael Rabiger's book* Directing the Documentary, *Second Edition (Boston: Focal Press, 1992).*

FURTHER RESOURCES

For those wishing to study documentary filmmaking in more detail, see Michael Rabiger's *Directing the Documentary*, Second Edition (Boston: Focal Press, 1992); Alan Rosenthal's *The Documentary Conscience: A Casebook in Film-Making* (Berkeley: University of California Press, 1980) and *Writing, Directing and Producing Documentary Films* (Carbondale: South Illinois University Press, 1990); and Eric Barnouw's *Documentary: A History of Non-Fiction Film* (Oxford: Oxford University Press, 1992).

In *Brink of Reality: New Canadian Documentary Film and Video* (Toronto: Between the Lines, 1993), Peter Steven provides an overview of an innovative kind of Canadian documentary filmmaking that he believes has emerged since 1980.

Also of interest may be Annette Kuhn's *Women's Pictures: Feminism and Cinema* (London: Routledge & Regan Paul, 1982); and Trin T. Minh-Ha's *When the Moon Waxes Red: Representation, Gender, and Cultural Politics* (New York: Routledge, 1991).

ways of storytelling

A work of art is a corner of nature seen through a temperament.
EMILE ZOLA

If documentary filmmaking is about telling stories with elements from real life, then a number of questions arise. How does a director take an idea, issue, or actual event and turn it into a film that is interesting to watch? How does the choice of narrator/storyteller affect the tone of the story being told? How are the rules of storytelling in documentary similar to — and different from — the rules of storytelling in drama?

The four films featured in this section offer a starting point for discussion of narrative in non-fiction film, and of the ways in which images and sound are used to heighten impact. Although very different from each other, all these films deal in some way with history and memory.

City of Gold was the first documentary to tell a story by using still photographs as its main visual source. Pierre Berton's narration, which begins as a personal reminiscence about growing up in Dawson City, leads into the heady days of the Klondike Gold Rush.

New Shoes consists of intriguing video clips and an interview with a woman whose ex-boyfriend tried to kill her. It functions on several levels — as an account of personal history, as an examination of how memory recreates an incident, and as a statement of how media productions can shape and distort experiences. In its form and content, *New Shoes* raises questions about the interview as a means of letting subjects tell their own stories, and about the effect of taking something familiar and giving it a twist.

Our Marilyn recreates the first crossing of Lake Ontario by marathon swimmer Marilyn Bell in such a way that it becomes an impressionistic meditation on heroism, Canadian identity, and cultural mythologies of the female body. The experimental use of sound and image lend a compelling, dreamlike quality to factual events.

All three films tell their stories in the first person. *New Shoes* and *Our Marilyn* stress the primacy of subjective experience. *Memorandum* uses a different device. Like *City of Gold* and *Our Marilyn*, it is about a journey, in this case that of a Holocaust survivor back to the concentration camp from which he was liberated almost 20 years earlier. This haunting inquiry into the "banality of evil" begins with Bernard Laufer's personal experience, but uses a compelling third-person narration, spoken by an "outsider", to widen the scope of the investigation.

city of gold

VIDEO LOCATION **20** IN *WAYS OF STORYTELLING*

22 MINUTES

BLACK & WHITE

1957

DIRECTORS: *WOLF KOENIG, COLIN LOW*

PRODUCER: *TOM DALY, NFB*

DISTRIBUTOR: *NFB*

SUGGESTIONS *for* USE

- *To maximize the film's impact, try "Before Viewing" Activity 1, involving work with still pictures, p. 13.*

- *Do the framing exercises, Activity 5, p. 21, after viewing the film and reading the interview with Tom Daly.*

In 1897 and 1898, more than 100,000 people stampeded the Klondike area of the Yukon, drawn by newspaper reports of "tons of gold" just waiting to be mined. The town of Dawson, at the mouth of the Klondike River, swelled into a city of 30,000 people lured by the promise of riches. Their failures, successes, hardships and triumphs were documented by the few intrepid photographers who backpacked camera equipment and 8"x10" glass plates up the notorious Chilkoot Pass. Their photos are the raw material from which the documentary *City of Gold* was fashioned.

When *City of Gold* appeared in 1957, it was unique, the first film to be based almost entirely on still pictures. Even more exciting than its considerable technical achievements, however, was the film's compelling narrative structure. Its weaving of pictures, words and music to tell the story of the Klondike Gold Rush still excites admiration. *City of Gold* won 21 awards, including first prize in the Short Documentary Features category at Cannes and an Oscar nomination.

City of Gold was produced before the development of lightweight sync-sound camera equipment which made it easy to record sound on location. Consequently, this documentary was constructed like a silent film: first, the visual elements of the film were edited to tell a story; then Pierre Berton's narration and Eldon Rathburn's music were added. (For information about the changes in equipment and the development of cinéma vérité filmmaking, see pp. 145-152.)

Before screening *City of Gold* in schools, we were uncertain how students would react to this classic: after all, the film was in black-and-white and more than 30 years old. We found, however, that they were riveted by the story, the pacing, and the music. Several described how moved they were by the symbolic nature of the quest these men had undertaken; many, particularly recent immigrants, were fascinated by this segment of Canadian history about which, as they told us, they knew virtually nothing. Finally, several young women wondered why the film focussed almost entirely on the experiences of men, thereby raising the issues of voice and point of view that have been so critical to the shaping of this collection.

an interview with Tom Daly,
editor and producer

The following excerpts are taken from an interview, conducted by Patricia Thorvaldson, that originally appeared in Pot Pourri, *a former NFB publication (Summer, 1977).*

City of Gold *was the first documentary to explore the filmic potential of still pictures in a sustained way. By doing so, it opened up photo archives of the nineteenth century to cinematic use, and showed documentary filmmakers that it was possible to fashion historical chronicles about periods that pre-dated moving pictures.*

In this interview, Tom Daly speaks about some of the experiments in camera movement undertaken by the City of Gold *team. He describes the effects these experiments were intended to achieve in terms of storytelling, stressing the primacy of the visuals: the film was structured so that narration and music follow the pictures, rather than the reverse.*

For *City of Gold*, Colin Low and Wolf Koenig, the directors, had collected hundreds of photographs. So the question was, how to make a story out of all those photos? We didn't want an illustrated lecture, we wanted to make the pictures tell the stories themselves, and have the sound added as a harmonizing element, an extra strand of the story. (So many films using stills are plodding and ineffective because the stills are really no more than an exaggerated form of inset illustrations for the text of an article or verbal story. If there was no text in most of these cases there would be no film, because you wouldn't know why the stills followed one another.)

In the case of *City of Gold*, Eldon Rathburn's music and Pierre Berton's commentary were added after the picture was completely cut. The film can be run without the sound track and you can follow it reasonably well. . . .

The main block of the film is made of still pictures only. The film begins and ends with some live action, but the block of stills in the middle was brought in without people much noticing whether they were stills or not. It was planned to be that way.

Everything was carefully calculated. First, we meticulously framed the best parts of each photograph. We also plotted movement from frame to frame within the shots in such a way that the movements worked as transitions, developments, changes of subject or location. And we never showed the edges of the photograph, so the illusion that the world went on in all directions beyond the camera frame was maintained at all times.

All the uses of panning or zooming were used, separately or together. Frequently, these mechanical movements, made on machines, feel mechanical and not like the movements made by real flesh-and-blood people. But one of our team, Roman Kroitor, invented a gadget that enabled animation-camera movement to be plotted live. This gadget was used a number of times throughout the film — for instance, near the beginning, where the camera pans over the snowy mountain tops and down their sides in a curved movement to pick up the line of incoming prospectors at the bottom and follow it up to the near foreground. And again, near the end of the film, when the combined July 1/July 4 celebration is being held in Dawson City, attended by 15,000-30,000 people, the camera explores the

crowd for interesting faces — just as you might explore it yourself. This visual passage, revealing sadness in the midst of celebration and loneliness in the thick of the multitude, is still, to me, one of the most moving moments in the film. It is so partly because the inventiveness of Roman Kroitor's gadget allows you to perceive it not only with your eyes and your mind, but with all your body as well.

We were also very careful about framing and composition, especially at the beginnings and endings of shots, to make certain that the viewer would know what the subject of the shot was. By subject, I mean the centre of attention of the framed composition.

Since most of the pictures for *City of Gold* had people looking in the direction of the camera, we had to find ways of turning that problem into an advantage, of using that fact dramatically. For instance, in one section of the film you have people looking at the camera in the gold fields, so we used it storywise, as if they were looking at you, the newcomers, arriving in the goldfields already staked by them. And, of course, you're looking at them too, to see what they're like. . . .

You can have a motion picture which is boring and flat, which has nothing to occupy your mind, something which you might call "static", or you can have *City of Gold*, where the images are static but where many people don't even realize when the motion picture shots changed to stills or when the still images changed back to motion. At the beginning of the film, after we had shown the live present-day activity, we gradually shifted the attention to the houses behind them, which were full of broken windows and empty doorways and boarded-up areas. Then we moved away to old locomotives in the forest, and decaying ferries aground, and then to a ship's rope that was thrown down carelessly and left rotting on the gangway. Without seeing him, you feel the presence of the person who once threw it there. Then we take you to the crosses in the cemetery, with the grass grown up around the graves. Again, you feel the individuals of those days in their numbers — though, of course, you do not expect them to move ever again. You know they are dead. So even the unconscious expectation of their moving is already ruled out by the order of the images up to this point in the picture. The next time you see these people, they are appropriately still, forming a line wending its way into the Yukon.

You can see that the effect was achieved not only by picture. It was also done by calculating the kind of progression of thought and feeling that would be generated in the audience from the order and progression of the images, gradually draining away the expectation of movement until there was no need for it any more, other than for camera movement over the stills. At the end of the film, we came back from past to present through a similar process in reverse, like coming out of a dream....

I think the team working on *City of Gold* actually did more searching work on the philosophy of it, the techniques and methods of it, the inventiveness of it, and the variations of its handling, than has probably ever been devoted to any other stills film before or since.

I don't know of another film using still photographs that is so thorough, so complete, so unified. A lot of the elements in it have perhaps, individually, been done as well or better since, but part of why I love that film and can still look at it with pleasure is because it seems an organic whole. All the parts hold together as if there were just the right amount of whatever it required. And that's pretty rare.

IDEAS *for* DISCUSSION

1

Share responses to the film. What did you like best? What do you remember most clearly? What do you think the filmmakers did, using a series of still pictures, to engage you in an event from the past, to make you feel strongly about the people and the place involved?

2

"After coming all this way, many of them never even bothered to look for gold at all. It was as if somehow they had already found what they were seeking." Discuss.

3

From whose point of view is this story being told? Does the fact that the narration is written and delivered by Pierre Berton, a person we know and presumably trust, make us believe in the mute people we see? Who else might have told the story?

ACTIVITIES

Before Viewing

1

An instant photographed can only acquire meaning insofar as the viewer can read into it a duration extending beyond itself. When we find a photograph meaningful, we are lending it a past and a future.

JOHN BERGER, *ANOTHER WAY OF TELLING*

For most of us, family photo albums function as an archive of personal history and a stimulus to memory: we know the people, we remember the events. Often we are flooded by emotions as we revisit the past in pictures. But what of photographs of people we have never met, living in times and places to which we don't belong? How do we "read" those pictures? What stories do they suggest to us?

Working individually or in groups, choose one or more of the photos on pages 14 and 15, and write about what you "see" in the pictures. You may want to create background notes about the people or settings, or write a poem or the outline of a story. What past, present or future do you see in the pictures? Who is telling the story? What feelings do the photos evoke in you? Do the stills suggest certain kinds of music? It is from these photos and hundreds of others that *City of Gold* was fashioned.

2

Screen a segment of the film without the soundtrack and consider the following questions: What do you think is happening here? Whose voice is telling this story? What would the voice be saying? What music or sound do you think would suit this sequence? You may want to try using different pieces of music with the visuals and compare the effects. (You may also want to use the excerpt *Study Extract from City of Gold* in the section SHAPING REALITY, video location 54.) Now screen the whole film.

ACTIVITIES

After Viewing

1

After viewing the complete film and reading Tom Daly's description of how it was made, look at a portion of the film with the sound turned off. Do you respond differently to the visuals now, when there is no music or voice? Knowing what music or voice went with the visuals, do you find it harder to think of other choices than you did before you had seen the film?

2

Screen the film again and note where the mood and tempo of the music change. Choose a few sequences (e.g., the climb up the Chilkoot Pass, the journey downstream to Dawson, the Independence Day celebrations) and discuss what the music adds to each scene.

3

After reading the interview with Tom Daly, re-screen the opening of the film to see how the filmmakers edited the visual material to prepare viewers for the stillness of the photos. Can you find the point at which the live-action footage switches to stills? (A hint: watch carefully when the camera moves down the side of the mountain to pick up the line of men struggling up the Chilkoot Pass.)

Can you find the point at which the stills move into the live-action footage of the present?

4

Screen the opening and closing sections of the film, shot in Dawson City during the 1950s. Notice the symmetrical way in which the material has been edited. The film opens with an aerial shot of the town, then moves to the streets, the restaurant, the old men, the children, the inanimate objects. How does it end?

5

After screening the film and reading the Tom Daly interview, try some framing exercises with the stills on pages 14 to 20. First, make a movable frame by cutting two L-shaped pieces of black card.

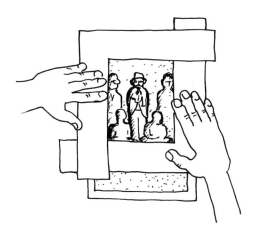

Experiment with various framings: focus on significant details in each photo; try moving from a specific detail to a larger context, as the filmmakers did in the shot of the women of Paradise Alley. What are some of the differences — in information and in feeling — that result from changing the framing on each picture?

Experiment with the concept of framing in other contexts: for instance, analyze the way in which a story is told or a news item reported. From whose perspective or point of view is the story or news item "framed"? What does it include? What does it leave out? Is it a close-up view? Does it try to suggest a larger picture?

6

History is, in part, telling stories of the past in a way that matters to us in the present. How are visual documents — drawings, photographs, film and video footage — useful in trying to reconstruct the past? Who has been recorded? Who has not? (See the quotation about history in the discussion of *Memorandum*, p. 35.)

Copy old photos from a family album. (Photocopies usually work well.) Arrange them to form a story about your family's history. If you have still pictures and film or video footage of the same event, compare them. What are the strengths and drawbacks of each medium in documenting actuality?

7

Compare *City of Gold* and *Our Marilyn* as recreations of a past event. Both use found footage, a first-person narration, and evocative music; and both were experimenting with the form and conventions of the documentaries of their day. What differences and similarities are there in the tone and feel of the films and in the use made of voice? In what ways are these documentaries both "creative treatments of actuality"?

8

An excerpt from *City of Gold*, entitled *Study Extract from "City of Gold"*, can be found in the section SHAPING REALITY, video location 54. See p. 104 for additional activities involving this film.

FURTHER RESOURCES

film/video

In this collection, *The Ballad of Crowfoot* and *Speak White* are also created from archival stills. *Of Lives Uprooted* comprises the animated drawings of refugee children from Central America. These three selections are found in the section VOICES OF EXPERIENCE, VOICES FOR CHANGE, PART 1, video locations 00, 64, and 71.

See Charlie Chaplin's silent classic, *The Gold Rush*.

Ken Burns's series *The Civil War* is a masterful recreation of the past using archival photos and extracts from writings of the time, including letters and journals. Available for purchase from PBS (Public Broadcasting Service) in the U.S.A.

print

For more information about the stampede for gold, see *The Gold Crusades: A Social History of Gold Rushes, 1849-1929* by Douglas Fetherling (Toronto: Macmillan, 1988).

Collections of archival photos provide a wealth of information about other times and, sometimes, other places. Among them are *Canadian Photography 1839-1920* by Ralph Greenhill and Andrew Birrell (Toronto: The Coach House Press, 1979); *A Harvest Yet to Reap: A History of Prairie Women* by Rasmussen et al. (Toronto: The Women's Press, 1976) and *Portraits of North American Indian Life* by Edward S. Curtis (Toronto: New Press, 1972).

For a thought-provoking book on working with images, see John Berger's and Jean Mohr's collaboration *Another Way of Telling* (London: Writers and Readers Publishing Co-op, 1982).

new shoes

VIDEO LOCATION 42 IN *WAYS OF STORYTELLING*

6 MINUTES

1990

DIRECTOR: *ANN MARIE FLEMING*

PRODUCER: *MARY ARMSTRONG*

DISTRIBUTOR: *CFMDC/CFMDC WEST*

Vancouver filmmaker Ann Marie Fleming made *New Shoes* (subtitled *An Interview in Exactly Five Minutes*) in 1990, shortly after graduating from the Emily Carr College of Art and Design, where she studied film animation. Originally produced for the collection *Five Feminist Minutes* by Studio D, the "women's studio" at the NFB, *New Shoes* is a provocative mixture. A straightforward but compelling documentary interview, in which a young woman talks about how her ex-boyfriend tried to kill her when she was a teenager, is intercut with animated sequences of a mysterious, princess-like figure.

The form and content of *New Shoes* raise a host of questions: How do we remember and recount the "stories" that have happened to us? How are personal and private experiences packaged by the media? What are our images of gender, of relations between the sexes? What is the value of creating something that sounds familiar, and then giving it a twist?

These concerns were further elaborated by Ann Marie Fleming in a feature film, also called *New Shoes*. The two productions give viewers an opportunity to compare two versions of the same event. An excerpt from the longer film is included in the video interview with Ann Marie Fleming that follows *New Shoes* (WAYS OF STORYTELLING, video location 48).

SUGGESTIONS *for* USE

- *This film usually provokes a lot of discussion. Give viewers time to work through their own responses and to read Ann Marie Fleming's original proposal for the film, before watching her interviewed on video.*

- *The film is so short that it easily lends itself to a second viewing.*

- *Because* New Shoes *deals, albeit in an unexpected fashion, with a violent incident between a young woman and a young man, be alert to student reactions.*

ABOUT *the* ANIMATION TECHNIQUE

New Shoes combines documentary footage of a talking-head interview, shot on film stock, with video images of a fairy princess figure surrounded by floating coloured shards.

Ann Marie Fleming achieved this effect by positioning a video monitor on its back underneath an animation camera. The images of the fairy princess were then manipulated frame by frame — forwards, backwards, freeze-framed — by means of a remote-control device. Fleming placed a sheet of clear glass over the video screen. On top of this sheet she arranged broken pieces of stained glass, which she also moved, frame by frame, around the images of the princess. All these movements were recorded by the animation camera, one frame at a time.

Below is the original proposal for New Shoes *submitted by Ann Marie Fleming to the Five Feminist Minutes committee. It is interesting to compare this proposal with Gaye Fowler's description of what actually happened once the filming began.*

Gaye, now a mother in her thirties living in Vancouver, as a teenager was chased down a Toronto alleyway and shot through her side by her ex-fiancé, who then turned the gun on himself.

This is true.

The film is about memory, vicariousness of experience, especially through the media, manipulation, control, and other "big" things. All of this centres around the story of Gaye Fowler, as told in this interview.

I originally heard Gaye's story over warm noodles and began turning around the idea of making a

film out of it, but was concerned about exploiting her own experience and recreating it in a way that was not authentic to her. We did an interview where Gaye was aware of the purpose and she did alter her storytelling — it became more linear and certain points changed — like things do in progressive memory, through telling and retelling.

What I want is to recreate the interview, prompting vocally and with the script, when Gaye goes off-track from the "official record", the interview I have already edited and transcribed, playing around with the constant newness of experience through memory and also the impossibility of capturing this on film.

While the "real" interview is going on, there will be flashbacks to a princess on a hill, with mattes of castles and clouds and starry skies animating to and fro, to emphasize the fairy tale quality of the story taking place, or at least that land of myth and make-believe where we relegate such horrific events that happen to other people, the mythologizing of personal histories.

The entire original interview takes approximately 10 minutes. Gaye will be cut off at precisely 5 minutes, to fit into the guidelines of the "Five Feminist Minutes" — not enough time to tell her whole story — to bring attention to the fact that her story lives outside the film and can only be partially represented by the medium, the format, the "Five Feminist Minutes".

It is a story of horror, of alienation, desensitization, urban violence, survival, and introspection told with a sense of humour.

It is never the whole story.

The whole experience of making a film was very foreign to me, even though the subject matter was obviously personal and I knew it very well. The only instructions I had got from Ann Marie were, "Show up and make it funny." I certainly felt like I could handle the situation — it was just telling my story one more time. And it was only going to take five minutes. But when the camera started to roll, I drew a blank. I did tell what had happened but in a flat, very factual way. I guess I hadn't realized that there were going to be so many people in the room, all of them focussed on me — I found that really disconcerting. Besides I was trying to keep track of all sorts of things. For instance, Ann Marie had said, "Make sure you remember to say 'I once had a boyfriend named Albert.'" I was trying to remember all the lines and fit everything in and do it all in five minutes. And on top of that, I wasn't allowed to move my head because they didn't have a boom mike and my earrings kept making a clicking sound. So I felt pretty restricted.

Then we took a break and while Ann Marie went off to make some tea, I looked at what we had shot on video. The crew started asking me all kinds of questions about what had happened and when Ann Marie came in and heard me talking, she said, "Now, that's what I wanted it to sound like — animated and natural." So we did it again, and the second time I felt very emotional. Maybe it was because I felt more intimacy with the crew.

Even before we made the short film of *New Shoes*, Ann Marie had already taped my story in all sorts of venues in Vancouver — in a restaurant, by the water, on a ferry. I must say that, in the longer film, I felt uncomfortable knowing that everything the actress said was taken directly from my words — but said in a very flip way. I felt as though someone was taking my experience and changing it.

I've only seen the short version of *New Shoes* once, and that was in a theatre screening. I was so busy thinking about how I looked on a big screen or how strange my voice sounded to me that I didn't really focus too much on what I said. Actually I've been amazed at how this film continues to be seen. You know, you think you'll be in a student film and that will be the end of it. But it hasn't happened with this one. . . .

When you do interviews, what comes out in the end is all in the hands of the director or the reporter, and it can be distorted. I remember when the attack on me was reported in the Toronto papers — they got everything wrong, even our ages. The only thing that was accurate was the date. And the incident was written up as a big revenge drama, which it wasn't. After that experience, I feel that if you give an interview, you should be clear and concise. And you shouldn't get emotional because that's what TV thrives on, especially tabloid TV.

I find that every time I tell the story, it's different for me. Mostly, it doesn't bother me to talk about what happened because it's a story of survival, not just destruction. Although I didn't feel that way about it for the first few years. And I still can't help wondering about what spurred Albert on to actually try and kill me. Was it something planned, was it something spontaneous?

I still think that a film needs to be made about what happened *after* the shooting — about how every detective and police officer I dealt with was male; about how they didn't know how to respond in a humane way; about how after the doctors had to cut away my clothes to find the entry point for the bullet, these officers all clustered around the door so they could get a look at a naked teenage girl; about how the nurse, trying to salvage my dignity, told them to get the hell out of there; about how I had to learn to walk again after my surgery; about how everyone who came to the hospital those first few days kept saying "Poor Albert" until I realized, a few days later, "What about poor me?" You still don't often get to hear about these experiences from the woman's perspective or to find out how justice plays itself out for *her*.

—VANCOUVER, 1992

IDEAS *for* DISCUSSION

1

What is this film about? As a group, document some of the issues raised. (There should be no judgments passed — by the teacher or by students — during this process.)

2

Do you think this is a true story? Why?

3

Would you have a different opinion if you thought the woman telling the story was an actor rather than a person who had lived through the experience she describes? Why? After watching the Ann Marie Fleming interview, which version of the story seemed more believable — that told by Gaye Fowler or the actress's portrayal?

4

Whose story is this? Whose voice is telling the story? Who shapes the story? How would you have reacted if someone else had told her story, or if it had been reported as a news item — by another woman's voice? by a man's voice?

5

Why do you think Ann Marie Fleming chose to set this interview in a kitchen?

6

We never see the interviewer, though we do hear her intervene. Why? As a member of the audience, who do you identify with in the film — the subject or the interviewer?

7

How did you react to the interviewer's laugh? Why? Why do you think Ann Marie Fleming kept the laugh in the film?

8

Why does the interviewer mention there are only 10 seconds left? What does New Shoes *say about the way in which the mass media — and news in particular — package events and experiences, particularly those involving violence against women?*

9

Why do you think the subject of the film noticed the new shoes? What does this reveal about how memory works? Can you think of a time when you or someone you know was in a major crisis? Was there anything bizarre — a small detail, perhaps — that stood out for you?

10

What does the woman jumping up and down make you think of? What does she add to the film?

11

What do the coloured bits falling around her remind you of?

12

What sounds do you recall hearing on the soundtrack? Why were they added in?

13

Ann Marie Fleming produced **New Shoes** *for less than $10,000, which is a tiny sum in the world of filmmaking. In an interview, she stated:*

> *The facilities that you have open to you and the money that you have affect the level that you work on and your method of working, but it doesn't make any difference as to whether you're making a good film or a bad film or an effective film. Maybe it's not so slick, but I don't think that's the measure of a good film anyhow.*

What do **you** *think is the measure of a good film?*

ACTIVITIES

1

Ask students, working in pairs, to do the following: Remember an incident that made you either very happy or very frightened. Try to recreate the feeling and tone as well as the facts of that situation. (Teachers may want to set up some safeguards for students when dealing with very emotional material.) One of you tell your story to the other, taking as long as you feel you need, responding to the interview questions as they arise. The interviewer should take notes or use an audio recorder, if one is available. Now switch roles, but this time the speaker has exactly five minutes to tell a story or describe an incident. The interviewer might also have some set questions to ask. Tape the second interview, too. Discuss the differences: in the stories and in your feelings about telling them, under the different circumstances. What other factors might influence the way a story is told during an interview? (Some students may want to record this activity on video and then play it back for the class.)

2

In pairs or small groups, come up with a list of the qualities you would look for when selecting someone as an interview subject. What is the difference between your reactions to Gaye Fowler as she tells her story, and your reactions to a politician, for instance, delivering a speech on television? What makes an interview subject seem credible and authentic?

3

Look at some media reports (radio, TV, newspaper, magazine) about an incident of violence against a woman. How was the report presented? From whose point of view? Who is depicted as the aggressor? Why? What assumptions about violence underlie the piece? In what other ways might the story have been told? Present it again in another voice, from another point of view.

Do you know people who have had their names in the newspaper? Did they feel that they, or the events with which they were associated, were fairly represented?

FURTHER RESOURCES

film/video

After the Montreal Massacre and *Not a Love Story* can be used when considering the issue of violence against women. *Media and Society* contains 11 minutes of excerpts from *Not a Love Story*. All available from the NFB.

print

The pop psychology book *The Cinderella Complex* by Colette Dowling (New York: Summit Books, 1981) might offer some comments on the fairy-princess figure.

Robert Munsch's children's book *The Paper Bag Princess* (Toronto: Annick Press, 1980) offers a delightful twist on the usual happily-ever-after scenario so often associated with the princess waiting for her prince.

memorandum

VIDEO LOCATION 55 IN *WAYS OF STORYTELLING*

COMPLETE FILM: *58 MINUTES*

EXCERPTED LENGTH: *30 MINUTES*

BLACK & WHITE

1965

DIRECTORS: *DONALD BRITTAIN, JOHN SPOTTON*

PRODUCER: *JOHN KEMENEY, NFB*

DISTRIBUTOR: *NFB*

It's astonishing and tragic that we, the common people, know virtually nothing firsthand of the thoughts and aspirations of our ancestors. Apart from their songs and tales, they left nothing because they owned nothing and could leave no personal record. Their history, practically the only one we have, was written for them by their masters.

Documentary filmmaking now allows the common man not only to publicly argue his case but to leave a highly sophisticated record of his mind, surroundings and vision. I like to think that future historians will find the documentarist's record of man and woman no less important than those of the chroniclers and diarists of old.

MICHAEL RABIGER, *DIRECTING THE DOCUMENTARY*

SUGGESTIONS *for* USE

- *There is a fade to black on the screen after each of the excerpts. You may want to stop and deal with each excerpt separately.*

- *See the "Before Viewing" activity, p. 40.*

When Donald Brittain set out for Germany in the summer of 1964 to make a film about the Holocaust, he was certain of only two elements. First, a Jewish glass cutter named Bernard Laufer was making his annual pilgrimage from Toronto to Germany to meet other survivors of Bergen-Belsen. This trip, however, 20 years after the liberation of the concentration camps, he was taking his teenaged son with him. Second, as part of his research for the film, Brittain had read Hannah Arendt's book *Eichmann in Jerusalem* and had been particularly struck by her discussion of the banality of evil. The notion that hideous actions could be performed by apparently decent folk seemed worth exploring.

During the three-week shoot in Germany, Brittain and his cinematographer and co-director, John Spotton, used newly developed lightweight cameras and sync-sound equipment to gather candid footage of Laufer's return to the camps. They also documented, in part, the trials of men accused of atrocities during the Holocaust, and collected images of a modern and affluent country only too happy to forget its haunted past.

The resulting documentary, *Memorandum*, is a superb example of a film fashioned in the editing room. Unlike a piece of reportage, *Memorandum* strove to understand the *meaning* of the events we call the Holocaust, rather than simply presenting those events. Laufer's story became the departure point for inquiries on history, memory, the complicity of "normal" people, the drive to remember, and the urge to forget. Disparate visuals, archival and contemporary footage of the camps, and cinéma vérité material of Laufer's journey were interwoven through a memorable narration and an evocative sound track. The voices of the survivors are included, but the commentary is written from the point of view of an outsider, an omniscient third-person narrator trying to understand what happened and why.

Donald Brittain is remembered particularly for his mastery of commentary writing and for his ability, through structuring, to meld seemingly unconnected fragments into a unified whole. To achieve his effects, he used a range of devices including irony, understatement, juxtaposition of sequences, and the counterpoint of words and images. In an interview in *Cinema Canada*, he described some of the difficulties he and John Spotton encountered during the editing of *Memorandum*:

> I don't know how many times we put that thing together. At one stage it was too predictable, at another it was too confusing. Certain things which laid an egg at the beginning of the film became wonderful at the end. We had cut ninety-two sequences which were never used in the final film. Nine months in the editing room and I never thought the thing would work.

But work it did. *Memorandum* won the Grand Prize, the Lion of St. Mark, at the XVII Exhibition of Documentary Film, Venice.

Our selection consists of three excerpts from the film.

One of the most compelling moments in *Memorandum* is the interview with the Polish Jew who "always carries the bones", bones that represent 700,000 people from the Treblinka death camp. He is a clear example of the power of documentary film to bear witness, to record and disseminate personal testimony. By recounting their experiences, such individuals challenge and contradict the versions of history set forth by the "masters". This tradition of the *testimony* has been particularly important in Latin American documentaries that chronicle the social and political upheavals of the last several decades. (Also see *Of Lives Uprooted* in Voices of Experience, Voices for Change, Part 1, video location 71, which presents the experiences of refugee children in El Salvador and Honduras.)

a note about narration

In his comprehensive and thoughtful book *Directing the Documentary*, Michael Rabiger describes some of the salient characteristics of film narration, its functions, and its effects.

On the positive side, narration can rapidly and effectively move the viewer into the heart of the situation and focus attention on aspects of the film that might otherwise go unnoticed.

Less desirable is the potential of narration to feel like an intrusion into the relationship between the audience and the participants in a film. Moreover, a third-person "voice-of-God" narration usually smacks of *authority* in a way that is all too familiar for viewers of television commercials and "factual" films.

In most cases, the narrator is considered by viewers to be the voice of the film itself.

Good commentary writing is an art and has its own rules:

- Narration has to be compressed, striving for maximum meaning in the fewest possible syllables. Simple, short and direct is usually best.

- As narration is meant to be spoken, it must sound balanced to the ear.

- The first word to fall on each new shot (or image) strongly influences the audience's interpretation of that shot.

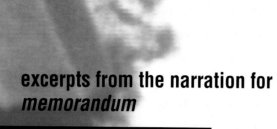

excerpts from the narration for *memorandum*

Video Image from *Memorandum*

It has been noted that Donald Brittain's commentary writing often has the cadence and density of poetry:

Early one morning in Munich in the summer of 1965. In a few days, Fraulein Mara Bellet will be celebrating her twenty-fourth birthday. She was born in 1941 -- the year that Hitler decided, among other things, that she should never see a Jew. But that's finished now, and there's enough to do, getting ready for the day ahead.

. . . .

Here they come now: seventeen of them, late of the Auschwitz adminstration. Some killed with gas and needle and club. And some with the pointing of a finger. Maltke, the adjutant, who kept track of things, and then went into the export trade. Capesius, the druggist, who helped in eight thousand murders, but said he was always polite. Papa Kaduk, who sat in his chapel, and admitted he had to occasionally pull himself together. Doctor Klehr who punctured hearts with a needle, and Bednarek who interrupted torture for prayer, and Wilhelm Boger, who beat men's testicles until they died.

. . . .

They rejoin the German crowd. And who will ever know who murdered by memorandum, who did the filing and the typing from nine o'clock to five, with an hour off for lunch.

And if it could happen in the fairyland of Hansel and Gretel, and the Pied Piper of Hamelin, could it not happen anywhere?

And could it not happen anywhere, if it could happen in the cultured land of Bach, Beethoven and Schiller?

And how could it happen in a land of churches? There were some martyrs, it's true -- but where were the other servants of Christ?

And where were the scholars of Heidelberg? They were with the captains of industry and among the first to play along.

And how could it all have started in the happy land of Bavaria? In this, the Hofbrau House of Munich, Adolf Hitler first laid out his program to the world. But why should that darken the festive summer night? A third of them are tourists, a third were too young, and the other third are sick and tired of the whole business.

IDEAS *for* DISCUSSION

1

What are your reactions while watching this film? Which images, sounds or moments do you most remember? What was it about them that compelled your attention?

2

Whose story is it?

3

Who tells the story? Why did Brittain not make Laufer the narrator of the film? Does the film gain anything by being narrated by an outside observer, someone conducting an inquiry?

4

Why did playwright and director Peter Weiss seat the actors who played the Nazi defendants in such a way that they were simply extensions of the audience? What does his intention have to do with the theme of the film? What is this film about?

5

Re-screen the segment of the film in which the narrator details the sentences handed out to the accused Nazis and then talks about those who murdered by memorandum (WAYS OF STORYTELLING, video location 55). What do you think the accompanying visuals add to those statements? Would you have chosen something else?

6

What is the difference between this film about the Holocaust and a factual news report about the same period?

7

Who in the film feels compelled to remember? Who would rather forget? Is it important to remember such a painful event? Why or why not?

8

Why would Donald Brittain have chosen to make a film about something that had happened 20 years earlier? Does the film have anything to say to us today, 50 years later? Does it have any relevance to events that have happened since — in Vietnam, El Salvador, Cambodia, Iraq, Bosnia Herzegovina, Somalia and a re-united Germany?

9

Is "I was just following orders" a justifiable defense? Research the topic of civil disobedience; two possible examples are the Innu occupying the runways in Labrador, and environmental protesters. What reasons do such people give for the stances they have chosen? Is resistance valuable? When? Why?

ACTIVITIES

Before Viewing

Without giving any background information about this documentary, show the opening sequences of the film until Bernard Laufer's arrival at the airport in Germany. Have the sound turned off. What do students think the film is about? Where does it take place? When? Concentrate on the images. What is the common thread between the music box, the soldiers, the sign, the funeral, and the group of arriving travellers? Now screen the segment with the sound to see how narration and music set the mood and themes of the piece.

After Viewing

Bring in a news item taped from television. Listen to the way the item has been presented. Screen it again without the sound. Ask students to write other commentaries for the item from different points of view — perhaps a first-person account by a participant or an "outside expert".

FURTHER RESOURCES

film/video

For other examples of "testimony" films in this collection, see *Of Lives Uprooted* in VOICES OF EXPERIENCE, VOICES FOR CHANGE, PART 1 (video location 71) and *Children of War* in VOICES OF EXPERIENCE, VOICES FOR CHANGE, PART 2 (video location 00) and *New Shoes* in WAYS OF STORYTELLING (video location 42).

See *Anybody's Son Will Do* (in THE CANDID EYE?, video location 52), particularly the sequence in which the Marine drill instructor is instructing the recruits on the attitude they should develop towards "the enemy". Relevant quotes from the film can be found on p. 171.

Speak White, based on a poem by Michèle Lalonde, marries a passionate, lyrical narration to black-and-white archival images. See VOICES OF EXPERIENCE, VOICES FOR CHANGE, PART 1 (video location 64).

Return to Dresden is a beautifully constructed documentary about a veteran going back, 40 years later, to the city he firebombed as an 18-year-old. There, struggling with the moral responsibility of having "followed orders", he is confronted by his former "enemies" with whom he finds common

ground in a longing for peace. Available from the NFB.

The NFB distributes a 13-part series *Brittain on Brittain* which was produced by ACCESS Alberta. Each tape consists of an interview with Brittain about a specific film, as well as the film itself. *Donald Brittain, Filmmaker* is a portrait of the celebrated documentarian that interweaves material from his films, footage of Brittain working on location, and portions of his biography. Available from the NFB.

print

Donald Brittain: Never the Ordinary Way contains articles about Brittain the man and Brittain the filmmaker; descriptions of his films; excerpts of some of his most memorable narrations; and a filmography and bibliography. Available from the NFB.

For a moving personal testimony see *I, Rigoberta Menchu: An Indian Woman in Guatemala* (London: Verso, 1984) by the 1992 winner of the Nobel Peace Prize. In a similar vein is *Let Me Speak*, by Domitila Barrios de Chungara with Moema Viezzer (New York: Monthly Review Press, 1978).

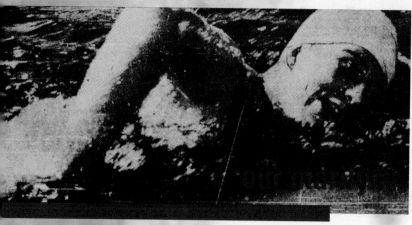

VIDEO LOCATION 85 IN *WAYS OF STORYTELLING*

27 MINUTES

COLOUR/BLACK & WHITE

1987

DIRECTOR: *BRENDA LONGFELLOW*

PRODUCER: *BRENDA LONGFELLOW*

DISTRIBUTOR: *FULL FRAME*

SUGGESTIONS *for* USE

- *It was our experience that students responded positively to experiments in documentary form: they tended to be both fascinated and challenged by fresh and unexpected approaches that left them scrabbling for answers.*

- *Before giving students copies of the interview with Brenda Longfellow to read, ask them to brainstorm what questions they might put to the filmmaker, were she present. After reading the interview, notice which questions remain unanswered. See if they can be dealt with in small group or class discussion.*

How does one re-create physical experience on film, so that viewers connect with it in a direct, visceral way? What images of women's bodies are we offered in the media and how do these images affect us? Who are our Canadian heroes and why? What different ways are there of remembering and recounting "historic" events or moments? What is the value of exploring these questions in an innovative manner?

In 1954, 17-year-old Marilyn Bell of Toronto became the first person to swim across Lake Ontario, thereby gaining a place in history and in the hearts of the nation. Using a mixture of elements culled from traditional documentary and experimental film, *Our Marilyn* explores some of the many meanings of this event in a way that strains against standard definitions of the documentary genre. The richly layered soundtrack uses an array of voices rather than the conventional voice-of-God narration, as well as music and sound effects. Images of the marathon swim are re-worked by a process known as optical printing. This produces a haunting, hallucinatory effect that suggests the psychic as well as the physical aspects of Marilyn Bell's feat. There is also a fictional narrator, a young woman named Marilyn, who tries to locate herself between two images and possiblities, Marilyn Bell and Marilyn Monroe. The result is an impressionistic meditation on cultural appropriation of the female body, heroism, and Canadian identity.

Our Marilyn is the second film made by independent filmmaker Brenda Longfellow. It was more than three years in the making, and was produced on a tiny budget, with some help from Studio D of the National Film Board and the Ontario Arts Council. *Our Marilyn* was awarded the Prix du Publique at the 4ième Festival international de film et vidéo de femmes de Montréal and a shared Grand Prix at the Oberhausen International Film Festival.

a note on experimental film

Conventional filmmaking, in both the documentary and dramatic genres, relies heavily on narrative — the unfolding of a plot or story line that culminates in a climax. (The Hollywood movie is the most widely known example of a narrative-driven film.) There is, however, another filmmaking tradition that plays with the formal elements of film — image, light, sound, temporal and spatial dislocations — to create works that sidestep our everyday categories of perception and understanding. Rather than dispensing information or telling stories, these films tend to have much in common with non-linear, associational states such as dream and memory. This tradition is usually referred to as "experimental filmmaking". The differences between the two approaches to filmmaking are analogous to the differences between figurative and non-figurative painting.

Our Marilyn borrows from both traditions. Its rather straightforward chronology — the beginning, middle and end of the marathon swim — forms the spine of the film; layered sound effects, visuals and voice move the story out of the objective realm of reportage.

feminist voice in documentary

During the 1970s, feminists became interested in using documentary as a means of preserving and disseminating previously hidden or unexplored aspects of women's history. Conscious that the personal, too, is political, they stressed the validity of personal voice and subjective experience in their films. The extended interview-as-testimony played an important role in the documentaries of this period, as did filmed conversations of groups of women discussing matters of personal and political importance to them. These films were a striking contrast to the "objective" documentaries driven by a single, authoritative, male narrator or the catch-life-on-the-fly approach of direct cinema.

Director Brenda Longfellow's decision to re-examine the story of Marilyn Bell through the filter of an individual woman's consciousness places her in the tradition of feminist filmmaking: in *Our Marilyn*, the "voice" of the film is that of a young woman who tries to understand what meaning the images of womanhood offered by the surrounding culture might have for *her*.

an interview with Brenda Longfellow, director

What was the genesis of *Our Marilyn*?

I had been trained as an historian and I really liked popular history. And I became very interested, via my studies and reading in feminism and film, in public images of women and what they mean in terms of how we construct certain mythologies about women. So I thought I would do something quirky about Marilyn Bell who was a 50s icon of ideal Canadian womanhood, young and virginal and full of stamina. I wanted to make something that was very hokey and tongue-in-cheek, but once I started to get into the material, I realized how fabulous her feat really was — to swim across Lake Ontario for 21 hours.

I did a lot of research with marathon swimmers, talked to them and tried to pull them back into

remembering what the experience had been like. Because in the archival material, there were images of Marilyn leaping off the dock and images of her being pulled out at the end, but there was no coverage of that whole middle process of the swim itself, for all sorts of reasons. The CBC didn't believe that she'd actually make it. The American swimmer Florence Chadwick was the one who was getting all the attention, and yet in the end it was this little girl who succeeded.

Luckily, I found a marathon swimmer who had actually swum the lake both ways, once against the current, and had kept an hour-by-hour diary: " At this point I had to do breaststroke, at this point I had to change strokes because my arm hurt. . .". I used a lot of that material when I tried to re-create the middle part of the swim.

I wasn't re-creating the actual event in some attempt to reproduce documentary reality. Instead, there seemed to me something compelling and hallucinatory and dreamlike in the details and images I worked with, something that speaks to people about the body and the unconscious and the dreamworld. And I've certainly been told that some of the images of swimming seem to have something to do with motherhood and, of course, that's set up in the beginning by the narrator as well.

Because the image of the swim is so ambiguous, people can project and draw on and develop it in all sorts of ways. When the film was first finished, I was often at screenings where a marathon swimmer or runner or athlete in a wheelchair would come up at the end and say, "Yes, you got it exactly right. It's just like that." I've certainly never had that kind of experience myself, other than doing the optical printing for it. I hadn't imagined it as a realistic film at all, and yet it seems to touch people in realistic kinds of ways.

What decisions did you make about how to re-create Marilyn's story?

We shot me swimming Lake Ontario in Super 8 film, transferred that to 16mm, and then re-worked the images in black-and-white film on the optical printer. I adore optical printing. We live in a world of media overload, we live in a world where every two seconds on televison, there's a cut. So there's something very substantial and fulfilling about optical printing because it slows things down, it lets you dream, it lets you discover.

I knew from the very beginning that these images of swimming would repeat and fragment over and over again to create that visceral feeling, that experience of swimming and hallucinating and losing control over your consciousness and losing control over your physical centre, becoming a part of the lake instead of having those very definite boundaries, me and lake. But even though I knew that was always a very important element, I had no idea how all of it would fit together. I had some tracks of narration that were done and I had bits of archival footage and bits of this and bits of that. I also knew that there would be a narrator who would try and pull everything together.

Using Marilyn Monroe was a complete accident. I was researching archival material and found 1954 newsreels: Marilyn Bell swims, Marilyn Monroe entertains troops in Korea. They were almost back to back, and I thought, "Wow, that's fantastic!" I started imagining how that could be put together, playing with ideas about "our Marilyn", "whose Marilyn", and so on.

I wanted to create a person in the present who would be reflecting on these historical images, now and from a feminist perspective. So I came up with the third Marilyn who is trying to discover where she fits in as a woman between the icon of Monroe, the beautiful sex goddess — blonde, vulnerable, weak, exploitable — and the Canadian icon of femininity, which is the little virginal person of stamina and endurance. For us, these are great Canadian qualities — not as snazzy as Monroe, but nevertheless they seem to be part of the way we collectively think about our heroes.

What about the uses you made of sound?

I wanted several layers of time in the film, and one of the layers I wanted was the voice breathing in time with the re-created, dissolving, fragmented, optically printed images of the swimmer swimming. It wasn't simply the way that it's represented in popular history — "Canada moves into nationhood with Marilyn Bell's swim" — but to imagine it and represent it as a very visceral, physical experience. So the voice — the breathing voice, the counting voice, the singing voice — was about bringing that bodied presence into the film but bringing it in via the soundtrack rather than via the images. I found a very young actress who was 16 or so, and we recorded her here in the basement, poor thing, breathing and singing and hyperventilating for hours.

We had a lot of trouble getting exactly the right sound of the waves. First, we tried going out on Lake Ontario and that was a disaster. All we got was scrunch, scrunch, rattle, rattle. Then we tried taping in swimming pools but that wasn't loud enough. Eventually, we went to a sound-effects library. We had five tracks of different kinds of waves — big ones, little ones, lapping ones, rough ones — and we used different bits from each to create the bodied sense of the waves that we wanted.

The music I found in the archives. Some of the radio bits were actually from that time as well. I wrote other snippets, like the stuff about the CNE and Florence Chadwick, or for moments when I felt we needed more information. I had an actor read those parts and tried to re-create them with the same kind of CBC intonation and the static and the beep.

When we showed the film, some students wanted to know why there was so much happening at certain moments. As Marilyn heads for shore, the creeper is scrolling up the screen, the music is playing, there's a voice-over . . .

That's one of my favourite moments. Pure sensory overload. It's a dramatic structural moment where we are coming to the end and this accumulation adds a sense of urgency about completion. It's there to take us from the slow lyrical imagery, building up to the climax. Also, I found the creeper very funny: at 10:10 she took orange juice, at 10:15 she went swimming, at 11:00 she was swimming 30 strokes a minute. It's a very scientific, rational order trying to impose itself on something that is completely other: the body, the unconscious and all that. So it's a moment when all these different narratives about Marilyn coalesce: there's my commentary, and the songs with their hokey kind of Canadian nationalism, and a scientific way of trying to explain everything very precisely in mathematical terms. And then, what does she swim into? Commodification and becoming something that sells products.

You seem to enjoy playing with a lot of the notions of conventional documentary.

In *Our Marilyn*, instead of trying to be objective and instead of trying to represent something as "reality" (and then at the end you see the credits — directed by, written by some individual sensibility), I chose to personalize the voice-over. As I said before, I wanted a presentation filtered through a contemporary consciousness and from a feminist perspective that was trying to work on problems of images of women, how you represent the body, what the body means. But, of course, the "I" in the film is a fictional "I", though she may be very close to me in certain ways. So that fictionalized voice is very distinct from the classical tradition of objective, realistic documentary. Besides, the images are clearly not presented as realistic images. It's apparent that they've been found and then worked and re-worked so they move into different realms.

There is a tendency now in a lot of writing about documentary to say that every image is a fictional image, that documentary itself is fiction. This view is in opposition to the tradition of the NFB or the tradition of the classical voice-of-God narration, which implied that the documentary image was reality, a window on the world. Now what you have are contemporary critics saying, "No, no, they've had it all wrong. Really, the documentary is as created and as fictional as the Hollywood film."

Personally, I think that's not true. One of the reasons why I feel found documentary footage is so compelling is because you know that it is a representation of something that did actually happen, that it's reportage. There's a range of response, a greater emotional investment in images of real people and real events that comes from our knowledge as viewers or as people who read history or as people who've heard of Marilyn Bell or Marilyn Monroe. If there had been a Hollywood film of a woman who swam across Lake Ontario, you'd have a very different response to those images. That's why I like to play with archival images and contrast them with dramatic re-creation or fiction. Then I can say, "Well, what is true? This is a documentary image but is it true? How does this fiction work against that one?" and so forth. It's those kinds of questions and those kinds of responses that intrigue me.

—Toronto, 1992

about optical printing

Optical printing is a process of rephotographing filmed material one frame at a time. This is done in the optical printer.

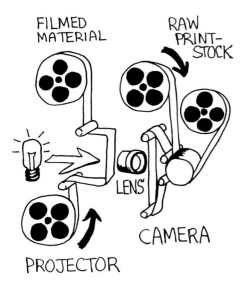

An optical printer consists of a movie camera and a projector. As the original filmed material moves through the projector gate, the camera, which faces the projector, rephotographs the original material frame by frame onto a new roll of film. During this process, it is possible to do a number of things:

- **STEP PRINTING:** print each frame a number of times. This slows the image down.

- **SUPERIMPOSITIONS AND DISSOLVES:** print more than one image on the same piece of film.

- **RE-PHOTOGRAPH THE SAME IMAGE OVER AND OVER:** In *Our Marilyn*, for example, the footage of Brenda Longfellow swimming was originally shot in Super 8 colour film and then transferred to 16mm black-and-white film. In the optical printer, the 16mm film was re-photographed on high-contrast black-and-white film stock, then photographed again. With each subsequent printing, the image became more and more "graphic": the formal elements were highlighted and details were lost in the build-up of contrast. This is very similar to the degradation of an image that occurs with successive passes through a photocopier.

IDEAS *for* DISCUSSION

1

Share reactions to Our Marilyn. *Were there specific moments, images or sequences that stood out for you? Were you responding to both sound and image, or were you more aware of one element than the other? What feelings did you have while watching the film? (You may want to do some of the activities related to sound, or re-screen particular sequences to examine in greater detail how each emotion was aroused.)*

2

Read the Brenda Longfellow interview about the making of Our Marilyn. *Were you surprised by her comments? Discuss the idea that the "meaning" of a film arises out of interaction between the individual viewer and the "text" of the film. Can you describe how that interaction took place in your particular case?*

3

What is the effect of the incomplete image, the mysterious dissolving image you can't quite make out? What difference would it have made if the middle of the swim had been represented by the coloured footage of the swimmer that you see at the beginning and end of the film?

4

Does Our Marilyn *fit your idea of a documentary? If not, in what ways does it differ? What might have been the standard way of representing Marilyn Bell's swim? Why did Brenda Longfellow choose to find another way, a different form? What kind of reality was she trying to represent that could not be contained by usual documentary conventions? What did you see or feel because of her fresh approach that you may not have become aware of otherwise?*

5

Do you agree or disagree with Brenda Longfellow's statement, "If there had been a Hollywood film of a woman who swam across Lake Ontario, you'd have a very different response to those images [than to images of an actual event]"? Why?

6

Marilyn, the narrator, says she grew up, in the 1950s, between the images of Marilyn Monroe and Marilyn Bell. What were the possibilities and choices represented by each of these images? What contemporary images would influence young women today? Whose images would influence young men? Screen Anybody's Son Will Do *(THE CANDID EYE?, video location 52) for a look at the image of manhood presented to the recruits.*

7

Do we have any Canadian heroes today? What kinds of achievements do we honor? What kinds of values do they represent?

ACTIVITIES

1

In 27 minutes, *Our Marilyn* tries to convey the experience of an agonizing marathon swim that lasted 21 hours. Re-screen the film, trying to pinpoint some of the devices Brenda Longfellow used to create a sense of duration.

2

With your eyes closed, listen to the soundtrack of the excerpt *Study Extract from "Our Marilyn"* (SHAPING REALITY, video location 59). (The image can also be turned off, but for maximum effect, your eyes should be shut.) What images or feelings did these sounds create for you? What elements make up the sound track? What voices are in the film? For further activities related to sound in this film, see p. 106.

3

This is a film about events that happened in Ontario in 1954. Re-screen *Our Marilyn* to see what elements of sound and picture the director used to establish the sense of that particular time and place.

4

Marilyn, the narrator, says, "Growing up between your bodies, I dreamed of another story." Who is this third Marilyn? What is she like? What might *her*

story be? Work with verbal and/or visual imagery to explore some of the possibilities the present-day Marilyn might want to construct for herself.

5

In her interview, Brenda Longfellow talks about several kinds of images, including media images and dream images produced by the unconscious. How do these differ from one another? Are they ever connected?

Think of yourself as a nocturnal image maker. Keep track of your dream images for a week. Choose one and try to reproduce its "feel" in sounds/music, colours, words, collaged images, slides. Can you think of other films that capture the dream-like quality of certain states? Do the images offered by the media ever speak to your dreaming self? What do they speak to?

6

Our Marilyn distinguishes between the public and private (or inside and outside) meanings of an event. What is the difference, for example, between the views of the swim given by Marilyn Bell and those given by the media reports? Have you ever been in a situation where you have felt such a dichotomy? Try to reproduce the different perspectives in writing or as ideas for film scenes. Or choose someone else who has been in this situation (for instance, Ben Johnson during the

Olympic Games), and with another person role-play the different points of view on the event.

7

Compare *Our Marilyn* and *City of Gold* (WAYS OF STORYTELLING, video locations 85 and 20) as films that recreate a past event. Both use found footage, a personal commentary, and evocative music, and both were experimenting with the documentary form and conventions of their time. What differences and similarities are there in the tone and feel of the films, in the voices used? How are both these films "creative treatments of actuality"?

8

Compare *Our Marilyn* and *The Kid Who Couldn't Miss* (available from the NFB; excerpts in THE POLITICS OF TRUTH, video location 25) in the light of myth making and the creation of heroes. In what sense can heroes — such as the two Marilyns and Billy Bishop — be seen as collective dream images?

9

Screen the swimming scene in *Our Marilyn* and the dance scenes in *Flamenco at 5:15* (THE POETRY OF MOTION, video location 56) to see different ways of conveying a sense of the body in motion.

1 0

Brenda Longfellow produced *Our Marilyn* with few technical or financial resources. Compare her situation with that of Cynthia Scott, an NFB staff filmmaker, as she describes it in her interview about the making of *Flamenco at 5:15*, page 244. Research the situation — in terms of financial support and distribution possibilities — of independent filmmakers in Canada today. Ask one to come speak to your class about the pros and cons of being an independent producer. Also see the interview with John Walker, p. 70.

FURTHER RESOURCES

film/video

For those who want to find out what other directors have done with optical printing, screen Norman McLaren's haunting dance film *Pas de deux* (available from NFB) and David Rimmer's mesmerizing *Variations on a Cellophane Wrapper.* *Variations* is available from Canadian Filmmakers Distribution Centre, 67A Portland St., Toronto, Ont., M5V 2M9, tel.: (416) 593-1808; and from Canadian Filmmakers Distribution West, 1131 Howe St., Suite 100, Vancouver, B.C., V6Z 2L7, tel.: (604) 684-3014.

Another production that contrasts Canadian and U.S. identities is the feature film *My American Cousin*, directed by Sandy Wilson, which focusses on a teenage girl growing up in the Okanagan Valley in the 1950s.

For a different perspective on women and their role in society, see *Mother of Many Children*, Alanis Obomsawin's respectful and loving tribute to native women. Available from the NFB. Also see *Black Mother, Black Daughter* in this collection (VOICES OF EXPERIENCE, VOICES FOR CHANGE, PART 2, video location 26).

In *Heroes: A Transformation Film* by Sarah Halpern, three of the filmmaker's friends tell their stories of ordinary heroism to the camera. Available in 16mm only, from Canadian Filmmakers' Distribution Centre, 67A Portland St., Toronto, Ont., M5V 2M9, tel.: (416) 593-1808.

print

Margaret Atwood's novel *Cat's Eye* (Toronto: McClelland & Stewart, 1988) is about growing up female in 1950s Toronto.

shaping reality

Art is not a mirror held up to reality but a hammer with which to shape it.
BERTOLT BRECHT

Filmmaking is a series of highly significant choices — of what to shoot, how to shoot it, and what to use in the end.
MICHAEL RABIGER

This section concentrates on film language, the tools that documentary film and video makers use to create an experience for an audience. They have at their disposal images, words, sound effects, music and silence. How those elements are selected and combined involves countless decisions made by those who work on a film: the researcher/writer, the director, the cinematographer, the picture editor, the sound recordist, the sound editor, the composer.

SHAPING REALITY is less a technical primer than an attempt to suggest some of the choices made in the process of "constructing reality". We have included a number of films that open up discussion on various aspects of filmmaking. *Ready When You Are* gives some sense of the logistics involved in setting up a documentary shoot, and also introduces the area of cinematography. *Techno-babies: The Making of a Television Documentary* is a behind-the-scenes look at making a program for a television series, and offers reflections on that process. The short dramatic film *The Edit* suggests how malleable film and video footage can be, and raises questions about the ethical issues implicit in manipulating material. *Track Stars*, about foley artists who create sound effects to match and extend the visuals, opens up discussion on the powerful and often overlooked contribution of sound to the total effect of a film or video.

Wherever possible, we have also tried to include print interviews with practitioners of some of the film crafts — cinematography, directing, editing and sound recording. We suggest that, as a rule, students be given these interviews *after* they've shared their own responses to the films.

Finally, this section contains a series of short study extracts selected from films included in this collection. These have been chosen for their potential as a springboard for activities involving shooting, sound, editing, narration and music.

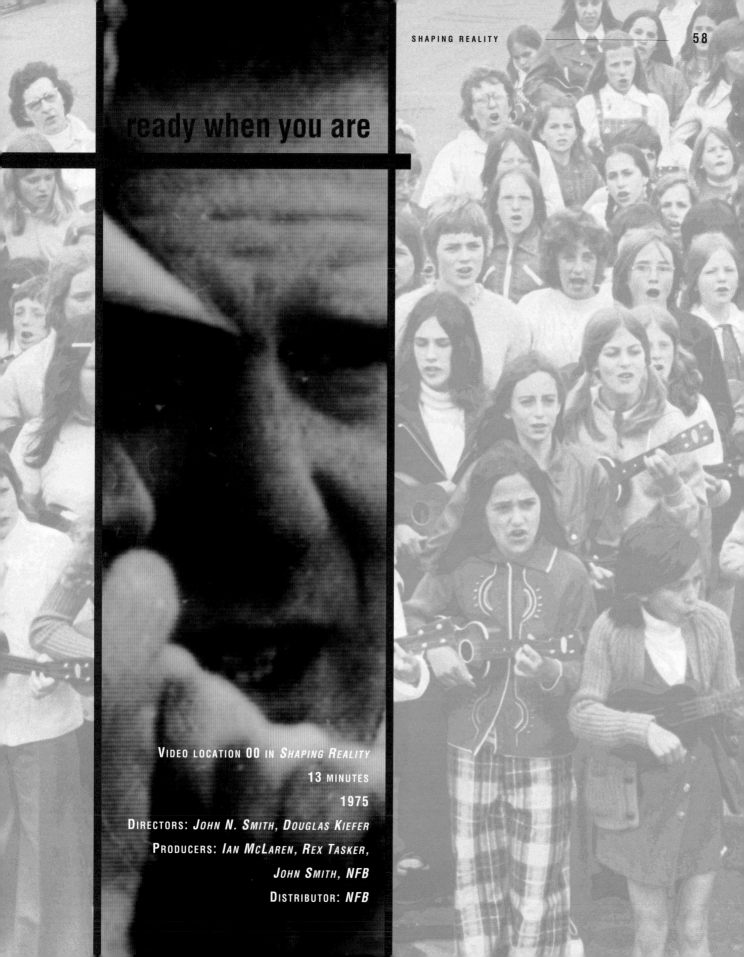

ready when you are

VIDEO LOCATION 00 IN *SHAPING REALITY*

13 MINUTES

1975

DIRECTORS: *JOHN N. SMITH, DOUGLAS KIEFER*

PRODUCERS: *IAN MCLAREN, REX TASKER,*

JOHN SMITH, NFB

DISTRIBUTOR: *NFB*

Ready When You Are is a light-hearted look at the logistics and potential pitfalls involved in a documentary shoot. In this case, the scene to be recorded — a segment for a TV special on Atlantic Canada — took place on a Halifax pier and involved several hundred schoolchildren standing on the dock in a bitterly raw wind and playing the ukelele. Getting proper coverage of the event involved the use of a helicopter, a couple of Navy destroyers, several tugboats, bullhorns and assorted walkie-talkies. High winds, the zoom shot that never happened, a critical lack of bathroom facilities: all these became factors with which the harassed crew and director had to deal.

Unlike most documentary films, the footage used in *Ready When You Are* was shot with more than one camera: there are close-ups, long shots, and medium shots from the bridge, from the helicopter, and from the pier itself. (See FILM AND VIDEO TERMS: AN INTRODUCTION, p. 260, for further explanation of these terms.) Track had to be laid the day before the shoot so that a camera, moving slowly along the track, could pan the faces of the children as they sang.

The children were on the pier for 3 to 4 hours, during which they were filmed and their singing was recorded. After the children left, with all their illusions about the glamor of filmmaking in tatters, the crew did pick-up shots of the location.

The film was put together in 3 to 4 weeks and changed dramatically in the editing room. It was originally conceived as a musical interlude in a television special, with some footage of the crew at work thrown in for good measure: but the shoot didn't produce the desired results. In a playful bit of problem solving, the directors and editor decided to focus on all the amusing mishaps that can — and do — befall a documentary crew. Once that final structure was decided upon, the little radio announcement that opens the film was manufactured, as a way of passing on necessary information without using an official narrator.

We have identified various crew members in this version of the film to give viewers an idea of who does what on a film shoot. Most documentary crews are very small, compared to crews on feature films, which can sometimes include several hundred people. In *Ready When You Are*, there were no lights, there were no costumes or props or backgrounds to prepare, but there were several cinematographers; consequently the crew numbered 10 to 15 people.

The Writer writes the script proposal, commentary and dialogue.

The Grip moves equipment, builds scaffolds, lays track.

The Line Producer coordinates all financial and scheduling aspects of the shooting phase of the production.

The Gaffer places lights where directed.

The Assistant Camera sets up the camera, keeps it clean, loads film, operates clapper board, keeps camera report sheet.

The Best Boy assists the gaffer, positions ca

The Composer composes the theme and music for the film.

The Narrator is the off camera voice of the film.

The Foley Artist makes sound effects in the studio for anything not recorded on location.

The Sound Editor synchronizes the sou track with the visuals, cuts in sound effe music and narration.

...ucer raises money, ...and is responsible for the ...oduction.

BANK

The Director (see below).

The Production Manager draws up the budgets and schedules, and manages them for the duration of the film.

The Boom Operator manoeuvres microphones.

The Sound Recordist records sounds and directs the boom operator.

The Director interprets the script or proposal into film, directs actors and production crew through the production manager and assistant director.

The Assistant Director maintains order on the set and makes sure actors are present when needed.

...nematographer or **Director of Photography** ...shots to the wishes of the director.

LAB

Illustration by Tracy Lewis

...e **Picture Editor** arranges the shots together into ...e visual form according to the director's vision of the ...m.

The Sound Mixer brings together all the individual sound tracks, combining them onto one cohesive master track.

Interview with Ali Kazimi
cinematographer/director

*The following material consists of excerpts from a
fairly lengthy interview. Kazimi was not part of the
crew on* Ready When You Are *but has worked as a
cinematographer and director in both film and video.*

What are some of the main differences between shooting documentary and shooting drama?

The main difference is in the degree of control one
has. When you're shooting a fiction film, you have
full control over lighting, over the set, even over the
way in which the actors move: should it be fast or
slow, should they walk into a shot, from which

direction should they come? In a documentary,
things can't usually be managed in the same way.

In documentary, you also have to remember that
you're not working with professional actors. That's
another crucial difference. You have to be aware
that the people you're photographing and asking to
repeat the same actions over and over again are not
used to this process. They soon discover that it's
very hard work (and usually they're not being paid
for it, either). Professional actors, on the other
hand, know exactly what's expected of them and
realize that they will have to keep doing something
until it's right for the director.

What happens when you're working in a cinéma vérité situation?

In cinéma vérité, you try to document real life as
it's unfolding. As the cinematographer you have to
be completely present and focussed. In a situation
like that, if somebody is having an argument and
you miss it, you can't ask them to stop and do it
again. So you have to know not only what's
happening but what may happen. That ability to
anticipate is based partly on a trust in your own
intuition and partly on experience.

In these situations, it's also very important that the
cinematographer, director and sound recordist all

Cinematographer, Tony Ianzelo

Another factor in a cinéma vérité situation is that you're often hand-holding the camera, which means that you have to be fairly fit physically. Veteran documentary cinematographers and sound recordists tend to have bad backs, because they're carrying fairly heavy loads on their shoulders for a long time and contorting themselves into all sorts of positions to try and get that shot — and then unwinding in complete agony.

In a documentary, especially an independent documentary, you try to keep the crew to a minumum. That means the director, the cinematographer and the sound recordist have to haul the cases of batteries, lights, camera magazines, film stock, tape stock. After you've exhausted yourself doing the shoot, it's not over. You still have to move these dozen cases back to the car, take them back to where you're staying, unload it all, lug it up to your room, unpack it, and check that everything is okay.

In drama, on the other hand, there are periods when you can walk away from the set. As director of photography, you have a mini-crew under you to whom you can delegate jobs. This gives you time to unwind between shots, and you also have full control of the situation.

be on the same wavelength; because once the flow of events is happening, you don't have time to stop and confer. That means that I have to know what the director's vision, concept, dream of the film is before we shoot. And I have to be in tune with the sound recordist, too. Say I'm on a shot that is framing the head and shoulders of someone who is talking. Now I want to move to a shot that includes six people around this person, which means that the shot will include more space above this person's head, where the microphone is. So, without stopping the camera, I have to develop a signalling system that lets the sound recordist know that I'm changing the shot size, so that the microphone will be moved to keep it out of the shot.

What is the job of a director of photography in a fiction film?

The director of photography's job is to design the visual look of the film. He or she works closely with the director to design shots and design camera movements, and also works with a lighting crew to design the lighting of the locations.

The director of photography (D.O.P.) works with a camera crew. Many D.O.P.'s do not operate the camera; instead, there's a camera operator who will actually run the camera. The director of photography will look through the viewfinder and set up the shot. There's another difference between documentary and drama: in a drama, a director can look through the viewfinder and know exactly what the camera is going to see. There's also a system whereby a video monitor is hooked up to a film camera so the director can see what the camera sees as the shot is being taken. In a documentary, however, the director has to have complete and implicit faith in the cinematographer, because the director has no way of seeing what is being photographed and how it's being photographed until the film comes back from the lab. So, during a cinéma vérité shoot, the cinematographer is actually sharing the role of the director.

What do you look for as a cinematographer?

I look for images that are rich and complex, with a certain emotional quality that goes beyond the obvious. Sometimes I like to have images that have a teasing quality to them so that you're revealing just enough to keep the viewer interested. This work is all about visual excitement; even it you're filming something very serious, you want to emphasize the notion that things are unfolding in front of the viewer, who is therefore motivated to be alert and pay attention.

Also, I'm trying to make an image that transcends the specific person or event that I'm photographing and somehow portrays an aspect of the universal human condition that everybody can identify with.

I'm very conscious of the ways things are represented visually, how people and situations are photographed. For example, I went to India to shoot the film *Song for Tibet* about two Tibetan-Canadians going back to Dharamsala, the seat of the Tibetan government-in-exile. The director Anne Henderson and I had talked about doing a montage about India to give viewers the sense of transition, of going from Canada to a different place.

Being from India myself, I'm very aware of the way India is usually represented. There are visual clichés associated with that country, a very romantic notion of an exotic land with the Taj Mahal, domes and minarets and temples and holy men, people in the Ganges, all the glamorous stuff. Then there's the other side, which is the urban squalor and the poverty and the destitution of the people.

I had to move beyond these stereotypes in terms of how I would shoot the montage in Delhi, the city where I grew up and spent most of my life. At the same time I didn't want to fall into a reactive mode in which I would dismiss all those images — the poverty, the Taj Mahal — and concentrate instead on suburban middle-class homes. I decided to be faithful to my own sense of the truth and reality of India, which is that things fall somewhere between the two stereotypes of destitution and romanticization.

That one-minute montage shows that there is, indeed, urban squalor, but at the same time, within that squalor I tried to present people as survivors, not victims. One of my favourite shots in that sequence is of a rickshaw driver. He's transporting a huge, impossibly heavy-looking load and he's pedalling like crazy. And yet, he's smiling, he's full of life. He's not a victim — he's empowered, he's there as a human being.

How do you deal with those concerns about representation when you are shooting in Canada?
I think it's critical to show the diverse and pluralistic nature of our society. And it's important that that be done visually, since we live in such a visually literate and image-dependent culture. And that can't be done in a tokenistic kind of way, where you sprinkle some non-white faces throughout a film. We need to have people from different races, ages, cultures being represented in a range of activities from kids playing in a sandbox to nuclear physicists meeting at a conference. I really think documentary filmmakers have a responsibility to get beyond the usual visual conventions, because they are reflecting the world around them. So it's important to address these issues: Who's being photographed? How are they being photographed? In what role are they being photographed?

—TORONTO, 1992

ACTIVITIES

1
camera angles

As you watch *Ready When You Are*, keep track of how many different places the cameras are shooting from. Usually in a documentary film there is only one camera; therefore, in order to cover an event from different angles, it is necessary to move the camera during the event or to film the event more than one time. Then, during the editing process, the shots from various angles are juxtaposed so it looks as though the filming was happening simultaneously rather than sequentially. Pick a person, event or situation and see how many different angles you can shoot it from.

2
mood creation — camera

Create a mood — threatening, inviting, humorous — by the way in which you photograph people or a situation. How close is the camera to the subject? From what angle (low angle, eye level, high angle) is the shot being taken? Is it in black-and-white or colour? What is included in the background or foreground of the shot? From whose point of view is the shooting being done? Experiment with these variables. How do they affect the mood of what is being shown? How do they influence the emotions of the viewers?

3
mood creation — lighting

The way in which a person or scene is lit greatly influences the effect of what is shot. Turn off the overhead lights and draw the curtains. Experiment by moving a light source around so the subject is lit in different ways — below, overhead, straight on, from the side, from the back. What different moods are created by the differences in lighting?

4
lighting

How would you light a person who has dark skin? Light skin? (Videotape different people with different skin tones in front of both dark and light backgrounds to see what problems might arise with the exposure. Try videotaping two people with contrasting skin tones in the same shot.)

5
point of view

The point of view from which one chooses to shoot a scene has a critical, though often ignored, influence on the audience. Try shooting an event (a football game, a school outing, a demonstration) from different points of view. For instance, a demonstration could be covered in close-ups; from the middle of the demonstration looking out; from the outside looking in; looking at the feet of the demonstrators; across police lines; from the point of view of a toddler in a stroller. See *The Journey* (THE POLITICS OF TRUTH, video location 54), which analyzes CBC coverage of an anti-nuclear demonstration. Also see Joyce Wieland's film *Solidarity* which documents a demonstration by shooting the legs and feet of all those who marched. (*Solidarity* is available from Canadian Filmmakers Distribution Centre, 67A Portland St., Toronto, Ont. M5V 2M9. Tel: (416) 593-1808.)

6

See the Activities section of "City of Gold", p. 21, for exercises related to framing. What do you choose to include in a shot? What do you leave out? How, for instance, would you frame a person who is deaf and signing?

7

Take five pictures of the school cafeteria. What was included? What was left out? Have the cafeteria staff take some pictures. What did they shoot? How were their images similar to and different from yours?

8

Using a camcorder, move with the camera as you shoot a scene. What does movement add to the shot, as you move towards, away from, or circle? What is the difference in feeling between zooming into a scene and actually moving the camera in closer?

9

You might want to examine the following films/videos included in this collection as particularly fine examples of cinematography: *Sandspit to Dildo, Flamenco at 5:15* (THE POETRY OF MOTION, video locations 86 and 56), *Anybody's Son Will Do* and *Lonely Boy* (THE CANDID EYE?, video locations 52 and 00).

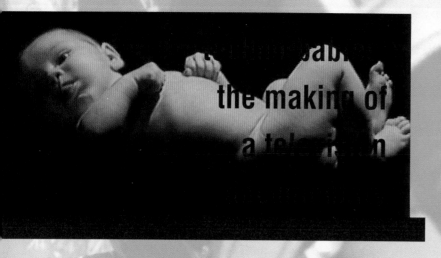

VIDEO LOCATION **13** IN *SHAPING REALITY*

18 MINUTES

1993

DIRECTOR: *DAVID ADKIN*

PRODUCER: *MICHAEL ALLDER, NFB*

This short video, created for *Constructing Reality*, offers a behind-the-scenes look at the making of a television documentary for the award-winning weekly CBC series *Man Alive*. As the show had a fairly quick turnaround time, we were able to document most stages of its production from beginning to end. In total, the TV program took about 2 1/2 months to produce. Research — finding the subjects and locations — was done over a two- to three-week period. The actual production — shooting and sound recording — took seven days, spread over four weeks. Another three weeks were devoted to post-production — editing, taping the host's narration, composing the music, preparing the relevant graphics.

The program was produced relatively quickly because it is part of a weekly TV series in the current affairs department. It therefore had a specific format that had to be followed — a host, a half-hour time slot — and tight deadlines that had to be met. F.M. Morrison, the director profiled in *Techno-babies*, commented on the demands of this kind of production: "I work for a weekly television series and, on the whole, it's a great maw that you feed. The odd time it turns out really well, and you get something that is better than you could hope for within the confines and limitations of working in television."

Not all shows, however, are put together in-house for a weekly air-date. Some network staff directors are given more time and resources to produce documentaries than is usual in current affairs or information programming, which needs to be fairly topical. Still other programs are co-produced by the networks with independent filmmakers, a variety of funding agencies, and broadcasters in other countries. Films and videos can also be purchased from independent filmmakers or from film-producing agencies, such as the National Film Board, after they have been completed. In this collection, most of the films and videos were made by independents or by directors working for the NFB.

Documentaries produced by independent filmmakers tend to be made under conditions that differ from those shown in our *Techno-babies* piece. Academy Award-winning independent director Barbara Kopple believes that five years constitutes the time-frame natural to documentary filmmaking. "You don't know what's going to happen but you know that it doesn't happen in quick moments. You have to be there [in a community] a long time . . . . That's my style of filmmaking, to struggle to get in there deep; to live, work, and immerse myself in a community."

Do the different kinds of conditions under which documentaries get made affect the kinds of films that are produced? What are some of the advantages and drawbacks of being an independent producer rather than a network employee? To discover some answers to these and other questions, we talked to John Walker, one of Canada's most accomplished documentary filmmakers, about why he chooses to follow the independent path.

the filmmaker as camel: interview with John Walker

Being an independent documentary filmmaker in Canada is a lot like being a camel: you get only a little bit of water and you have to sustain yourself on it forever. And you're a funny-looking creature, not particularly attractive to most broadcasters. They're not quite sure what to do with you.

There are certainly major differences between being an independent filmmaker and working as an employee for a network. If you're willing to take the financial risks, as an independent you can make the films you want, the way you want to make them. In my case, for instance, I can control how much time I spend researching, how much time I spend with the subjects of my films, how much time I spend editing.

Having that control means you don't have to deliver a finished film in a very short period. You can create your own pace, you can spend much more time in pre-production, and you can get to know your subjects really well before you do the actual shooting. And that's important because usually the more time you spend on a film, the greater the richness of what you produce. For example, knowing your subjects is going to help enormously in terms of how you see them and how you film them. Because if you know them well, then you know when they're being silly or doing something on camera that's not really authentic. You know when it's a superficial rather than a genuine portrait.

All this you cannot do in television because there simply isn't time. Instead, you have a researcher calling up people, you go film them, and in 2 to 3 weeks you have a show; that makes it hard to do something with meaning. It took me six years to make the film *Strand: Under the Dark Cloth*. For the *Hand of Stalin* series I spent six months researching — doing background reading, thinking, spending time with subjects in the field.

Another reason for being an independent is that as long as a broadcaster isn't involved in the production funding, nobody else has to approve what you do. You don't have to deal with an executive producer who can say, "I don't like this or that", which is when you get disagreements erupting over content.

You often hear filmmakers say, "I'm making something for television." What does that mean? Television is nothing, it's just a means to broadcast a piece of film. The ideal way to work is to make your films as an independent and then sell them to television. Then you're not making them "for television", you're making them for yourself and if someone wants to broadcast them, great. Luckily, there are networks like Channel 4 in Britain that are open to letting you work the way you need to.

The down side is that funding is a big part of every independent filmmaker's life. It can be very frustrating, slogging away to raise the money you need. In Canada, there's no longer any single source of money, so, as an independent, you're forced to pull together various bits of funding. That means if you have an idea, you take it to the CBC, you take it to the NFB, in England to Channel 4 or the BBC, to other international broadcasters and to provincial broadcasters like TVO. You can end up

with ten different sources of funding, and that can get very complicated: there are a lot of different masters to please. For instance, you might find yourself in a situation where nine funders like what you've produced but the tenth refuses to broadcast it. In that case, what you usually try to do is to make a version specifically for that funder.

Why do I keep doing it? I think that what drives you as a filmmaker is the love of the medium. Ultimately, there's something very addicting — and compelling, too — about telling stories with sounds and images. It may be a lot of hard work but it's also just so much fun to do.

—TORONTO, 1992

IDEAS *for* DISCUSSION

1

Was there any information about the making of the program **Techno-babies** *that surprised you, that you hadn't known about?*

2

In her comment quoted on p. 69, F.M. Morrison mentions the confines and limitations of working in television, at least for a weekly series. What do you think these restrictions might be? What might be the advantages of working in this context?

3

What do the terms "the independent voice" and "the independent eye" suggest to you? After reading John Walker's interview, discuss which factors about working as an independent seemed to you most important and most appealing? What drawbacks did you see? (For further background information about different conditions under which filmmakers work, see the interviews with directors Cynthia Scott, p. 244, and Brenda Longfellow, p. 45. Also, see the material in THE POLITICS OF TRUTH, *p. 113, about objectivity, subjectivity and point of view in filmmaking.)*

4

Another reason for being an independent is that, as long as a broadcaster isn't involved in the production funding, nobody else has to approve what you do.
JOHN WALKER

What do you think the term "self-censorship" might mean? How do you think it might operate in filmmaking? Do you think independent filmmakers might also censor themselves? How and why?

5

Discuss Peter Downie's comment, "I'm really leery about how superficial television can be, and how it can present everything in a 30-second sound bite and how it's all slick. Well, life isn't slick and life isn't a 30-second sound bite. That's the hardest part for me, to try and remember that these are people's lives." Do you agree or disagree with his statement? Give reasons for your position.

For further ideas and activities related to time restrictions in the media and what they can mean for the portrayal of persons, events, and situations, see "New Shoes", *p. 24, and* "The Journey", *p. 134. A relevant film on the subject is* Only the News that Fits, *available in the collection* Media & Society, *or as a separate film, from the NFB.*

ACTIVITIES

Before Viewing

Ask viewers to keep track, as they watch, of how many people are involved in the making of this program, what jobs they are doing, and the different stages the program goes through from beginning to end.

After Viewing

1

One of the prerequisites for making a documentary is being granted access to the people or events you want to film. In *Techno-babies: The Making of a Television Documentary*, F.M. Morrison talks about some of the difficulties she faced in gaining such access. List two or three subjects about which you would like to make a documentary. Working in pairs, present your ideas to another person who asks you the following questions: To tell your story, who, where and what would you want to shoot? Whose permission would you have to get? How do you think you would do that? Which idea appeals to you most? Which idea do you think has the most possibility of being made?

2

In her interview with us, Louise Lore, executive producer of *Man Alive*, commented: "Realistically, a program doesn't survive in the CBC prime-time schedule unless it can prove that it has a wide audience appeal, particularly when we appear on a night when commercial sales are important." F.M. Morrison stated, in regard to the question of ratings, "We want people to watch this stuff. I don't think any of us particularly wants to program for small minorities. We're working on a national network and we hope to deliver an audience for that network."

How do these attitudes differ from that of Sylvia Hamilton, director of *Black Mother, Black Daughter*? She stated: "I wanted to [make the film] for the younger generation and for the women too [in the Black community], so they could really see themselves. These groups were my core audience. *Black Mother, Black Daughter* wasn't made to educate white people about the Black community, although if that happened, it was marvellous."

Choose a topic — a person, an issue, an event, a place — about which you would like to make a film. Who are you making it for? How does your idea of the film's audience (or audiences) affect what you do and how you do it? Assuming that you have made your film or video as an independent producer, how will you ensure that people get to see it?

the edit

VIDEO LOCATION 31 IN *SHAPING REALITY*

14 MINUTES

1982

DIRECTOR: *MICHAEL TODD*

PRODUCER: *MIRUS COMMUNICATIONS*

DISTRIBUTOR: *KINETIC*

An editor interviewed for *Constructing Reality* commented that many people think that film editing involves snipping out the bad parts and joining together the good ones. In fact, editing — the process by which structure and meaning are created by juxtaposing individual shots as well as whole sequences — plays a crucial role in the shaping of any film. This is especially true of documentaries that are shot without scripted dialogue and without the control over sound, picture and performance that are associated with fiction filmmaking. It is not unusual for the makers of a cinéma vérité documentary, committed to recording the hurly-burly of events as they unfold, to have to transform at least 20 hours of raw footage into 60-90 minutes of finished film. Clearly, choices have to be made: material has to be selected and shaped, devices to compress the narrative have to be settled upon, and the most effective way of telling the story has to be found.

Much of the work of editing documentaries involves building sequences (or scenes) and then moving them around to see where they are most powerful and resonant. Many of these shifts influence the emerging meaning of the film, as viewers "read" a particular sequence in terms of what precedes and follows it. It is the ability, through editing, to make the same material mean different things in different places that both gives rise to perplexing ethical questions, and creates serendipitous pleasure when something totally unforeseen suddenly "works".

The Edit, a drama with comic overtones, is premised upon the malleability of film / video footage, and the consequent potential pitfalls for overzealous filmmakers and unwary viewers. A television news reporter, determined to nail a political candidate for apparently shady business practices, gleefully cuts and shapes the interview he conducted in order to make as damning a case as possible. Not to be outwitted, the unscrupulous financier sends in a mole who re-edits the same material to create very different evidence.

In this film, the manipulation and ethical dilemmas have been thrown into high relief. Most of the perplexing decisions that editors and directors commonly face tend to be more subtle, as both John Walker and Steve Weslak discuss in interviews.

To give people a chance to experience for themselves how editing can shape (and re-shape) meaning through juxtaposition, we have included a series of stills at the end of this section (pp. 83-86) to be used in editing exercises.

interview with Roushell Goldstein, editor

In this excerpted interview, Roushell Goldstein explains the stages a film goes through during the editing process. Though different technology is involved in editing videotape, the stages are basically the same.

Right now, I'm working on a one-hour film about welfare mothers, which will take me a number of months to edit. There's a lot of footage to get through — maybe 25 to 30 hours — and it can take a long time to build up the story. In documentary, you're not working with professional actors, so any awkward moments have to be compensated for during the editing.

When I first begin to work on a film, I look at all the footage with the director. We have lots of conversations about her vision of the film because I have to understand what she's trying to achieve. But I also have to relate to the material myself because I need to choose the shots and the performances that will go into the film.

I make stacks of notes about what I'm seeing and hearing. Then we discuss some sort of possible structure. This structure comes out of the material and shouldn't be imposed upon it. (It reminds me of the Inuit notion of sculpture, where you search for the spirit of the figure contained within the stone and then you work to set it free.)

The first cut is called an *assembly* and contains all the shots that you would like to see in the film. In this case, the assembly is five hours long and has a structure of sequences [or scenes] loosely strung together. Each sequence is noted on a separate index card. I describe the visual sequence in black ink and the idea behind that sequence in red. These cards are then stuck up on a wall in the order we'd like to see them. Once we've got that far, we start moving the cards around like pieces of a jigsaw puzzle.

For instance, in this film we might have the following sequences about one particular woman: getting breakfast, sending her kids to school, being at the laundromat, going to Legal Aid, arriving at the food bank, waiting to have her documents verified, getting the food.

As we look at these visuals, I'm also having to decide what she will be saying. I can use sound that was recorded at the same time as the picture and/or I can choose to insert, as a voice-over, part of a conversation that might have been recorded at a separate time. So sound and picture are both malleable elements, and I can use them to complement or counterpoint one another.

After we look at the assembly two to three times, we begin to see a structure emerging. Some sequences seem more important, others less. For instance, in the film on welfare mothers, three women independently talk about how they feel when others accuse them of being lazy or of cheating the system. We try to choose the one who is the strongest. Sequences and themes start to emerge and we end up with a *rough cut,* which can be between two and three hours.

The next challenge comes when you have to start whittling and trimming. The chiselling becomes much more specific and detailed. It may involve cutting down the visuals or taking out sentences or phrases that seem superfluous. Finally, we arrive at a *fine cut,* which often runs just over an hour.

When we're all agreed that there is no more to be done in terms of changing, adding to, or deleting shots, and the credits have been included, then the picture is locked. This means that no more picture changes should be made and the sound editing can begin. *(See p. 93 for a description of the sound editing process.)*

—TORONTO, 1992

interview with John Walker, independent documentary filmmaker

During this excerpt from an interview, John Walker talks about how the selection and juxtaposition of footage during the editing process can shape an audience's perception of the person or situation on the screen. This power can lead to ethical problems for the filmmaker, who may find herself in the position of having to make some critical choices.

When you're making a documentary, you're moulding people's opinions and feelings about the material they're looking at. That's the nature of film. During editing, you can really shape a character; in that way, it's like drama. You do that by what you put in and by what you leave out. You can also create your subjects as good guys or bad guys in terms of how they're contextualized in the overall story — who they come before, who they come after, all that has an impact on how you perceive those people.

The most difficult situation is when you're portraying a character that could be perceived as negative. That's hard because you have a responsibility to those people whose trust you've gained, those people who've allowed you to film them. For example, in the series of films I made about Russia, we learn how during the Stalin period, people got deported and millions of them died. We had this one character who was a member of the Communist Party and he deported 5000 people from his little town. The weight of how good or bad, how innocent or guilty this person seemed was totally in our hands — just by placement. In this case, if we had placed him near the beginning of the film before we had spelled out the horror caused by the deportations, his actions would have seemed much less culpable than if we placed his story later, in the context of what actually happened.

In the end, I did place his story later for dramatic effect, but I was careful, through other choices I made in the interview, to show that the blame lay with him not as an individual but as a member of a totalitarian regime. It's too simple to point a finger and say, "It's all his fault". Finally, you have to decide: how hard do you want to come down on him?

These are the kind of ongoing debates you, as a director, have with the editor as you try to work through these problems. Because it's the exact same material, but how you shift around your bits of film — the order in which you present them — can totally change an audience's perception of how good or bad someone is. That's the worst part of the process for me. I much prefer when I'm not in the position of having to make those kind of judgments about people's character.

I do use guidelines. They're based on spending time with my subjects, on getting a sense of who they are. For instance, you never use all of an interview. You may have talked together for a couple of hours in research and a couple of hours on film. So out of a minimum of three to four hours conversation with someone, you may end up with five to ten minutes on screen. During editing, I try to make sure that the piece I have chosen to include is a fair representation, that I haven't selected the one bit that is totally out of character with everything else that the person has said. And I use my own intuitions, because as a documentary filmmaker you get very sensitive about understanding people; your intuitions become attuned to how people tell stories, and you have to trust that kind of knowledge, too.

—TORONTO, 1992

interview with Steve Weslak, editor

In this interview, Steve Weslak talks about the differences between editing documentary and drama, the role of the editor, and ethical considerations that arise during the course of cutting a film.

What's the main difference between editing drama and editing documentary?

With drama, you're following a script which is being produced under very controlled conditions. The lighting is controlled, the sound is controlled, the story is there. So, as an editor, your first cut can be a fine cut. You can begin working immediately on all sorts of subtle details.

With documentary, you often have to spend months figuring out what is this film about? What is its structure? Where does it start? Where does it end? It may sound surprising but in a documentary you actually have more choices about what you can do with the material. You can take a moment and expand it and really examine it in a way you can't in a drama where the story has to get told. For instance, in the film I'm working on about gay and lesbian youth, there's a demonstration on Yonge Street in Toronto. We could step-print that footage and slow it down. [For further information about step printing, see the section on optical printing in "*Our Marilyn*", p. 49.] We could freeze-frame the images or do effects that would make them look like photographs. We could have people talk about the incident and then cut to the scene itself. In a drama, even if the time sequence is very disjointed, you're telling a story and, essentially, you just tell it once. You do it, and you get out of it, and you're on to something else.

What's your role as an editor?

The main thing that an editor brings to a production is that he or she is supposed to be an outsider. I always think that I have to help the director see things the way an audience might see them. The other aspect that interests me is coming to realize the difference between what a film seems to be about and what it's really about.

For instance, let's say you're doing a film that is apparently about mountain climbing. Anyone looking at the film sees people packing in supplies, setting up a camp, climbing, setting up another camp, weathering out a storm. But, in fact, what the film is more likely about is the human spirit that can triumph over adversity. So there's a subtext running through the film that's never made explicit, but nevertheless everyone understands that this is what it's about.

As an editor, you also have to put the material together in such a way that you pique the audience's interest. A film may be very slow to start, perhaps because you're meeting characters or learning about the situation; somehow you need to get the audience through that portion of the film. Say it's the mountain climbing film. You might have people in England packing their bags, going off to buy some piece of equipment, making sure that they've got their shots, and going out to the airport. You want to show all this material because it's part of the process of leaving home, but it doesn't make for an exciting opening. So what you might do to make the film more interesting is to

take the final few minutes of the film — the climbers struggling the last hundred yards up the top of the mountain when a raging storm hits them — and show that at the very beginning. Just as the storm hits and everything wipes out, the screen would go white, you'd come up with the title, you'd come out of white, and see the skyline of London with a line over it saying "London, Six Months Earlier". Then the audience knows they're going to end up in a really exciting situation on a mountain somewhere.

That's a very simple example of how you could manipulate material to a dramatic end or for pacing, for instance. Because when you're editing documentaries, basically what you're doing is moving all the scenes around constantly until you find the best combination.

I guess another way to look at editing or structuring a film is that it's a lot like composing. The main story of the film is like a melody that's running through it. Then the way that you pace a certain scene, the kind of music that you put in, how rapid the dialogue is, how long the shots run, all these elements play on the melody line.

Does the manipulation involved in editing ever lead to ethical dilemmas?

Sometimes. I'll give you an example from a

documentary I worked on, called *Deadly Currents,* set in Israel. We wanted to include part of an interview with an Israeli soldier whose face had been badly burned, but we had no visuals we could use as he described the accident. Clearly we hadn't been there at the time of the incident.

In the interview, the soldier says, "We were going through an Arab village, we were moving slowly, I was sitting in the back of a jeep." It so happened that our cinematographer, from a jeep, had shot some footage of the backs of soldiers in an Arab village so those images fit very well. Then the soldier continues: "A grenade or a bomb was thrown into the jeep and it burst into flames."

At one point during the shoot, the crew had passed a car wreck at night. The car was on fire and the cinematographer got a close-up of the flames coming out of the car windows. So I cut that image in, along with some shots of a Molotov cocktail being made.

Now, if you really wanted to, you could say that we were cheating. We totally fabricated this incident, visually. After all, here we were making a real documentary about real people and real events and we shouldn't do this. Both the director and I thought long and hard about this, and finally we decided what we would do was to show the film to an audience and question them about that scene. Did they have any trouble with it? Did it bother them that we did that? We obviously weren't with the man making the molotov cocktail and we weren't with the soldiers.

So we showed the film and virtually everyone that saw the film had no problem with it. When we asked them why, they said they realized that, because of the way we had approached the footage, the incident was like a dream, that what they were seeing was someone's memories of an incident. No one took it literally, no one believed that we had had a camera in three different places shooting the event. And, in fact, if you look carefully at the film, you'll see that the fire is at night and the other shots are during the daytime. But the impact of seeing the flames pouring out the car windows is so powerful that no one even noticed. Since the audience reacted that way, we felt totally justified in running the scene.

When there is an ethical consideration like the example I just described, I think you have to bring it up, try it with an audience, and see how they're interpreting the scene. You can't keep it quiet.

—Toronto, 1992

IDEAS *for* DISCUSSION

1

How much manipulation of raw footage is fair? Does "fair" matter? When does manipulation seem acceptable and when not? Have you ever manipulated material while editing a video you have shot? (You might want to refer to the presentation of this idea in the Steve Weslak interview (p. 79). Also see the material on reconstruction and fiction/fact in "Docudrama: Fact and Fiction", p. 124).

2

Discuss Roushell Goldstein's comment, "structure comes out of the material and shouldn't be imposed upon it." Can you think of other areas — of art, of film, of life — in which this attitude or approach would apply as well?

3

What responsibilities do you think documentary filmmakers and editors have to the people in their films? To the film itself? In what kinds of situations might the two come in conflict?

4

In his interview, Steve Weslak stated that his role was "to help the director see things the way an audience might see them." Discuss.

ACTIVITIES

1

In groups of four or five people, look at photocopies of the stills on pages 83-86. Construct a story using 7 of the 16 photographs. Decide on dialogue, narration, music and sound effects where these seem called for. Have each group present to the others your sequences/stories, and explain why you chose those particular photos. What conclusions can you draw from this experience?

After doing this activity, discuss John Walker's comment: "You can create your subjects as good guys or bad guys in terms of how they're contextualized in the overall story: who they come before, who they come after has an impact on how you perceive those people."

2

Have students choose a series of photographs from old family albums. Ask them to arrange photocopies of these pictures so they form a story line. They can experiment with copying the photos at different sizes, so as to emphasize some and downplay the importance of others. Are words needed to expand upon the meaning inherent in the arrangement of the visuals? If so, write a narration (first person? third person?) to lace the images together.

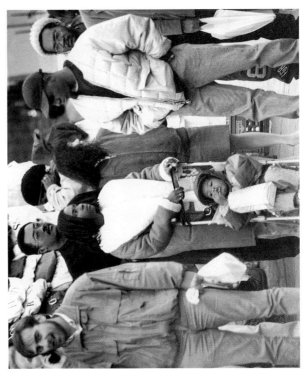

3

For interesting examples of editing in this collection, see *Memorandum* (WAYS OF STORYTELLING, video location 55), *Lonely Boy* (THE CANDID EYE?, video location 00), *Flamenco at 5:15* and *Sandspit to Dildo* (THE POETRY OF MOTION, video locations 56 and 86). Also check the Study Extracts (SHAPING REALITY, video location 54) for examples related to editing.

FURTHER RESOURCES

print

For discussion of some of the ethical questions involved in documentary filmmaking, see Michael Rabiger's *Directing the Documentary*, Second Edition (Boston: Focal Press, 1992).

track stars

VIDEO LOCATION 45 IN *SHAPING REALITY*

8 MINUTES

1978

DIRECTOR: *TERRY BURKE*

PRODUCER: *MOVEMENT FILMS/FILM ARTS*

DISTRIBUTOR: *KINETIC INC.*

Track Stars shows two foley artists in a studio, flinging themselves about as they create sound effects appropriate to the action unfolding on the screen. The film was originally shot in 35mm as a theatrical short, so the image, on video, is obviously greatly reduced. Since *Track Stars* uses a split-screen technique, some of the details, on video, may be hard to spot from the back of a room. However the constructed nature of movie sound is clear, as is the exuberance with which these two men attack their work.

We have included *Track Stars* in this section to open discussion on the role of sound in film and video. Though sound seems "invisible" to most people's appreciation of a film, it is, in fact, a crucial factor in shaping viewers' emotional responses to the images they see on the screen. The rest of this section includes an interview with a sound recordist, some background information on the work of foley artists, and a description of the stages involved in producing a finished soundtrack.

Some general suggestions for sound-related activities are included here; others appear in the discussions of individual films. These activities can connect with sound in poetry and with descriptive- writing exercises. Also see notes on the Study Extracts (pp. 98), which present ideas for specific sound activities.

SOME SOUND TERMS

MOS: *picture recorded without sound ("mit out sound")*

WILD SOUND: *sound recorded without picture (can be used for sound effects, ambience, voice-over)*

SYNC SOUND: *sound and picture recorded simultaneously*

interview with Brian Avery, sound recordist

What's your job as a sound recordist?

In a documentary, usually you're dealing with people — and the people do things and, mostly, they talk. So your job as a sound recordist is to bring back the most intelligible dialogue recording that you can, technically. Because conditions in a documentary are often uncontrolled, you have to strive against very bad odds to do that.

If you want ideal sound, you have to remove all background noise, have fairly acoustically dead environments, and get mikes pretty close. The real world, however, isn't an acoustic studio; in fact, it's usually extremely noisy. To compensate, you have to use the best possible mike for the person and put it in the right position. So that's the first level: technical expertise.

Then you've also got to be aware of your impact on the people whom you're filming, which means being laid-back and fairly chameleon-like in your approach to them. Sensitivity is required, and a great deal of trust, because people will be much more open if they have faith in you and your project.

People often tend to say more things when the camera is switched off than when it's on. If you're an alert recordist and you study human nature, you can often get material on tape which will later add a lot to the film's content. And there are things happening in every environment in the soundscape which, when you pull them out and focus a mike on them, can add a terrific flavour to what you're doing. It can be simple background sound effects or content material like car radios or taxi radios or intercoms or walkie-talkies or kids playing on the street.

These are all audio vignettes which can be laid on the soundtrack. Sometimes they don't even have to have visuals. In fact, sound in documentaries is especially exciting when subtle sound cues are used not only as reinforcement for the picture but also as counterpoint to the picture.

Can you give an example?

I once worked on a film about population explosion. Normally when you have crowds on the screen, you would have crowd noises on the soundtrack. In this case, we used silence and the sound of a metronome ticking away with the shot of a crowd scene. The visual of millions of people with only the sound of a ticking clock, used for symbolic rather than literal purposes, was a very potent counterpoint of sound and picture.

Because we live in a world that is filled with sounds, if you leave periods of silence, the next sound that you hear after the silence is very telling. I did sound for a film called *North of Superior*. For about a week and a half, I spent every day on location recording tons and tons and tons of fire sound effects, everything from a single leaf burning to a branch to a tree to a whole tree to a whole tree exploding, and all from different perspectives and different distances. Luckily, the sound editor was a really skilled person and had enormous patience. He catalogued all those sounds. So when the forest-fire sequence was edited, every time a little detail happened on this enormous IMAX screen — for instance a tree flaring up in one corner — he had cut the sound to match the picture beautifully. But the point of my story is that, having built up a huge forest-fire sequence from the tiniest beginnings to a raging inferno, the director at that point decided to cut from an enormous crescendo to silence. Then we see trees being planted to symbolize the rebirth of the forest. At the same time we hear minute insects, mosquitoes, emerging out of the silence. So that was a very poetic use of sound.

What are some of the differences between doing sound for drama and sound for documentary?
Working on a TV series or a feature film, you're usually part of a large team, 25-50 people, all jumping around and running like crazy. In a documentary crew, on the other hand, which usually runs three to four people, when the times are right you become a wee little family.

Doing sound for a drama is a purely technical job, whereas documentaries I find much more energizing and interesting because of the input I can have in terms of the content and the esthetics of the piece. For example, in terms of sound, I'd ask the director: Do you want it to be a perfectly linear film? Do you want to introduce some craziness? Do you want to use found sound? We'd talk about if and where music is going to be used, if and where narration is going to be used. Is the film going to be narrator-driven with the voice of God intoning away, or will it be interview-driven? These decisions affect how, what and where you tape. For instance, if you film something with jet planes in the background and you see the jet planes on the screen, there's no problem. If, however, you film an interview which you know may be used for voice-over and it's got jet planes on the sound track, you're out of luck — because you can't add jet planes into a picture of the marshes at the top of the Don Valley. You have to consider these factors before choosing your locations. All these decisions have to be carefully thought out before shooting or else the resulting problems have to be solved in the editing room later.

I do think it's important to realize when you watch television or go to the theatre to see a film that very rarely are the things that you hear the things that were there when the original recording was made. Almost always there's a lot of artifice involved in setting up what you hear.

—TORONTO, 1992

constructing sound:
how soundtracks are made

The foley artist is only one of many unsung heroes and heroines of movie sound. The making of a film or TV soundtrack is a creative and technical process involving many people. During the post-production period (after the actual shooting has been completed), sound effects must be found or created, music must be composed and performed, narration must be written and recorded. All of these elements must then be edited and "synchronized" to the picture, to create a listening experience that will complement the experience of watching the film.

Much of the sound we hear in a film — even in a documentary — was not recorded at the time of filming; instead, it has been added by the filmmakers during the sound-editing stage. Sound editing ensures that the soundtrack is clear and understandable. It allows the filmmakers to enhance or counterpoint what we see and hear, and to create a mood and atmosphere for the action on the screen. Sound editing begins only after the picture editing is finished, and may take weeks or months, depending on the length and complexity of the film.

The steps involved in finishing a soundtrack are described below. For a visual reference, please refer to the illustration depicting the various stages and people involved in filmmaking, p. 60.

preparing for the sound edit

First, the sound editors meet with the director to watch the film and to discuss ideas for the soundtrack. What mood does the director wish to create in each scene? What sound effects might be used to create this mood? At this stage the director also meets with the music composer to discuss which scenes require music and what kind of music might be appropriate. (Filmmakers who cannot afford to hire a composer and musicians can buy pre-recorded music from a "stock music library" — a company that makes and sells music specifically for films and commercials.)

After meeting with the director, the sound editors view the film again, scene by scene, to make a detailed list of all the effects ("FX") that will be needed. These FX must then be found or created. Many can be found in "sound FX libraries" — pre-recorded collections of sound that can be purchased on disc or tape. The sound team may also go out on location to record or create specific FX.

Once all sound FX have been collected and transferred to videotape or magnetic-film stock for editing, the actual sound edit begins.

the sound edit

The sound editor's first, basic job is to make sure the sound, especially the dialogue, is clear and understandable (unless the director wants it otherwise). This may involve replacing words obliterated by such background noises as door slams, microphone bumps or other accidents. Sometimes lines of dialogue must be re-recorded by the actors or participants, and re-synchronized with the picture. Sounds that were missing at the time of shooting must be added; sounds that were unclear, replaced.

Certain sounds, such as those of movement (for example, footsteps, scuffles) may be given to foley artists to re-create in the foley studio. This is often less time-consuming and expensive than trying to collect and edit-in each effect individually.

By adding background or "ambient" sounds, the sound editor can heighten the sense of time and place in a scene. An ordinary shot of a neighbourhood street can be brought to life by adding the sounds of dogs barking and children playing. A downtown scene might require traffic noise and ambulance sirens wailing in the distance.

Sound can also be used to create a particular mood or atmosphere. An ominous rumble of thunder in the distance, a ticking clock in a lonely room, church bells tolling, or children laughing in a playground all carry different, often subliminal, emotional meanings for an audience.

The various sound elements — voices of different characters, FX, ambience, music — are separated on different "tracks" or reels, in preparation for the final sound mix.

the sound mix

The sound mix is the point at which the final creative touches are added to the film. In the sound mixing studio, all the individual sound elements are blended into the finished soundtrack that will be heard by the audience.

During the mix, the sound mixer works from "cue sheets" that show, in chart form, the sound effects or elements on each separate track, and the order in which they occur. (It is the equivalent of the conductor's score for an orchestral composition). Using the cue sheets as a guide, the sound mixer can control the volume of each element, deciding which sounds at a given moment will be loud and prominent, and which will be soft or background. Sound fade-ins and dissolves are also done. The number of tracks that need to be mixed depends on the type of film and the complexity of the soundtrack: how many characters are speaking, how many sound FX are happening at the same time, whether there is music, and so on. The simplest film may involve the mixing of only two or three tracks, while a large feature may involve 60 or more.

Once mixed, the soundtrack is ready to be sent to the lab to be combined with the finished picture. Then the film is complete.

the work of the foley artist

When we did test screenings of Track Stars *in various high-school classrooms, the students had a number of questions about how foley artists worked. Andy Malcolm, one of the foley artists involved with the film, gave the following information.*

You might ask, why are foley artists needed anyhow? Why isn't all sound recorded right on location? The main problem with location sound is that you cannot control the sound elements separately. To create a rich, layered soundtrack, each element must be separate, distinct and controllable. Only then can the mixer effectively combine all the sound elements in the final track. Usually during a shoot, the sound recordist is

concentrating on a single bit of action, most often the dialogue, trying to make sure that it's clearly audible. Almost everything else is added at a later date.

Foley artists are named after Jack Foley, who worked at Universal Pictures in Hollywood during the '30s and '40s. He developed a system to add synchronous sound to movies and felt strongly that while he was creating the sounds, the foley artist had to act out the scene to get into the spirit of the story, just like the actors did on the set. He once estimated that he had walked 5000 miles in the studio, just doing footsteps.

A foley theatre is acoustically designed for recording extremely quiet sounds. The picture is projected onto a large screen or played on a video monitor. The foley artist watches the picture and performs sound in sync with the action. Usually, you can create sound for about 10 minutes of film per day.

A foley theatre looks much like a junkyard. Along one wall is a series of doors: screen doors, metal doors, sliding doors. Along another, oil drums, chains, metal pipes, car parts, office chairs, broken chairs, squeaky chairs — and anything else that has been brought in for the session.

The floor has been divided into various surfaces:

hardwood, linoleum, parquet, concrete, crushed stone, grass and sand, as well as a large water tank. I've heard it said that a foley artist has more shoes than Imelda Marcos: high heels, work boots, cowboy boots, rubber boots, slippers, running shoes — all to re-create the footsteps of every character on the screen.

To do this work, you need a good sense of timing. I've noticed that quite a few foley artists I know have studied mime. The work is done by both men and women, but there aren't that many of us. There are no foley schools; you learn by apprenticing with another foley artist.

Foley is a collaborative effort between the foley artist and the recording engineer. And the best foley tracks are invisible: the action has been so perfectly created, the movements so perfectly interpreted that the viewer is drawn into the scene. The final mixed sound just washes over the audience.

ACTIVITIES

Before Viewing

Try the following exercise to explore how carefully motion is choreographed in film, and how consciously sound is manipulated to enhance the emotional effect of the action. Ask two people to create a motion sequence at the front of the room. Create eight images or tableaux of what happens during the sequence. (If you can record the sequence of movements with a polaroid camera, so much the better.) Ask the group, on the count of three, to re-create the sound of impact. (Most will begin by clapping hands but will soon realize that is not satisfactory.) What else might do the trick? Now screen *Track Stars* to see how sound is made for film. Ask viewers to keep track of the different materials used for various punches in the course of the film.

After Viewing
1

Creating sound effects is usually an exercise in problem solving. As the following examples indicate, the solution is not always what one would expect:

FIRE: scrunching up saran wrap, bubble wrap

WALKING IN SNOW: fingers in cornstarch and coffee whitener

BODY PUNCHES: punching piece of meat

HEAD PUNCHES: punching cabbage

GORING: squishing of watermelon

BIRDS IN TREES: waving feather duster

Take a sequence or scene from a film or novel and make a list of all the sounds that might be needed — from footsteps to the opening of a door to the running of a faucet. Try to re-create those sounds, using a simple cassette tape recorder. Is the recording of the actual sound always the most effective? What alternatives might create an illusion of that sound that's better than the original?

2

Create a sound collage of some area in the school — for example, the cafeteria, the gym, the hallway lockers — by recording at least five sounds that would suggest the flavour of the location.

3

Choose a film, turn off the sound, and watch the picture. What kind of track do you think it has? What does it include? Choose a piece of music to go with the images. Working in groups of three, look at the images together with each person's music selection. Decide as a group which seems most appropriate and why. Now screen the film with its original soundtrack. (Some of the films in this collection with especially interesting soundtracks are *Our Marilyn, Sandspit to Dildo, Lonely Boy* and *Of Lives Uprooted.*)

4

Listen to the soundtrack of a film, with the picture turned off. What kinds of images do you "see"? Screen the film again. How did the sounds shape what you expected to see?

FURTHER RESOURCES

Nails, an award-winning NFB film with no words, uses an evocative soundtrack to heighten the effect of its poetically shot and edited images.

The Sound Collector, a delightful animated film, examines sound's ability to spur the imagination. Available from the NFB.

A Sense of Sound, made for a young audience, features a kaleidoscope of everyday visual images, accompanied by a sometimes realistic, sometimes playful soundtrack. The juxtaposition of expected and nonsense associations encourages viewers to examine how we interpret auditory messages. Available from the NFB.

See *Our Marilyn* (WAYS OF STORYTELLING, video location 85), *Memorandum* (WAYS OF STORYTELLING, video location 55) and *Of Lives Uprooted* (VOICES OF EXPERIENCE, VOICES FOR CHANGE, PART 1, video location 71) for examples of evocative soundtracks.

study extracts

A number of excerpts from films in this collection lend themselves to close study of the elements of film language — cinematography, editing, voice, sound and music. These segments have been assembled at the end of the video SHAPING REALITY and labelled "Study Extracts". The Study Extract material also provides a jumping-off point for a number of suggested activities. For further ideas and information related to each film as a whole, see the entry devoted to that particular documentary.

study extract from *city of gold*

VIDEO LOCATION 54 IN *SHAPING REALITY*

EXCERPTED LENGTH: *2 MINUTES 39 SECONDS*

(THE COMPLETE FILM CAN BE FOUND IN *WAYS OF STORYTELLING*, VIDEO LOCATION 20.)

This excerpt is the ghost-town sequence from the opening of a classic documentary about the Klondike Gold Rush. The shot breakdown below can be used for analysis and narration writing exercises. In the video presentation the shots have been numbered in the lower left-hand corner of the screen. The original commentary, spoken by Pierre Berton in the film, is included at the right.

SHOT BREAKDOWN

ORIGINAL COMMENTARY BY PIERRE BERTON

[T]his town where I spent my childhood isn't really like any other town in the world.

1. TILT UP side of abandoned sawmill

This is Dawson City: the centre of the Klondike Gold Rush. History will never see its like again.

2. LONG SHOT: Yukon Hotel

Every summer, when the seeds of fireweed drifted across the valley of the Yukon River, we kids used to roam through these decaying buildings.

3.   PAN from saloon to blacksmith shop

Some of them had been locked and barred for almost half a century.

4.   TILT DOWN: door latch and padlock

You could buy anything in Dawson City in its heyday, I remember my father telling me. Anything from oysters to opera glasses. You could buy a dancehall queen for her weight in gold — and one man did. His name was Chris Johannson, and he lived on Whiskey Hill.

5.   PAN: across balcony of hardware store

6.   WIDE SHOT of abandoned house

For a child, Dawson was a bit like a giant play yard full of enormous dolls' houses, each one crammed with the trinkets of the stampede: hundreds of picks and shovels, old magazines, bedsteads, pictures, furniture, bric-a-brac.

7.   TILT DOWN side of house and PAN to buildings behind it

We used to play locomotive engineer on the old Bonanza Creek Railway, almost to the very spot where

8.   LONG SHOT: abandoned locomotive

George Washington Carmack picked up the nugget that started it all.

9.   CLOSER SHOT: two locomotives

10.   MEDIUM CLOSEUP of locomotive wheel

We played steamboat captain, too. These deserted sternwheelers are part of a fleet of, oh, there'd be 250, that steamed up the Yukon in the stampede days. Floating palaces,

11. TILT UP from name of steamboat to upper decks

brightly painted, loaded with champagne and dancing girls — and gold. Today there isn't a single one left on the river.

12. TILT DOWN from name *Julia B* to steps and rope; DISSOLVE TO

Most of the men are gone with the steamboats. Of the tens of thousands who came here,

13. CLOSEUP: cemetery grave marker

only a handful found the gold they were seeking. And yet

14. MEDIUM SHOT: CROSS

15. LONG SHOT: grave markers

very few, I think, regretted the journey to Dawson City, for the great stampede was the high point of their life.

ACTIVITIES

- *Play the sequence once without sound. What do the images suggest? Is someone speaking? Male, female, from what cultural group or background? What might this person be saying? What kind of music would suit these images?*

- *Screen the excerpt with sound. Is the narration what you expected? How does the music help establish a sense of time, place, and mood for the story being told? (Notice the points where the music changes to underscore a change in the visuals or a new idea in the commentary.)*

- *Using the shot breakdown at the left, write a different commentary to go with this sequence — perhaps from the point of view of a woman, or an old-timer, or a traveller who comes upon a ghost town. (See rules of commentary writing, p. 37.) Where is breathing room left? Read the different narrations aloud with the images on the screen and the music track. Have a range of voices — women, men, people with different inflections and different accents — read the same narration to the same images. How does each voice color the feeling of the narration?*

study extract from *of lives uprooted*

Video location 57 in *Shaping Reality*

Excerpted length: *2 minutes 26 seconds*

(The complete film can be found in *Voices of Experience, Voices for Change,*

Part 1, video location 71.)

The experiences of children escaping the horrors of civil war in Central America are portrayed through their drawings and words. The stack of drawings has been animated and given depth by an evocative soundtrack. The excerpt begins with an attack that occurred during the crossing of the river Lempa; it ends in the refugee camp.

ACTIVITIES

- *Screen the segment without sound. What do the images convey to you? What do you think the excerpt is about? What do you imagine the soundtrack would be? You may want to choose music, create sound effects, write a narration. Whose voice (s) would you include? How — first person, third person? What would the voice(s) be saying?*

- *Screen the segment with sound. What elements do you notice on the soundtrack? What functions does the music fulfill? How does it suggest a place and culture? How does it add resonance to the scene? Where are sound effects and music used? If you feel the voices are effective, what makes them so? If not, why?*

study extract from *our marilyn*

Video location 59 in *Shaping Reality*

Excerpted length: *4 minutes 34 seconds*

(The complete film can be found in *Ways of Storytelling*, video location 85.)

This excerpt consists of the swim sequence from a film about, among other things, marathon swimmer Marilyn Bell.

A C T I V I T I E S

- *Screen the excerpt with the sound turned off. What rhythm do the images suggest? Create a soundtrack to go with those images; consider using music, sound effects, voice. Do you need to have someone talking? If so, what will the person be saying? Will it be a man talking or a woman? Why?*

- *After listening to one another's tracks, play the sequence again with its original sound. List the different sound elements used by the filmmaker. (For a list of sound elements, see p. 47.) How effective do you think her choices were?*

SHOT BREAKDOWN

1. CLOSEUP of Anka's hand rising, moving to microphone in other hand

2. MEDIUM SHOT: girl screaming

3. MEDIUM SHOT: girl with open mouth

4. LONG SHOT: female fan being lifted on stage

study extract from *lonely boy*

VIDEO LOCATION **64** IN *SHAPING REALITY*

EXCERPTED LENGTH: *1 MINUTE 57 SECONDS*

(THE COMPLETE FILM CAN BE FOUND IN *THE CANDID EYE?*, VIDEO LOCATION **00**.)

This classic documentary is a candid portrait of pop star Paul Anka as a young man. We have chosen an excerpt which offers an interesting example of documentary shooting and editing. To facilitate analysis, a shot breakdown is included here. The shots on the video have been numbered in the lower left-hand corner of the screen.

The sequence of shots beginning at left, which shows the climax of the Freedom Land concert near the end of the film, offers an outstanding example of the use of the *cutaway* or *reaction shot*. Dramatic interest is created, through editing, by the juxtaposition of the main action onstage and the reactions — shot with a carefully observant eye — of the audience members. Note that these so-called "reaction" shots of the onlookers may have been filmed at any time during the concert, but have been selected and used by the editors at specific points in this scene to illustrate the young star's effect on his fans.

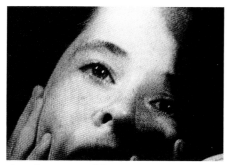

5.   CLOSEUP: girl fainting

9.   PAN UP from female fan to Anka, then back down as he places her head against his shoulder

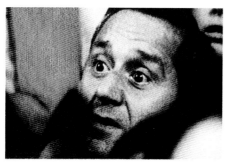

6.   CLOSEUP: man chewing gum

10.   CLOSEUP: young woman gasping

7.   LOW ANGLE SHOT of female fan clutching Anka's hand

11.   CLOSEUP: Anka's hand holding microphone, moving to girl's face as she is removed from stage

8.   CUTAWAY of policeman watching

12.   CLOSEUP PAN of female faces, envious, enthralled

13. CLOSEUP of young woman bursting into tears. CUT TO:

14. TRAVELLING SHOT: car speeds past as woman with cigarette looks out the window

ACTIVITIES

- *Screen the sequence without sound. What kind of track do you imagine it would have? Now screen it again with the original track. What's the effect of having only the music (ie., no screaming) accompanying the shots of the screaming girls?*

- *As you watch the sequence, notice the camera's (and therefore the viewer's) point of view: is the camera part of the audience or part of the action on stage? From what angles is this sequence being shot, from how close up or far away? What is the effect of the close-up shots? The low-angle shots of Anka? What perspective do you think the filmmakers might be encouraging us to take toward this situation, if any?*

study extract from *anybody's son will do*

VIDEO LOCATION **66** IN *SHAPING REALITY*

EXCERPTED LENGTH: *2 MINUTES 40 SECONDS*

(THE COMPLETE FILM CAN BE FOUND IN *THE CANDID EYE?*, VIDEO LOCATION **52**.)

The training process that turns young civilians into ardent Marines is the focus of *Anybody's Son Will Do*. (For more information about the content and ideology underlying the film, see p. 166.) This sequence, about one young aspirant's failure to make the grade, is a striking example of how gripping direct cinema (more commonly known as cinéma vérité) can be.

ACTIVITIES

- *As you watch the sequence the first time, notice how you react, and to what. Do your feelings change? At which points? Are there any images or sounds that have a particular impact on you? How would you describe the shooting style? Where are you in the scene? Are you an involved or a detached observer? Do you feel close to the action or as if observing it from a distance?*

study extract from *Sandspit to Dildo*

VIDEO LOCATION **69** IN *SHAPING REALITY*

EXCERPTED LENGTH: *2 MINUTES 41 SECONDS*

(THE COMPLETE FILM CAN BE FOUND IN *THE POETRY OF MOTION*, VIDEO LOCATION 86.)

This skateboarding sequence from a playful, high-spirited cross-country look at Canada was shot on Hi8 video. We included the segment because of the opportunities it offers to consider shooting, editing and sound. (For further information on how the video was made, see the interview with director Chris Mullington, p. 254.)

ACTIVITIES

- *What strikes you about the shooting? (You may want to watch the sequence first without the sound, in order to concentrate on the visuals.) Does it capture the feeling of movement? How? Where has the camera been placed? At what angle? Would you describe the the sequence as serious, inventive, playful? Why? What effect is created by switching between black-and-white and color?*

- *In* Sandspit, *certain sound and visual elements are repeated again and again, often with slight alterations. What effect does this repetition have?*

- *Screen the sequence with the soundtrack. Voices have been used as a malleable sound/musical element, rather than for any information they might convey. What voices do you hear? Is there a narrator? Is one necessary? Are there connections between the visual and sound rhythms in the video?*

the politics of youth

When we first began planning this collection, we asked students for their definition of a documentary. The responses came thick and fast: documentaries were boring, educational, black-and-white and, above all, true. It was then we knew we had our work cut out for us.

In fact, the issue of truth is particularly complex in documentary filmmaking. Comprising footage of real-life events, people, places and situations, a documentary can appear to be a transparent, unmediated "window on the world". However, like all film and video productions, documentaries are constructions — highly compressed and shaped versions of "real" space and "real" time. They are the result of countless decisions made by people working under many constraints and influences, including time, money and resources, institutional editorial policies, and the ideology of the culture that they and their affiliated institutions transmit, consciously or unconsciously.

Nonetheless, there is undoubtedly something compelling about watching actual people in actual situations — glimpsing "the real thing". It is because of the attraction of "the real" that the ideology implicit in how documentaries are put together can seem invisible.

This section contains material that raises questions about "fact", "truth", point of view, and bias. In the light of the growth of "reality-based" television offerings, docudramas, infotainment, and the increasing proportion of people who receive their information about and view of the world from broadcast news, these issues are ever more pressing.

The Spaghetti Story parodies documentary conventions of authoritative authenticity. The segment from *Has Anybody Here Seen Canada?* provides background on the the National Film Board under its first film commissioner John Grierson, and focusses on the creation of propaganda films during World War II. It should also stimulate discussion of the media's role in manufacturing consent, and of the possible political and economic consequences of producing films that question the status quo.

An excerpt from *Docudrama: Fact and Fiction* focusses on the rights and responsibilities of filmmakers who combine fact and fiction in one work. It highlights the controversy surrounding Paul Cowan's documentary about World War I flying ace Billy Bishop. *The Journey* confronts the notion of objectivity head-on, both in its content and its style. The excerpts from *The Journey* examine some of the biases involved in the construction of television news programs, and the resulting implications for the public's access to political information.

We have found that students' first reaction upon learning how media material is structured is to think in terms of conspiracy. There are, undoubtedly, ideological factors at work in almost everything produced; yet the fact that film/video productions are shaped constructions does not assume a deliberate intent to deceive. In fact, documentary filmmakers are more often than not spurred by a determination to challenge the accepted "truth" of a given situation and to share the results of their investigations, interpretations and vision with an audience.

But truth is multifaceted so, as one filmmaker profiled in this package warns: "Let the viewer beware".

For further exploration of these issues and concerns, also see SHAPING REALITY, pp. 55, and THE CANDID EYE?, pp. 144.

the spaghetti story

VIDEO LOCATION **00** IN *THE POLITICS OF TRUTH*

3 MINUTES

BLACK & WHITE

1957

PRODUCER: *BBC*

DISTRIBUTOR: *BBC*

How do we know that what we see on the screen is true? *The Spaghetti Story*, a purportedly serious documentary piece about the Swiss spaghetti harvest, aired on April Fools Day, 1957, as part of the weekly BBC newsmagazine program *Panorama*. Crammed full of the documentary conventions used to assure viewers that what they are watching is authentic, *The Spaghetti Story* is narrated by Richard Dimbleby who, for many British viewers, was the media voice of credibility itself.

This short spoof on the travelogue/nature documentary/process film is a lighthearted starting point from which to examine the presentation of truth in the documentary format. It also raises questions about the audience's attitude, critical or otherwise, to what is seen on the screen. Does *The Spaghetti Story* expose the cozy conspiracy between filmmaker and audience which involves the willing suspension of disbelief on the part of the audience? Do viewers have a responsibility to question what they watch?

SUGGESTIONS *for* USE

- *See the sections on truth in the introductory video piece* WHAT IS A DOCUMENTARY?

- *Try introducing the film in different ways: for instance, you may want to screen it without giving viewers any background at all. Alternatively, you could tell them they are going to see an older documentary made for a BBC newsmagazine program rather like* W5 *or* Fifth Estate. *Before students view the item, ask them what conventions they expect to see. Note any differences in the group's response to the presentation, given that information.*

spot the conventions

The Spaghetti Story deftly parodies many of the truth-assuring techniques used in documentary. Some of the most obvious that are sent up here include:

- authoritative male narrator, "the voice of God"
- "seeing is believing": actuality, "on the spot" footage
- references to experts
- references to facts, particularly of a scientific nature
- "authentic" music — to create a feeling of place, locale
- stereotypes of the happy (but silent) subjects of a travelogue piece, "local colour"

I D E A S *for* D I S C U S S I O N

1

At what point did you realize that this was a send-up? What tipped you off?

2

Until that realization, what characteristics of this film made you assume that it was true? Do you automatically assume that what you see on the screen is authentic? Are you more likely to do so if an appeal is made to facts? Why?

3

Would it be possible to watch this film and not realize that it's a parody? What do you need to know about how spaghetti is made in order to evaluate this presentation? What if the film were not about spaghetti but the Gulf War, for instance, or the 1992 riot in Los Angeles? Could you know if what you were hearing and seeing were true or accurate if you had no other frame of reference or sources of information?

4

Travelogues, ethnographic documentaries and many news reports focus on people and events in other cultures. Often, information, impressions and interpretations — the "truth" about those cultures — are conveyed to viewers not by the people of the culture themselves but by an outside commentator, a third-person narrator who assumes the right to speak authoritatively about the subject. Though there is only one voice in **The Spaghetti Story** *— that of a male outsider explaining to an audience of outsiders the truth about spaghetti in the Ticino area — quite a few people with different perspectives appear on the screen: cultivators, harvesters, cooks, waiters and guests. How might the film be different if presented from the point of view of one of these people?*

ACTIVITIES

1

Look at *The Spaghetti Story* again to spot the "conventions of truth". Then screen another "regular" documentary you may have seen before, perhaps on a scientific subject, and see how many of those conventions you can recognize.

2

It's clear that *The Spaghetti Story* includes staged "authentic footage" of the spaghetti harvest. Not all re-creations are so obvious (or so amusing). See DOCUDRAMA: FACT AND FICTION, p. 124, for activities related to the issue of re-creation.

3

Develop a treatment for your own process film. What activity or process would you choose to depict? What stages in the process would you show? What kind of shots would you use? What kind of music would you choose? Would there be a narrator? Try creating a storyboard for your process film, with a thumbnail sketch for each shot or scene, and a few words describing the actions and sound.

FURTHER RESOURCES

film/video

Other parodies of documentary form and techniques include *The Bronswik Affair* (available from the NFB as a stand-alone film or as part of *Media & Society*), which spoofs the conventions of documentary investigative journalism; *This Is Spinal Tap*, a take-off on the behind-the-scenes and in-front-of-the footlights films about rock musicians; Woody Allen's *Zelig*; and the Movietone News parody "News on the March" at the beginning of *Citizen Kane*.

Those with a particular fondness for scientific documentaries should look at *In Search of the Edge*, in which members of the Flat Earth Society seek to disprove the myth of the earth's roundness perpetuated by globularists. (Available from McNabb & Connolly, 60 Briarwood Road, Port Credit, Ont., L5G 3N6. Tel: (416) 278-0566.)

Only the News that Fits (*Media & Society*, NFB), about the way in which mainstream media in the U.S. and Britain reported on events in Central America, contains some telling examples of outsiders commenting on events in a culture that is not their own.

For a lyrically beautiful process film without commentary, see *Nails*. Available from the NFB.

has anybody here seen Canada? a history of Canadian movies 1939-1953

VIDEO LOCATION **03** IN *THE POLITICS OF TRUTH*

COMPLETE FILM: *85 MINUTES*

BLACK & WHITE

1978

EXCERPTED LENGTH: *22 MINUTES*

DIRECTOR: *JOHN KRAMER*

PRODUCERS: *KIRWAN COX, MICHAEL MCKENNIREY,*
          ARTHUR HAMMOND, NFB

DISTRIBUTOR: *NFB*

For many people the word *documentary* conjures up memories of war-time propaganda films: images of black-and-white battles, generous helpings of stirring music, a wall-to-wall commentary delivered in booming tones by an unidentified but apparently omniscient narrator. *Has Anybody Here Seen Canada?* focusses, among other things, on some of these productions made during World War II.

The excerpts we have chosen deal overtly with the propaganda issue and show how malleable visual images can be. We see, for example, how footage from the Nazi masterwork *Triumph of the Will*, by Leni Riefenstahl, was recut and a new narration added, to buttress the Allies's "war for men's minds".

As well, these excerpts present material about the early days of the National Film Board, the influence of its first film commissioner, John Grierson, and the way in which his career was destroyed by allegations of Communist affiliation made in the wake of the Igor Gouzenko affair during the mid-1940s.

■ ■ ■

In his excellent book *Documentary: A History of the Non-Fiction Film*, Erik Barnouw describes the documentarian's role during World War II as being like that of a bugler. The moral and strategic issues then seemed clear, and many filmmakers willingly deployed their skills to meet the aims of the state. In those pre-

television days, short newsreels screened in theatres before the feature presentation were a crucial means of informing the masses and ensuring their participation in the war effort.

However, all-too-present was the threat of political intervention when filmmakers overstepped the boundaries of the permissible, as Grierson was soon to discover.

Though the excerpts from *Has Anybody Here Seen Canada?* deal with events of the 1940s, the issues they raise are still relevant today. First, they suggest that there are times when works produced by filmmakers and broadcast journalists can be used to manufacture consent within a democracy. The most striking recent example is the debate concerning the media coverage of the Gulf War. (For an example of consensus-making at work, see "Mad Dogs and Englishmen", p. 139, which analyzes the language used in the British press to describe the actions of both sides in the conflict.) Propaganda, in the sense of consensus creation, may also operate through omission — the events not covered, the probing critical inquiries not made.

Questions about journalistic bias, historical truth and censorship raised in *Has Anybody Here Seen Canada?* are also dealt with in *Docudrama: Fact and Fiction* and *The Journey* (The POLITICS OF TRUTH, video locations 25 and 54).

IDEAS *for* DISCUSSION

After you have come up with a definition of what constitutes propaganda (see Activity 3, below), consider some of the following questions: Can you describe any examples of propaganda that you have experienced? Is propaganda restricted to wartime? Is there a difference between a film with a strong point of view and a piece of propaganda? Is every documentary with a point of view propaganda?

ACTIVITIES

1

Re-screen some of the clips from World War II films, paying particular attention to the language used to describe "our" side and "their" side. Compare your findings with "Mad Dogs and Englishmen", p. 139.

2

Compare the versions of war and fighting given by the clips in *Has Anybody Here Seen Canada?* and the clips from *The Kid Who Couldn't Miss* in the selection *Docudrama: Fact and Fiction* (THE POLITICS OF TRUTH, video location 25). Describe the point of view in the wartime films, and the one in the production about Billy Bishop.

3

Research the characteristics of propaganda and the techniques employed in its creation. To explore the way in which propaganda might function today, it is useful not only to consider television coverage of conflicts, such as those in Central America and the Middle East, but also to examine the role and techniques of advertising.

Business and government are among the most consistent creators/sponsors of propaganda material. View government ads on a current political, economic, or social issue. Campaigns promoting social issues, such as the dangers of drinking, drugs, and unsafe sex, should not be hard to find.

4

See the activities related to editing in SHAPING REALITY, p. 55.

FURTHER RESOURCES

film/video

See the excerpts from *The Journey* (in THE POLITICS OF TRUTH, video location 54). They examine how the media shape political consensus, as does *Only the News that Fits*, available from the NFB either individually or as part of the *Media & Society* collection.

For further investigation of the malleability of film and video footage, see *The Edit* (in SHAPING REALITY, video location 31).

The Life and Times of Rosie the Riveter is a wonderfully incisive and entertaining look at the propaganda techniques used to entice women into U.S. factories during World War II — and to usher them right back home again when the men returned. (Available from Full Frame Film and Video, 394 Euclid Ave., Toronto, Ont. M6G 2S9. Tel: (416) 925-9338.)

Manufacturing Consent explores the political life and ideas of the controversial author, linguist and radical philosopher Noam Chomsky. Highlighting Chomsky's analysis of the media, the film focusses on democratic societies in which populations not disciplined by force are subjected to more subtle forms of ideological control. Available from the NFB.

print

The Age of Propaganda: The Everyday Use and Abuse of Persuasion (New York: W.H. Freeman, 1992), by Anthony R. Pratkam and Elliot Aronson, deals with such topics as the psychology of persuasion, public opinion, advertising, and television in relation to propaganda.

Gary Evans' book *John Grierson and the National Film Board: The Politics of War-time Propaganda* (Toronto: University of Toronto Press, 1984) expands on some of the material covered in *Has Anybody Here Seen Canada?*

docudrama:
fact and fiction

VIDEO LOCATION **25** IN *THE POLITICS OF TRUTH*

COMPLETE FILM: *119* MINUTES

1987

EXCERPTED LENGTH: *29* MINUTES

DIRECTOR: *MICHEL CHOQUETTE*

PRODUCER: *NFB*

On February 1, 1986, a public forum was held at McGill University to explore the complex issues raised by the emergence of the hybrid form known as docudrama. Ten NFB filmmakers took part, among them Donald Brittain, Jacques Godbout, Anne Claire Poirier and Paul Cowan. A question-and-answer session between the audience and members of the panel alternated with screenings of excerpts from some pertinent NFB films. The event was moderated by Michel Choquette, filmmaker, author and teacher. From the videotaped proceedings of the forum, we chose a segment that includes excerpts from the film *The Kid Who Couldn't Miss*, and portions of the ensuing discussion.

The Kid Who Couldn't Miss, about World War I flying ace Billy Bishop, has been the focus of heated debate since its release in 1983. In part an examination of the process of legend-building and hero-making so common in wartime, the film aired doubts about the veracity of Bishop's credited "kills". Members of the Canadian Air Force Association considered the film's arguments spurious and its findings inaccurate; they succeeded in having the matter raised in the Senate Sub-Committee on Veterans' Affairs.

We have included the debate between Colonel Bauer of the Air Force Association and the film's director, Paul Cowan, because of the number of important issues raised by the controversy that swirled about this film:

- Are "facts" and "truth" necessarily congruent?
- What are a filmmaker's responsibilities when creating re-enactments?
- Is there a single true version of historical events? Can our understanding of an historical event change over time?
- Does a filmmaker have the right or responsibility to present an unpopular or dissenting point of view?

These are but a few of the many questions that might be discussed after screening the selection from *Docudrama: Fact and Fiction.*

SUGGESTIONS *for* USE

- *It is important that viewers know that the 13 minutes of excerpts from* The Kid Who Couldn't Miss *are actually part of a 79-minute film.*
- *In addition to looking at this selection in its entirety, you might want to try the following: Stop the video after screening the excerpt from* The Kid Who Couldn't Miss. *Encourage students to discuss their responses to what they have seen. Once they've screened the rest of the material about accuracy and point of view, ask them if their initial reactions have changed. If so, how and why?*
- *See the sections on "truth" and "objectivity" in the introductory piece,* WHAT IS A DOCUMENTARY?

the question of re-enactments

Filmmaker Paul Cowan at McGill symposium on docudrama

In documentaries, there's always staging to some degree. It ranges from somebody saying "look, could you just turn that way a little" to restaging a whole scene. If somebody tells you there isn't, I think they're not telling you the truth.

PAUL COWAN, FILMMAKER

Even conventional documentaries often resort to small amounts of re-creation in the absence of existing footage, particularly when some exposition is needed in order to set up the "story" of the film. Such small-scale re-staging of events is usually not made known to the audience. (See editor Steve Weslak's interview, p. 79, for elaboration of this point.)

There are cases, however, in which the filmmaker's failure to acknowledge a reconstruction can lead to confusion for the viewer and, possibly, misinterpretation, as the boundaries between fact

and fiction begin to blur. This is especially true of the current crop of reality-based crime shows which function as quasi-documentaries or quasi-dramas. For many people, the "look of reality" suggests that the depiction has an intimate connection with the truth. (See *The Spaghetti Story*, p. 116, for a discussion of some of the "conventions of truth" used in documentaries.)

Quasi-dramas tend to:

- draw on actual transcripts and research material for their re-enactments
- use stock footage (previously shot actuality material that is held in stock-footage libraries and is available for sale)
- use hand-held camera techniques (often seen in news reports) to convey a sense of immediacy and action
- script scenes beforehand but instruct actors to play them improvisationally
- edit interviews with actual participants in an event into re-creations that use actors.

Quasi-documentaries tend to use sound or picture of actual events, adding re-enactments where necessary. They, too, rarely indicate the differences between the two.

In *The Kid Who Couldn't Miss,* the opening sequence shows a young boy, presumably Billy Bishop, shooting ducks in 1904. The footage certainly looks authentic: the film is black-and-white, the motion is jerky, and the image appears to "jump" as it would in archival footage of the time. In fact, however, this material was created specifically for the film. The footage was shot at silent speed (about 18 frames per second), which is slower than the "normal" rate. When projected at normal speed (24 frames per second), the images appear to be speeded up, as do most very early moving pictures. The filmmaker Paul Cowan scratched the film, threw dirt on it, and cut out frames so that the images seemed choppy and discontinous. The resulting "old" footage is quite convincing; however, there is no indication that the scene is a reconstruction. Screen the opening scene of the excerpt again. Do you think Cowan should have made it clear that this was not authentic footage of Billy Bishop? Why or why not?

The following article by Howard Green appeared in the *Globe and Mail* July 23, 1992:

TELEVISION

Enough with the shakycam in commercials, Howard Green says

YOU might not have noticed it, but it rears its shaky head about every 10 minutes in prime time. I refer to the inordinate number of television commercials that look as though they were shot by someone with a hand tremor. Watch Dini Petty, all gussied up, parked in the middle of a gym, talking about the miracle of Pears Shampoo. The shot's just a-shakin' away, enough to make you reach for a dose of Gravol. And for what? Same with the good old Bank of Montreal and the old woman who's been storing her loot there since Canada was divided into Upper and Lower. If it's such a rock-solid place to do business, why not shoot the ad on a tripod instead of making us all dizzy?

This is, of course, the age of so-called "reality television," with current affairs and trash TV programs reaching back to the halcyon days of *vérité* shooting style. The message is simple. A shaky camera means we didn't set anything up, therefore you're getting the straight goods. If it shakes and it's out of focus, who cares? It's the truth.

Well, the folks who make the ads know a good gimmick when they see it and they're determined to bludgeon us with it.

Even Madonna, music's star marketeer, knows what's going on. Her ersatz documentary, *Truth or Dare*, was a two-hour ad for someone who didn't need an ad. And she did it in the guise of a documentary, using black and white, backstage shakycam with dirty grain and all.

Too bad it was obvious that her backstage scenes were meticulously pre-lit by highly experienced gaffers which made the grainy look very questionable.

Same goes for the TV ads. Although they strive for the grittiness of a documentary, they just miss. The camera is shaky, but it doesn't shake quite right. Someone's shaking it on purpose and it shows.

What really worries me about this foolishness is that the next ads to utilize "the technique" will be a vital part of the election campaign in the United States and will no doubt be imported by Canadian campaign mangers to show us the "real" Brian, Jean and Audrey.

I quote from a recent issue of Harpers magazine:

"I would do it — and all the Bush ads — with a handheld camera. That gives it a more documentary feel," says Stuart Stevens, who worked on the campaign of Massachusetts Governor William Weld.

Yikes, says me. And so should you. When you see an ad with a whole-lotta-shakin'-goin'-on, beware. It's not real. It's fake. Change the channel and watch a documentary.

Howard Green is a Toronto-based freelance broadcaster/producer.

IDEAS *for* DISCUSSION

1

What were your reactions to the excerpt from **The Kid Who Couldn't Miss?** *What were its most striking features and ideas?*

2

What did you find persuasive about Colonel Bauer's arguments? About Paul Cowan's responses? Did you feel differently about the film after you heard each of their arguments?

3

Define each of these terms: fact, truth, accuracy, point of view. What do you think the issues are in the debate generated by this film?

4

"Valour and horror: not politically correct?", an article written by Pierre Berton, was published in its entirety in the Toronto Star *on May 30, 1992. The partially edited version reproduced below is included because of the useful distinction it makes between factual accuracy and point of view. Discuss.*

Pierre Berton
Valour and horror: not politically correct?

On the 22nd of next month, a Senate subcommittee on veterans' affairs will sit in judgment on the CBC, the National Film Board and the McKenna Brothers, Terence and Brian, over a recent documentary series, *The Valour and the Horror*.

The McKennas — writer and director — will be subjected to an intensive grilling, because a powerful lobby group doesn't like the revisionist history the series represents. It is not "politically correct".

Forget about wartime nostalgia. This one questions the mass bombing of German cities, charging that Canadian pilots were led to believe they were attacking strategic targets, when the real purpose was the mass murder of civilians to lower the German morale. The documentary says that didn't work, and hundreds of Canadian flyers died needlessly.

It questions the training of Canadian soldiers, examines their generalship and finds it wanting and makes clear that some German prisoners were killed after surrender. It concentrates on the senseless and badly planned attack on Verrière Ridge, near Caen — the one that all but wiped out the entire Black Watch — and it charges that the facts were covered up by General Guy Simonds and other higher-ups, who laid the blame on a junior officer.

Much of this will be new to many Canadians, spoon-fed on the mythology of wartime and by the jingoist drivel that followed. The Canadians were perfect soldiers, their generals exemplary and noble, the battles tactically brilliant — that has been the party line.

The man behind the lobby is Cliff Chadderton, head of the War Amputations of Canada, and chairman of the National Council of Veterans Associations.

Although the War Amps is a charitable organization, supported by public donations, Chadderton has used its letterhead to mount an expensive advertising and lobby campaign to discredit the series.

He wants to prevent it ever being shown again on television. He wants the book that accompanies the series to be removed from the schools and the libraries. He wants to put a chill on the CBC and the NFB that will prevent any further revisionist documentaries of this kind.

He has come up with the long list of what he calls "inaccuracies." The producers answered them all. Some are picayune. He claims, for instance, they got the soldiers' hair cuts all wrong. In fact, they worked from wartime photographs and had a barber on the set to make sure they got it right.

More serious is his charge that "there is absolutely no evidence to back up the innuendos concerning the shooting of prisoners and many other incidents which did not make the Canadian soldier look too good."

Actually, the ordinary soldiers look very good indeed in the series. It is their leadership that doesn't look so good. As for PoW treatment, General Jacques Dextrase, the former chief of the Canadian general staff, makes that very point on camera. And one has only to read Tony Foster's *Meeting of the Generals*, to find other specific incidents.

There are times in all wars when the order is given to take no prisoners. Dextrase has said that if we lost the war, our own leaders would have had to stand trial.

What we are talking about here is an ongoing and healthy debate about war in general and this one in particular. It's not new. The debate on the value and morality of mass bombing, for example, is old stuff in Britain. Nobody there has tried to censor it.

Now, at last, the debate has arrived on our doorstep. A host of other Allied generals have long been subjected to critical scrutiny. Why not Guy Simonds? Is it because until this moment he has been presented as a paragon of military efficiency?

The McKennas' critical view of the war won't please everyone, but is that a reason to ban it? Nobody has yet been able to point to a single inaccuracy. It's the *point of view* that disturbs people like Chadderton. It doesn't tell "the other side".

But we already know the other side — the one expressed in all those *Canada Carries On* films, in the recruiting posters, in Matthew Halton's wartime broadcasts, in the memoirs of retired commanders, in the media deification of men like Simonds, and "Bomber" Harris, and in all that overheated oratory about gallantry and cowardice, patriotism and sacrifice. . . .

Let us hope that, in rejecting [Chadderton's] diatribe, [the Senate Committee] will go a step further and urge that every schoolchild be given the chance to see this documentary so that they may realize the horror, the misery, the cynicism — yes, and the incompetence too — that accompanies every war.

5

The term docudrama *does not mean that what the film says is not true. What it does imply is that certain parts of the material are dramatized and that material is woven in with more conventional documentary material.*

PAUL COWAN, FILMMAKER.

Does the filmmaker have certain responsibilities when working in the area of docudrama? If so, what are they, and to whom is she or he responsible? Should dramatic re-creations be labelled as such? Under what circumstances might it be essential to be clear which elements are which?

6

We could claim to put the truth in our films, but if you don't want to believe it you won't believe it, so where does that leave us? Where does that leave documentary footage?

JACQUES LEDUC, FILMMAKER

In the spring of 1992, a California jury found several police officers not guilty of using excessive force against an African-American man, Rodney King, in spite of the fact that the prosecution submitted as evidence 81 seconds of videotape that clearly showed the defendants beating King. Discuss Jacques Leduc's quote in the light of this event. What does the Rodney King incident suggest about the so-called passive viewer? What other factors might cause people to accept or reject visual evidence?

ACTIVITIES

1

In order to explore the contention that facts and truth are not necessarily synonymous, try the following exercise: Take five minutes to jot down all the verifiable facts about yourself and your life that you can think of. Look over the list. Do you feel that your collection of facts, if shown to a stranger, would give her a sense of the truth of your life? Why or why not? Is anything missing? What?

2

I suppose the next step is pure documentary with cops shooting their stories themselves. Can't you just see them jumping out of their cars with those lights going, and a camera in one hand and a gun in the other?

SONNY GROSSO, EXECUTIVE PRODUCER, *TOP COPS*

What do you think Sonny Grosso means by "pure documentary"? Analyze a number of reality-based TV crime shows, using some of the following questions as guidelines:

- What story is being told?
- From whose point of view or perspective is it presented?

- From whose point of view is it filmed?
- Who narrates the story?
- What sort of music is used, if any?
- What other sounds are used?
- What is the resulting message?
- Choose another person from whose perspective the events could have been presented. How would that story have been different?

3

Any country that sets its history in cement will wither.

MAGGIE SIGGINS, AUTHOR

Research the term *revisionist history*. What does it mean? Find some examples of the re-telling of history that have occurred either in print or in film. (Some of the films in VOICES OF EXPERIENCE, VOICES FOR CHANGE are pertinent here. Particularly relevant are the controversies surrounding *The Kid Who Couldn't Miss* and *The Valour and the Horror*.) What might be some of the reasons behind the re-visioning of past events? Who has the right to speak of those events? Who owns history?

4

Do you have a particular point of view on some topic about which you feel strongly? Present arguments to back up your interpretation. How would you make a film that presents this point of view? What strategies or techniques would you use to make your case as convincing as possible?

5

Compare the excerpts from *The Kid Who Couldn't Miss* with *Our Marilyn* (WAYS OF STORYTELLING, video location 85), in the light of myth-making and the creation of heroes. In what sense can heroes — such as Billy Bishop and the two Marilyns — be seen as collective dream images?

6

Imagine that a documentary is going to be made of your life from the point of view of: your mother, a close friend, a teacher, someone with whom you do not get along, someone who is in love with you, or think of some others. Choose two or three points of view. Jot down scenes from your life that you imagine each would show and describe the point of view you believe each would take. What differences would there be in these re-presentations of you and your life?

FURTHER RESOURCES

film/video

See *The Journey* (in THE POLITICS OF TRUTH, video location 54) for further discussion of objectivity and point of view.

See *Has Anybody Here Seen Canada?* (in THE POLITICS OF TRUTH, video location 03) for another look at films about war and soldiers, and the relationship between filmmakers and their political masters.

See *Richard Cardinal: Cry from a Diary of a Métis Child* (in VOICES OF EXPERIENCE, VOICES FOR CHANGE, PART 1, video location 11) which explores the meaning of a life — rather than merely presenting the facts of that life — using actors and re-creations.

The Ballad of Crowfoot and *Black Mother, Black Daughter* (in VOICES OF EXPERIENCE, VOICES FOR CHANGE, PART 1, video location 00, and VOICES OF EXPERIENCE, VOICES FOR CHANGE, PART 2, video location 26) re-tell stories of history from the point of view of Aboriginal people and Black women from Nova Scotia.

The three-part series *The Valour and the Horror*, about Canadian soldiers and their commanders during World War II, triggered a debate on controversial issues such as the ownership of history, point of view and the use of dramatic re-creations. Available from the NFB.

The hostile reaction of the mainstream press to Oliver Stone's *JFK* was almost as interesting as the film itself, which mixed documentary footage of Kennedy's assassination with dramatic re-creations to propose a conspiracy theory. Also see *JFK: The Book of the Film* by Oliver Stone and Zachary Sklar, a compilation of 97 reactions and commentaries.

print

There are a number of examples of "real-life fiction" (or "faction") available, including Capote's *In Cold Blood*, Doctorow's *Ragtime*, and de Lillo's *Libra*.

the journey

VIDEO LOCATION 54 IN *THE POLITICS OF TRUTH*

COMPLETE FILM: *14 HOURS 30 MINUTES*

1988

EXCERPTED LENGTH: *19 MINUTES*

DIRECTOR: *PETER WATKINS*

DISTRIBUTOR: *FULL FRAME*

The Journey is an epic documentary that shows what happens when "ordinary" people are given the chance to scrutinize detailed information about the arms race and the struggle for peace. Shot in a dozen countries, on five continents, in eight languages, the film's themes include war and peace, the social and economic consequences of militarism, the role of the media and education systems in distorting or fragmenting information, and the process and possibility of change.

From its 14 1/2 hours, we have chosen three excerpts, totalling 19 minutes. Clearly, these sequences give little sense of the whole film; they are, however, relevant to the discussion about truth in film, as they analyze the way in which television news is constructed. In addition The Journey, by virtue of its unique form and style, questions documentary conventions of truth, particularly objectivity, subjectivity, and bias.

The Journey was directed by Peter Watkins, an innovative British filmmaker renowned for his influential and controversial productions. The War Game, his best-known work, netted him an Oscar in 1966; but for twenty years, the BBC felt it was "too strong" to appear on network television, though they had commissioned the production.

SUGGESTIONS *for* USE

- *You may find it useful to initiate discussion after each excerpt.*

- *See the sections on truth and objectivity in the introductory video piece* WHAT IS A DOCUMENTARY?

- *You might also want to look at the interview with Alanis Obomsawin (in* VOICES OF EXPERIENCE, VOICES FOR CHANGE, *part 1, video location 41) in which she talks about why she prefers an advocacy approach to filmmaking.*

the excerpts

excerpt 1

The opening minute of the film makes clear that this is no ordinary documentary. As viewers gaze at a black screen, Peter Watkins introduces himself in a conversational tone of voice and emphasizes his subjective approach to the material to be presented. Unlike many documentary films that use an authoritative, third-person narrator with a supposedly objective point of view, *The Journey* immediately posits a different relation of filmmaker to audience.

Text of the opening narration

"Well, hello. My name is Peter Watkins. I'm English, an English filmmaker, at this time living in Sweden. And it will be my voice you hear from time to time during *The Journey* as narrator. It's my intention to give you some additional information and also to comment on the process of the film.

"I do hope that you will not feel that there is anything objective about the information that I'll give you. Certainly, all of us working on *The Journey* have tried very hard with our research to make the information as accurate as possible. But I must emphasize that our presentation of the information is biased, due to our very strong feelings about the subject of the film."

excerpt 2

Because of Watkins' interest in examining the access of ordinary citizens to political information, he focusses in this second excerpt on current television public-affairs coverage, particularly the evening news. The example he uses is Radio-Canada's reporting of the "Shamrock Summit" between Brian Mulroney and Ronald Reagan which took place in Quebec City in March 1985.

Watkins explains and illustrates the terms *edit* or *cut, cutaway* and *topo*; he then emphasizes that each cut represents a specific news judgment about form and content, and points out that a rapid cutting pace fragments information. In his brief discussion of the role of the Prime Minister's press secretary, he suggests that the goals of the media and politicans tend to mesh: the media need newsworthy events to cover and access to those events; the politicians long for publicity but want to ensure that it be positive.

excerpt 3

The final segment opens with a Radio-Canada planning meeting about the Summit gala; it then scrutinizes the CBC/Radio Canada coverage of demonstrators protesting U.S. and Canadian foreign policy. Watkins raises questions about the agenda-setting aspect of the news (what gets covered and what gets ignored?), editorial policy, objectivity, and bias.

objectivity, subjectivity and point of view

The evening news is subjective. You've taken one day in the world and you've boiled it down to 22 minutes. To do that, you've had to make all kinds of choices. Who can say that's not subjective?

PAUL COWAN, FILMMAKER

Objectivity is much touted in some journalistic circles. Richard Salant, former president of CBS News, was once quoted as saying, "Our reporters do not cover stories from *their* point of view. They are presenting them from *nobody's* point of view." This, then, seems to be one understanding of the term "objective": the intention, à la Dragnet, to give "just the facts, Ma'am" from some neutral position, unsullied by the taint of human subjectivity.

In practice, of course, such a stance is almost impossible. Scientists have concluded that there is no such thing as "pure measurement", since any measurement is be affected by the instrument doing the measuring. As in the world of science, so in the world of media representations.

■ ■ ■

All films and TV productions embody points of view. These viewpoints may be consciously intended or not, explicitly articulated or not; yet they manifest themselves through the ideological and aesthetic choices made by the filmmakers and producers:

- What story will be told (or reported)?
- From whose perspective will it be presented?
- How will it be filmed (camera placement, movement, framing)?
- How will it be edited?
- What music will be used (if any)?
- Whose voice(s) will we hear?
- What will the resulting message be?

It is helpful to remember that filmmakers and producers do not function solely as autonomous individuals. They operate within a framework that may include the conventions of documentary filmmaking, the editorial policies of the institutions to which they are connected, and the underlying ideology of their particular society.

The fact of a media point of view leads us to ask: What are the commercial pressures on filmmakers? What are the practical and aesthetic considerations? Who owns or controls the medium? And what is our role as spectator in identifying with — or rejecting — what we see and hear?

The alluring notion that a camera can ever record anything objectively begins to disintegrate the moment one confronts a few practical considerations.

What, for instance, is an "objective" camera position — since the camera must be placed somewhere? How does one "objectively" decide when to turn the camera on and off? And when one views the resulting material, how does one measure which parts most represent "objective truth", and should therefore be used?

These are all editorial decisions that are inextricably bound up with the film's need to compress lengthy, diffuse events into a relatively brief and meaningful essence. Quite simply, filmmaking is a series of highly signficant choices — of what to shoot, how to shoot it, and what to use in the end.

MICHAEL RABIGER, *DIRECTING THE DOCUMENTARY*

The implicit ideological burr that clings to the notion of objectivity is underlined by a comment reported to us by one of our educator consultants: "Is this film from a left-wing point of view or is it objective? "

Films and television programs (including those on such apparently neutral topics as science and nature) that reproduce the status-quo view tend to be seen as "objective"; those which challenge prevailing conventions as "subjective" and "biased".

In an attempt to achieve "fairness and balance" in public affairs programming and broadcast news coverage, television journalists and documentarians are often instructed to "tell both sides of the story". That journalists not become mouthpieces for one point of view, but allow the audience to make up its own mind from the material presented, may be laudable, in theory. In practice, however, it does little to ensure that the full range of opinion is represented.

For instance, who is to say that there are only two sides to an issue? If one holds to the notion of truth as multifaceted and complex rather than as a single, unified view to which everyone assents, perhaps a story has six sides or even ten. If the idea that there may be many sides to a story is accepted, one must also consider voice (Who gets to speak? Who doesn't get to speak?) when examining point of view. For further material on voice, see WAYS OF STORYTELLING, p. 5, and VOICES OF EXPERIENCE, VOICES FOR CHANGE, p. 177.

jingoism
Mad Dogs and Englishmen

Discussion of issues such as "truth" and "point of view" in documentary and reportage requires precise definitions of the terms used and a critical appreciation of the role of language. The article below, reprinted in the Globe and Mail *during the Gulf War, originally appeared in the* Guardian *in London, England.*

The following terms have all been used by the British press to report on the war in the Persian Gulf:

THEY HAVE	WE HAVE
A war machine	Army, Navy and
Censorship	Air Force
Propaganda	Reporting guidelines
	Press briefings

THEY	WE
Destroy	Take out
Destroy	Suppress
Kill	Eliminate
Kill	Neutralise
Kill	Decapitate
Cower in their foxholes	Dig in

THEY LAUNCH	WE LAUNCH
Sneak missile attacks	First strikes
Without provocation	Pre-emptively

THEIR MEN ARE	OUR MEN ARE
Troops	Boys
Hordes	Lads

THEY ARE	OUR BOYS ARE
Brainwashed	Professional
Paper tigers	Lionhearted
Cowardly	Cautious
Desperate	Confident
Cornered	Heroes
Cannon fodder	Dare devils
Bastards of Baghdad	Young knights
Blindly obedient	of the skies
Mad dogs	Loyal
Ruthless	Desert rats
Fanatical	Resolute
	Brave

THEIR BOYS ARE MOTIVATED BY	OUR BOYS ARE MOTIVATED BY
Fear of Saddam	Old-fashioned sense of duty

THEIR BOYS	OUR BOYS
Cower in concrete bunkers	Fly into the jaws of hell

IRAQI SHIPS ARE	OUR SHIPS ARE
A navy	An Armada

IRAQI	ISRAELI
NON-RETALIATION IS	NON-RETALIATION IS
Blundering/Cowardly statesmanship	An act of great courage

THEIR MISSILES ARE	OUR MISSILES ARE
Aging duds (rhymes with Scuds)	Like Luke Skywalker zapping Darth Vader

THEIR MISSILES CAUSE	OUR MISSILES CAUSE
Civilian casualties	Collateral damage

THEY	WE
fire wildly at anything	Precision bomb

THEIR POWS ARE	OUR POWS ARE
Overgrown schoolchildren	Gallant boys

SADDAM HUSSEIN IS	GEORGE BUSH IS
Demented	At peace with himself
A crackpot monster	Resolute
Defiant	Statesmanlike
An evil tyrant	Assured

THEIR PLANES	OUR PLANES
Are shot out of the sky	Suffer a high rate of attrition
Are zapped	Fail to return from missions

IDEAS *for* DISCUSSION

1

"Excerpt One", a 60-second sequence, occurs at the beginning of a 14 1/2–hour film. What reactions do you have to this opening?

2

How does Watkins' use of voice differ from the voice you've heard in other documentaries in content (what's being said) and in delivery (pacing, tone of voice)?

3

What is the effect of looking at a black screen while Watkins is speaking? Why might he have chosen this device?

4

Screen a segment of a more conventional documentary that uses a "voice-of-God" narration style. Network television and film libraries are replete with examples. (The Spaghetti Story, in THE POLITICS OF TRUTH, video location 00, is a parody of this approach. Has Anybody Here Seen Canada?, in THE POLITICS OF TRUTH, video location 03, contains clips from World War II propaganda films in which the voice is at its most strident and hectoring. Memorandum, in WAYS OF STORYTELLING, video location 55, uses a third-person omniscient narrator, albeit in a profound and moving way.) Who does this voice belong to? From where does its authority derive? Do you tend to believe what this voice says? Why?

5

Are you more inclined or less inclined to listen seriously to what Peter Watkins has to say once he has made it clear that he has a strong point of view, that he is not "objective"? What do you think is his attitude towards his audience? What would you feel if you heard a statement like this before the television news? Does something seem more likely to be true if it is presented as objective?

6

Peter Watkins distinguishes between objectivity/subjectivity (i.e., point of view) and factual accuracy. Discuss the difference. (Also see Pierre Berton's column, p. 129, Paul Cowan's comments about docudrama, p. 168, and Alanis Obomsawin's defence of advocacy filmmaking in VOICES OF EXPERIENCE, VOICES FOR CHANGE, PART 1, *video location 41.)*

ACTIVITIES

1

Peter Watkins stated that *The Journey* is partly about the way we use money and time on this planet. Look at a taped TV news program. How long is the program? How many stories are presented in that time? How long is the shortest item? The longest? How is each story presented visually? Are there certain patterns of visual presentation that emerge? Analyze one news item. How many cuts (i.e., changes of visual information) occurred? Compare a national newscast on CBC with one on a major U.S. television network and one created by a privately owned Canadian station. Are there noticeable differences in style, pacing, types of stories, and commercial content?

2

Investigate the ways in which several daily newspapers in the same city present the same news story. Compare the content, the headlines, the photos used, the juxtaposition of items on the page, the length of articles, their placement in the paper.

3

Analyze the language used in a newspaper story or television news item. What words are used to describe persons, organizations or events? Does the choice of words reveal assumptions or biases on the part of the writer? (See article on jingoism, p. 139.) Re-write the story to "colour" it a different way.

4

Our reporters do not cover stories from their point of view. They are presenting them from nobody's point of view.

RICHARD SOLANT, FORMER PRESIDENT, CBS NEWS

Take a newspaper story or television news item and re-present it from somebody's point of view. (An individual reporter's or writer's point of view is influenced by the editorial policies of the paper or network, and by the commercial and ideological forces that determine those policies.)

5

See p. 66, Activity 5, in SHAPING REALITY, which suggests different ways in which to shoot and "cover" a demonstration.

6

Current affairs TV is generally heavy on narration. It tells you what to see, how to interpret it and —at least implicitly — what to think about it. It relies heavily on officials and experts, decision-makers and spokespeople. Whenever ordinary people get to speak, they are usually edited down to fragments. While authority figures are treated with great respect, whether they deserve it or not (except in some good investigative reports), people without power or "expertise" are not granted much credibility. Whenever social criticism is expressed, it's well within "reasonable" limits.

MAGNUS ISAACSON, "THE FATE OF DOCUMENTARY IN A TV AGE", *CINEMA CANADA* #123, OCT. 1985.

Screen a newscast or current affairs program to test Isaacson's statement. Substantiate your position, using examples.

FURTHER RESOURCES

film/video

Only the News that Fits (available in the NFB's *Media & Society* package or as an individual film) examines the ways in which the ideological and formal constraints of television news (time, access, editorial policy, etc.) shape the information we receive about the world — in this case, the situation in Nicaragua.

Getting the Story, part of the series *Consuming Hunger*, examines the way in which the Western media reported on the famine in Ethiopia. (Available from Full Frame Film and Video Distribution, 397 Euclid Ave., Toronto, Ont., M6G 2S9. Tel: (416) 925-9338.)

Distress Signals considers the threat to cultural sovereignty posed by the globalization of broadcasting technology; it suggests a resulting Americanization of production and homogenizing of cultures, a matter that is also of great concern to Peter Watkins. Available from NFB.

The Journey is available for rental or purchase from Full Frame Film and Video, 394 Euclid Ave., Toronto, Ont., M6G 2S9. Tel. (416) 925-9338.

The Edit (in SHAPING REALITY, video location 31) shows how malleable footage can be and suggests that our ability to cut and shape what was apparently seen and said can lead to troubling ethical dilemmas.

Manufacturing Consent explores the political life and ideas of the controversial author, linguist and radical philosopher Noam Chomsky. Chomsky analyzes the media in democratic societies, which exert subtle forms of ideological control on the inhabitants. Available from the NFB.

print

In *Manufacturing Consent: The Political Economy of the Mass Media* (Pantheon, 1988), Edward S. Herman and Noam Chomsky contend that a pervasive elite consensus structures almost all facets of the news.

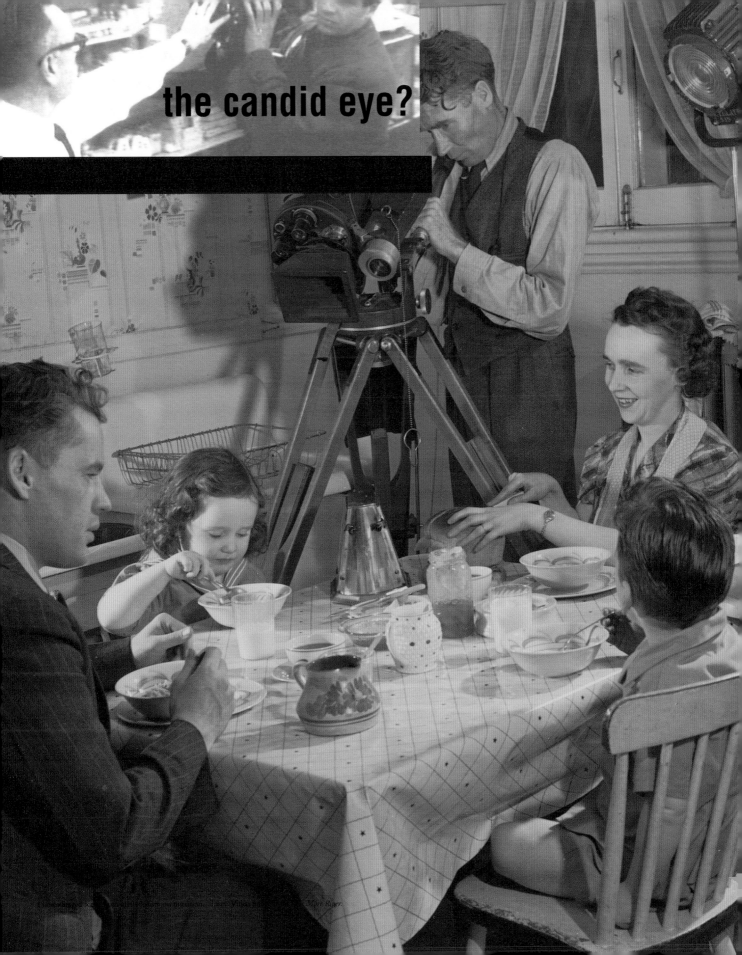

the candid eye?

Until the 1950s, documentary filmmakers interested in capturing what French photographer Henri Cartier-Bresson called "the decisive moment" — that spontaneous revelatory instant that illuminates our understanding of a person, event or experience — were thwarted by the tools of their trade. Cameras were bulky and noisy. Sound recording equipment was so large and cumbersome that any dialogue filmed on location almost inevitably appeared stilted, as human interaction had to be "managed" to conform to the dictates of the technology.

The development of lightweight portable cameras and sync-sound recorders during this decade soon made it logistically feasible to record dialogue on location, using a minimum of personnel and equipment. Suddenly, it seemed possible to catch life as it unfolded.

The new opportunities for intimacy, spontaneity, mobility and flexibility were seized upon by a number of filmmakers anxious for change and who had already been pushing for technological improvements. The resulting philosophies of how to handle the new equipment tended to break down into two camps.

Adherents of direct cinema saw themselves as detached, objective observers who believed that their fly-on-the-wall stance would let them record life as it happened, without affecting or altering it. They operated "witnessing cameras".

The other stream, cinéma vérité, began with the work of French anthropologist and ethnographic filmmaker Jean Rouch, who had worked extensively in Africa recording cultures not his own. For Rouch, the filmmaker made things happen or intervened in events as they occurred. In his view, those who wielded cameras were engaged participants and catalysts, not invisible recorders.

These two different approaches still exist, although the term cinéma vérité tends to be applied indiscriminately to both.

The films in this section are early and current examples of direct cinema and cinéma vérité practices. *Lonely Boy*, a classic from the early 1960s, is a candid portrait of pop star Paul Anka as a young man and of the adoring female teens who attend his concerts. In the excerpt from *Ladies and Gentlemen: Mr. Leonard Cohen*, the poet is looking at rushes of a scene of himself in the bath and commenting on the supposedly candid nature of the footage. *One More River*, like *Lonely Boy*, was made for television; in this investigation of the battle to integrate Mississippi during the 1960s, the journalists/filmmakers are clearly involved in the action: they appear on the screen, they are summarily thrown out of a store. The sense of immediacy is powerful and direct. Finally, *Anybody's Son Will Do* is a relatively recent example of a direct cinema film, made for television, which uses a host. This documentary, about the experiences undergone by 18-year-old Marine recruits during boot camp at Parris Island, raises interesting questions about access and point of view.

lonely boy

Lonely Boy, made in 1961, was one of the first "candid" film portraits of a pop star. The filmmakers were able to capture revealing glimpses of teen idol Paul Anka behind the scenes and in front of the footlights, partly because the recent development of lightweight, portable sync-sound equipment made it possible to record sound and image on location with a minimal crew and little interference in the flow of events. (See "The Evolution of Sound in Documentary", p. 151 , for further information.)

This particular style of filmmaking, which stresses immediacy and mobility, is most commonly known as cinéma vérité; however, the makers of *Lonely Boy* saw themselves as detached, ironic, journalistic observers in the tradition of direct cinema.

The footage in *Lonely Boy* was shot with one camera. The tape recorder was connected by a cable to the camera when it was necessary to record sound that synchronized with the picture. On other occasions, the sound recordist Marcel Carrière disconnected the tape recorder and went off to record *wild sound* (ie., non-sync sound) to be combined with images during editing. As there is virtually no narration in the film, the filmmakers' point of view or attitude toward the material had to be suggested by the juxtapositions (image/image or image/sound) created during the editing process. (For further information on and suggested activities related to sound and editing, see SHAPING REALITY p. 55.)

SUGGESTIONS *for* USE

- *To be used effectively, this film requires a context. See Before Viewing suggestions in "Ideas for Discussion", p. 154.*

- *Use* Lonely Boy *in conjunction with the excerpt from* Ladies and Gentlemen, Mr. Leonard Cohen *to explore questions of truth and candor in "candid" documentaries.*

- *Comments by students have been included here to serve as a jumping-off point for further discussion.*

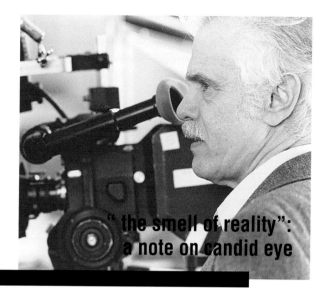

"the smell of reality":
a note on candid eye

Candid Eye films when we first thought of making them. There were many precedents: war–time documentaries like *Listen to Britain, Desert Victory, The True Glory.* Classics like *Drifters, Nanoo, Man of Aran, Night Mail.* A brilliant British post-war documentary particularly impressed us: *Thursday's Child,* a film about deaf children. There were even moments in feature films like *Kameradschaft* and *Naked City.* They all had the smell of reality about them, and this was what we wanted to get into our work too.

Wolf Koenig, shown above, worked as cinematographer and co-director on the NFB classics City of Gold *and* Lonely Boy, *as well as on many other films. In excerpts from a 1967 article about the NFB series* Candid Eye, *which produced some early and striking examples of direct cinema for television, Koenig talks about the factors that influenced the young turks in the Film Board's Unit B to push for a new kind of filmmaking. Intimacy, immediacy and spontaneity were to be the hallmarks of this new kind of documentary. It was to be a far cry from the rather stilted and carefully arranged productions that seemed to be the norm for NFB fare in those days, including such memorable films as* Why Grow Fat Hogs? *and* Teeth are to Keep.

There's nothing new under the sun. This seems to be true of everything. It certainly was true of the

In those days, television was demanding a lot of films. TV hadn't yet developed its own film production potential so it fell to the Film Board to produce much material for showing on the CBC. Here, we thought, was our chance. The audience was there and there was money for films. We were confident that we could do at least as well as everyone else — secretly we thought we could do better — so we went to see management.

This is roughly what we proposed: Record life as it happens, unscripted and unrehearsed; capture it in sync sound, indoors or out, without asking it to pose or repeat its lines; edit it into moving films that would make the audience laugh and cry (preferably at the same time); show it on TV for millions and change the world by making people realize that life is real, beautiful and meaningful, etc. Management was understandably puzzled by this proposal. We were told that films cannot be made like this — that there would be difficulties....

This unconventional kind of documentary film presented new and disconcerting problems. For instance: how does one get an audience to look at a film that doesn't have a story or even a conventional message? Worse: how does one get script approval from management for a film without a script? Or: how can one get close to the subject with all those clumsy cameras and lights and microphones without scaring him off? And how in God's name could we be sure of being present when the moment of truth arrives? We couldn't very well shoot every boring minute of the hero's life waiting for his soul to reveal itself (although at times we did). There were many such questions...

the evolution of sound in documentary

• The first documentaries were made with no sound.

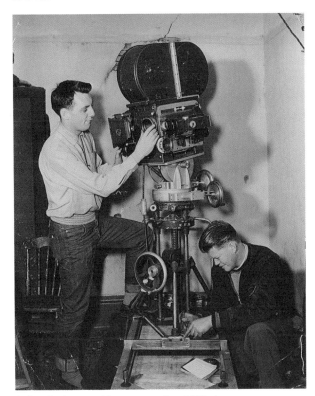

Before: Setting up a 35mm camera for a 1950s documentary

• Sound equipment came into general use in the late 1920s but was so cumbersome and required such a large crew that most documentaries, including *City of Gold*, were shot like silent film. Sound — voice, music, sound effects — was added later in a studio. When Colin Low and Wolf Koenig went to the Yukon in 1956 to shoot live-action footage for *City of Gold*, they were extremely frustrated by their inability to record the old-timers' stories in sync sound, on location. In fact, *City of Gold* was produced like a silent film, with the soundtrack added later. So great was their desire to be able to work in a different way that, upon their return from Dawson City, they, like other documentary filmmakers, began to press for technical innovations.

- The development of lightweight portable tape recorders and noiseless 16mm cameras in the late 1950s made it possible to record *sync sound* on location. These changes stimulated the development of direct cinema and cinéma vérité styles of filmmaking and the rise of the on-location interview during the early 1960s.

After: By the early 1960s, lightweight 16mm cameras made it possible to shoot almost anywhere

- The recent introduction of video camcorders has made documentary even more portable because, with a highly directional mike mounted on a camcorder, one person can shoot, and at the same time, record sound of fairly high quality. (*Sandspit to Dildo*, in THE POETRY IN MOTION, video location 86, was shot in this way.) It is also possible to record and play back without difficulty stereo sound on video equipment.

who is Paul Anka anyhow?

For all those students who asked us this question, here is a short biographical note about the subject of the film.

Singer/songwriter Paul Anka was born in Ottawa in 1941. His first hit single "Diana" was released when he was only 15 years old; it sold more than 20 million copies. From 1957 to 1962, he had 20 more hit singles. As taste in pop music changed and his popularity waned, he began to concentrate on songwriting. More than 400 of his songs have been recorded and he has, in his time, sold more than 100 million records. In the 1980s, he made a comeback as a singer with the hit song "You're Having My Baby". *Lonely Boy* was shot in 1961 when Anka was 20 years old.

students' comments

It was interesting to compare early 60s concerts to today. Besides, documentaries on rock stars are always worth seeing, what with interviews, concert footage and peeks behind the scenes.
17-YEAR-OLD VIEWER

It's a piece of history. I liked the way he made all his fans feel important.
17-YEAR-OLD VIEWER

Film critics are right. Black-and-white film has an intriguing quality. You tend not to get distracted by background colour.
18-YEAR-OLD VIEWER

It was boring because it was black-and-white.
18-YEAR-OLD VIEWER

The way it was filmed was great. It didn't seem like a documentary.
16-YEAR-OLD VIEWER

The whole thing seems fake, not like it's real life.
16-YEAR-OLD VIEWER

I liked Paul Anka's story about his days as an ugly, fat kid in high school and how he worked to change his appearance and overall image.
18-YEAR-OLD VIEWER

IDEAS *for* DISCUSSION

Before Viewing

1

What film about a rock star or a musician have you seen lately? What were the elements that made up the film (concert footage, behind-the-scenes material, interview with the star, family, entourage, etc.)? Was it completely flattering or did it show the performer's warts as well? What is the difference between a promotional film about a star, and a documentary?

Lonely Boy, *made in 1961, was one of the first "candid" portraits of a pop idol. The filmmakers used the newly available lightweight film techology to capture aspects of Paul Anka's life behind the scenes and in front of the footlights.*

After Viewing

1

How do you react to this portrait of Paul Anka? Did you find him likable? What aspect of the film made the biggest impression on you?

2

This film is supposed to be a candid look at a performer, someone wearing a mask. What does "candid" mean in this context? Do you feel his mask ever drops? If so, when? (To explore further how candid a "candid" film can be, see the following selection, **Ladies and Gentlemen, Mr. Leonard Cohen,** THE CANDID EYE, *video location 27.)*

3

How do you feel about the film being in black-and-white? Does that add to or detract from its effectiveness for you? What qualities do you associate with black-and-white footage? (The film was shot in black-and-white for a number of reasons: it was being produced for television, which, in those days, was only black-and-white; black-and-white stock gave the filmmakers more freedom to work under variable light conditions; and finally, black-and-white film stock was less expensive than colour. This was an important consideration, as direct cinema or cinéma vérité filmmaking often involves shooting a lot of footage and then trying to find its structure in the editing room.)

4

Why was the film called Lonely Boy?

5

Like most films, Lonely Boy *is a document of the values and customs of the time in which it was made. As you watch the film today, what seems foreign to you, what familiar?*

6

Discuss the following comment from Barbara

Ehrenreich's book Re-making Love: The Feminization of Sex *(New York: Anchor Press/Doubleday, 1986):*

In a highly sexualized society (one sociologist found that the number of explicitly sexual references in the mass media had doubled between 1950 and 1960), teens and preteen girls were expected to be not only "good" and "pure" but to be the enforcers of purity within their teen society — drawing the line for over-eager boys and ostracizing girls who failed in this responsibility. To abandon control — to scream, faint, dash about in mobs — was, in form if not in conscious intent, to protest the sexual repressiveness, the rigid double standard of female teen culture. It was the first and most dramatic uprising of women's sexual revolution.

ACTIVITIES

1

We give ourselves away in all our gestures, and the good documentaries watch for that. The landscape of the face, that's where the real action is.... There is transmission of message in body language, by the intonation or tone of voice which often has nothing to do with what the words are saying, and that's what you try to show — the nature of the human animal.

WOLF KOENIG, FILMMAKER

Pick a sequence or two from this film (perhaps the concert scene, the last sequence in the car, the scene with the Copa club owner) and see how you are given the kind of "under the surface" information Koenig describes.

2

Were you aware of the filmmakers or their attitudes toward Paul Anka while looking at the film? Do you think the filmmakers liked Paul Anka? Did they seem detached, critical, or accepting of him at face value? What makes you think so?

Re-screen a sequence or two (perhaps the interview with Anka's manager, the scene in the car, the fans' faces during his concert) to see how mood, humor, point of view have been constructed through juxtaposition — of shots and of visuals and sound.

3

To suggest how technological advances affected documentary filmmaking, compare the use of sound in *Lonely Boy* and *City of Gold*.

4

Our Marilyn (WAYS OF STORYTELLING, video location 85) and *Lonely Boy* are both about teenagers who become famous. Compare the ways in which the films present and examine the mythologizing involved in celebrity. Are there differences between Brenda Longfellow's attitudes towards the two Marilyns and those of Wolf Koenig and Roman Kroitor towards Paul Anka?

5

Compare a contemporary film about a rock star, musical performer, or group with *Lonely Boy.* Aside from the music itself, do they use similar elements in a similar way? What are the differences? Consider shots, angles, editing, use of colour and/or black-and-white, music and narration on the soundtrack. Do they seem to be candid portraits, too?

6

If you were to make a *Lonely Boy* today, who would you choose as your subject? What kinds of sequences would you want to shoot? Who would you want to interview and include in the film? Would it be a concert film or would you want to do something different? If so, what? Do you think access (getting permission to research and film) would be a problem? With whom would you have to negotiate access? What conditions might be attached to gaining access?

7

Explore the factors affecting candor in an interview situation. (You might want to do this activity in pairs or larger groups.) Choose a character you want to be and create a background for that person: who you are, how old, what you do, where you live, what kind of family you come from, etc. Write out a series of questions you want to be asked about yourself and give them to a "friendly" interviewer. Then, pass on the information you have developed for your character to a "skeptical" interviewer, who will ask questions she thinks of herself. (The resulting interviews can be role-played, and videotaped if equipment is available.) How did you feel doing those interviews? What differences did you notice in your character's reactions to each situation? Did you divulge the same amount or the same kind of information to both interviewers? If a film were going to be made about your character, what scenes should be shot?

8

In the 1950s and 1960s, filmmaking was revolutionized by the introduction of lightweight 16mm camera and sound equipment that allowed greater flexibility, mobility and accessibility. A similar upheaval is happening today with the development of low-end video. Research some of the new uses of video — for example, *America's Funniest Home Videos* — that have happened in the last five years or so. Also see the interview with Chris Mullington, director of *Sandspit to Dildo,* (pp. 254) who shot his production in Hi8 video.

9

Paul Anka was being carefully packaged as a

celebrity. The following exercise about fame was devised by media specialist George Ventura at West Toronto Collegiate:

CELEBRITIES: THE ELEMENTS OF STYLE

In chart form, list the following elements of style as they apply to five different celebrities. You may select the celebrities of your choice, but you should include at least one of these celebrities from the past: Marilyn Monroe, Elvis Presley, John Belushi.

Elements to consider:

a. appearance

b. style of dress

c. mannerisms

d. speech patterns

e. favorite expressions

f. typical settings or props with which they are identified

g. what you think their values and/or lifestyles are like

h. which "How to be famous" criteria apply:

> have talent
>
> have handlers (assistants, agents, publicists)
>
> have a unique look
>
> stay contemporary
>
> seem intelligent
>
> be your best celebrity self

FURTHER RESOURCES

film/video

There are any number of films about musical performers who are also icons of popular culture: *Madonna: Truth or Dare; The Decline of Western Civilization, Part. 2; The Metal Years* by Penelope Spheeris; *This Is Spinal Tap*, Rob Reiner's hilarious parody of a "rockumentary"; *The Last Waltz* by Martin Scorsese; and the classics such as *Gimme Shelter* and *Monterey Pop* by the Maysles brothers, as well as the fictional feature *Performance* by Nicholas Roeg.

print

Rockonomics: The Money behind the Music by Marc Eliot (New York: Watts, 1989) examines the business side of the recording industry.

ladies and gentlemen,
Mr. Leonard Cohen

VIDEO LOCATION 27 IN *THE CANDID EYE?*

COMPLETE FILM: *44 MINUTES*

BLACK & WHITE

1965

EXCERPTED LENGTH: *11 MINUTES*

DIRECTORS: *DONALD BRITTAIN, DON OWEN*

PRODUCER: *JOHN KEMENY, NFB*

DISTRIBUTOR: *NFB*

00:43:09

This selection consists of scenes from a jazzy, 1965 black-and-white film portrait of a young Leonard Cohen, then in his heyday as poet and novelist, before the blossoming of his career as songwriter/performer. The selection includes some candid footage of Cohen on the stage, in the bath, on the street and in his bed. He and writer/co-director Donald Brittain are then seen sitting in a screening room looking at rushes of the above scenes, while subject and filmmaker muse about being part of a so-called candid documentary.

The excerpt works well in conjunction with *Lonely Boy* (THE CANDID EYE?, video location 00) which also sets out to be a behind-the-scenes look at a person with a public persona.

IDEAS *for* DISCUSSION

1

What effect do you think the camera has on those who are being filmed?

2

How "true" and candid can a candid film actually be?

3

What difference does it make to have the presence of the camera acknowledged by those who are being filmed?

4

What do you think that Cohen's warning "Caveat emptor" — "Let the buyer beware" — means for a viewer? What does that idea make you feel — challenged, resentful, manipulated?

ACTIVITIES

Compare this segment of the film with a sequence from a current film or video about a celebrity, for example, *Madonna: Truth or Dare*. Is there any point in that video where the presence of the camera is acknowledged by the subject or where people talk about how they feel about being filmed?

WHITE
Rest Rooms
MEN & LADIES

one more river

VIDEO LOCATION 38 IN *THE CANDID EYE?*

COMPLETE FILM: *56 MINUTES*

BLACK & WHITE

1964

EXCERPTED LENGTH: *14 MINUTES*

DIRECTORS: *DOUGLAS LEITERMAN, BERYL FOX*

PRODUCER: *DOUGLAS LEITERMAN, CBC*

DISTRIBUTOR: *CBC*

One More River was made in 1964 for the CBC public affairs program *This Hour Has Seven Days*. A report on the status of racial integration in the American South, the film was shot over a period of two weeks with a crew of two — cinematographer Richard Leiterman, and either Beryl Fox or Doug Leiterman doing sound and conducting interviews. The filmmaking team collected dispatches for their viewers from behind the front lines, as it were.

In these dispatches, dogged segregationists and equally determined integrationists spoke in their own voices about the current situation and the forces fighting for and against change to the status quo. As Doug Leiterman mentions in his interview, he and his colleagues were determined to catch the gritty reality of the situation by focussing on the material itself, rather than worrying about technical niceties such as pure unblemished sound.

When the film first appeared, it was clear to its producers — and to its audience — that something new was being tried in television journalism. *One More River* did away with the voice-of-God narrator in order to let viewers interact directly with the material and make up their own minds about the cinéma vérité footage with which they were presented. In this film, the filmmakers intervene in some events and set others in motion, appearing on screen as a catalyst for what is to follow.

As the documentary has no narrator delivering an explicit commentary, the filmmakers' point of view had to be suggested by the way in which scenes were juxtaposed. Clearly the choices made were highly selective: a one-hour documentary was created from more than 30 hours of footage shot on location; the excerpts we have chosen total 14 minutes.

interview with Doug Leiterman, co-director and producer

As a television journalist, one's objective is to get at the facts in the best way possible, to get to the bottom of the situation. The intention of *One More River* was to try and assess the feeling in the Deep South nine years after the U.S. Supreme Court had ordered integration "with all due speed". We wanted to take the emotional temperature of the South, delve into the emotional intensities that flourished there, show people what it was like to be black in that part of the States. There was little in-depth coverage about the racial situation in the U.S. at the time so the public had no context to help them understand what was going on.

Only the full-length documentary allows you the luxury of examining a situation like that in some depth, of running more than simply clips of what people say. For example, we wanted to give people the flavor of Malcolm X. Who was he, what was he saying, why was his message so appealing to so many people? You can't possibly capture that in a 40-second clip on the nightly news. So the task of a documentary is to spend time (which means money) on a subject and pursue it in depth.

When we started making the film, we went first to all the "Negro" churches and "Negro" organizations and asked the leaders of the protest movement for ideas and names of people to speak to. To find those on the "other side", all you had to do usually was go speak to the mayor of the town. For instance, the guy at the opening of the show we actually heard on the car radio. He was a broadcaster in a small town in Georgia. I must say making that film was a pretty scarey experience at times. People weren't too well disposed to camera crews: some cameramen had already been shot at down there, and threats were made against Beryl [Fox]. The scene in the cafeteria was set up, in that we talked to a black woman and her son about what it was like trying to get served in restaurants and then we decided to go in and film what happened in these situations. Beryl had a small hand-held camera that she used to film the scene of the man lunging at Richard's camera at the lunch counter.

As for the movie house scene, we were curious to know what the ticket seller would do since, by law, she was obligated to let them in. So we decided to find out. We put wireless mikes on Beryl and the fellow she was with, and Richard was on the sidewalk, shooting away.

We recorded music on the spot whenever we could. The technology was just emerging then for actuality sound. We might do a 20-minute interview and 40 minutes of wild sound [sound not tied to any particular image], which could be used later as voice-over.

We shot 100,000 feet of film [about 33 hours] over a two-week period, which gave us enough footage to tell the story in a way that was gripping for the viewer as well as being fair to our understanding of the situation.

Don [Haig, the editor] had a real feel for juxtaposition, for how to put the material together without an omniscient narrator telling the audience what to think. We wanted to let the story tell itself, to let viewers draw their own conclusions about

where the truth lay. We felt quite thrilled by what we were doing. It was a breakthrough. We didn't worry if some of the sound was inferior, if there was background noise. For us, it had authenticity rather than a studio feel.

We had the notion of capturing events as they actually happened, even if the results were technically a bit rough. This was difficult in an organization like the CBC, which had a department of technical standards. Their response when they saw the film was, "Throw it out." We, on the other hand, weren't devoted to the technical quality, we were after the material.

We were conscious that we were riding the crest of the technology. Doors were opened for us that hadn't been open before, when it took eight people and two station wagons full of equipment to do a simple interview. You had to take along a lighting crew and gaffer to do all sorts of complicated things with the electricity wherever you happened to be. It made it impossible to get at reality, especially for people like me who wanted to practise journalism skills in film.

Instead you were always having to use feature-film tactics: telling people to sit up straight, blasting the light into their eyes. But these people weren't actors; we needed to create an environment in which they were comfortable. So we devised all kinds of tactics: we never used a slate to mark the beginning of an interview, we gave the cinematographer hand signals about when to start the camera rolling, and we would gradually slide into the actual interview so the subject wouldn't become self-conscious about suddenly being "on camera".

And with this new technology you could be incredibly mobile. *One More River* was made with no more than two people at a time: Richard Leiterman was the cinematographer and either Beryl or I did sound and conducted the interviews. And that was it.

When *One More River* finally came out, Westinghouse wouldn't run the program in the States and Alphonse Ouimet, who was head of the CBC at the time, insisted that we preface the film with a disclaimer stating, "We're sorry if this film offends anybody. It doesn't present the whole story." We also had to follow the film with a discussion group.

Later the next year, Ouimet presented us with a Wilderness Award for best documentary of the year.
—TORONTO, 1992

IDEAS *for* DISCUSSION

1

This film about racism was made in 1964. What is your response to this material? Does it seem dated, gripping, relevant? What images, sounds, people, or situations particularly caught your attention?

2

What if this film had a third-person narrator? Would you respond in a different way to the material?

3

While being interviewed, Doug Leiterman commented, "We didn't want to make a polemic. We didn't want to end up preaching to the converted but to let everyone involved have their say." Compare this point of view with that of Alanis Obomsawin (see her interview in VOICES OF EXPERIENCE, VOICES FOR CHANGE, PART 1, video location 41) who discusses her decision to make advocacy films, that is, films with a very definite purpose and definite point of view.

4

In his interview, Doug Leiterman comments, "Don [Haig, the editor] had a real feel for juxtaposition, for how to put the material together without an omniscient narrator telling the audience what to think. We wanted to let the story tell itself, to let viewers draw their own conclusions about where the truth lay." Filmmaker Paul Cowan questions this notion of objectivity and "truth" in documentary filmmaking when he says (in the video selection WHAT IS A DOCUMENTARY?): "As soon as you make a cut, you are no longer objective. You are imposing your intelligence, wisdom, perversity on the material and you're creating another reality out of it." Discuss the differences between these two positions.

ACTIVITIES

Compare this film with *The Ballad of Crowfoot* and/or *Speak White* (in VOICES OF EXPERIENCE, VOICES FOR CHANGE, PART 1, video locations 00 and 64), which also examine issues of race (and class), but from the perspective of an insider.

FURTHER RESOURCES

film/video

See *Black Mother, Black Daughter* (in VOICES OF EXPERIENCE, VOICES FOR CHANGE, PART 2, video location 26), which uses interviews and the techniques of oral history to build up a picture of the role played by Black women in Nova Scotia in the preservation of their culture.

print

See the discussion of ojectivity, subjectivity, and point of view in THE POLITICS OF TRUTH, p. 113.

anybody's son will do

VIDEO LOCATION 52 IN *THE CANDID EYE?*
57 MINUTES
1983
DIRECTOR: *PAUL COWAN*
PRODUCERS: *WILLIAM BRIND, JOHN KRAMER,*
　　　　　　BARRIE HOWELLS, NFB
DISTRIBUTOR: *NFB*

SUGGESTIONS *for* USE

- *This film has been prepared for classroom use in two parts, with titles announcing "Part 1" and "Part 2".*

- *The film will probably require several class periods since it raises a number of complex issues.*

- *Because of the length of the film, you may want to screen the entire film once and then go back and look at specific sequences.*

- *The students' comments have been included, page 172, to serve as a jumping-off point for further discussion. What, for instance, are the differences implied in the distinction made between documentaries and "real movies", i.e., fiction?*

Anybody's Son Will Do is an exploration of the rituals of basic training by which young civilians, mostly male, are turned into soldiers — people who kill and are killed. Shot at the Parris Island Marine Recruit Training Depot in South Carolina, this documentary consists of several elements: direct cinema or cinéma vérité sequences (candid shooting of actual events), interviews with veteran Marines, and a rather ironic commentary by host-commentator Gwynne Dyer, a journalist specializing in military affairs. The format was shaped by the fact that *Anybody's Son*, the second film in a six-part series entitled *War*, was produced for broadcast television which often uses the convention of an on-screen host.

Viewers' reactions to *Anybody's Son* tend to be polarized: some are appalled by the process the young men undergo, others are suffused with patriotism. Consequently, the documentary gives viewers an opportunity to differentiate between their own responses and the film's point of view, as constructed by the director.

For a fuller discussion of the characteristics and development of cinéma vérité and direct cinema, in which viewers have the sensation of seeing events as they unfold in a spontaneous and unmediated way, see the introduction to The Candid Eye?, pp. 145.

about the making of the film: an interview with Paul Cowan, director

background

Anybody's Son Will Do is part of the *War* series, which was a massive undertaking. The people working on the project had already decided to shoot a film on basic training at Parris Island, which they then asked me to direct. So a lot of the negotiations around gaining access were completed before I ever became involved.

I didn't really have any preconceived ideas before I made the film. I didn't know any Marines. I'd lived in the States for 10 years in the '60s and learned, like everybody else, to dislike the military. But still I didn't have any intimate contact with them. In fact, when I went to study at Cornell University, I tried to sign up for ROTC, the Reserve Officers Training Corps. They wouldn't have me because I was a foreigner; but I thought it would be great, climbing up and down mountains and ropes — that's how naive I was.

Basically, I knew nothing about the military. So I went to Parris Island with a blank slate. In fact, I didn't even make a research trip before we started shooting. I just went down there, got the lay of the land and figured out how I was going to do the film, which was essentially to follow one platoon through the training process. And then we dove right in. There were four of us — myself, an assistant cameraman, a sound man and a production manager — and we stayed five weeks. We probably shot 20 or 25:1. That means that for every hour of completed film, we had 25 hours of unedited footage.

We slept in a motel just outside the base because there was no room for us to sleep on the base. But we were on call 24 hours a day. Lots of times we would work through the night or we'd get a call in the middle of the night that something was happening and to come on over right away.

We did everything with those guys. We were up the tower and went down the ropes, which scared the hell out of me. We ran with them. We did push-ups with them. You have to do that. I consider it a condition of being a documentary filmmaker that you become like the people you're filming for a period of time. You have to enjoy them that much.

access

When we first got there, we had a press liaison person who was following us around saying, "Oh, I don't think you ought to film this" and "I'm not sure about that, either." By the end of the first week, we were filming anything and everything we wanted. They were even suggesting things that we ought to shoot. Remember that gut-wrenching scene where the guy is telling the recruit he's going to send him home and the kid is crying? Well, they phoned me up in the middle of the night and said, "You ought to come down and film this." They thought that scene was great because it showed how tough the Marines were: a third of those who start don't finish, and here was an example of someone who can't make it.

I don't think that kid even knew that we were there. And if he did, we were such a minor problem compared to this staff sergeant who was chewing him out that we were inconsequential. There wasn't one person who said, "Whoa, wait a second, what are you doing? You can't film me." First of all, the recruits are so scared that they would have assumed that if we were there, it was because the general knew we were there. And if the general knew we were there, that's all they had to know. Period. Anyhow, they're so involved in what they're doing and what they're doing is so intense that we very quickly became irrelevant.

So access was definitely not a problem. When I first arrived, I met the commandant of that base and he said, "We've got nothing to hide." The brass didn't see the film until it was finished and they never asked to screen a cut [an edited version before the film is finally completed] or demanded any rights to censor the film. To this day I don't know how they reacted to it. Even though, at the highest level, there were probably some sequences in there that Marines might have wished we hadn't filmed.

For instance, I think the general was quite embarrassed about the scene where the instructor is talking about women in a very crude and sexist way. But he couldn't really say anything because the sexual analogy is a constant theme. That guy knew we were filming and I don't think he changed anything for us, one way or the other. While we were there, the first batch of women recruits were going through basic training and we filmed a little bit with them. The Marines were quite insulted that there were women on the base. They seemed to have this very odd feeling towards women. They looked down on them; but, at the same time, protecting the weak womenfolk back home is a motivation which is used constantly with them. They tend to view women as whores or saints. It's totally neanderthal but it's one of the buttons they press in these young 18-year-olds.

structuring the footage

We worked on the editing for about six months. The film was simple to structure because it has a clear chronological line: the kids arrive on a bus in the middle of the night from Savannah, Georgia, they're yanked off the bus, their heads are shaved, and eleven weeks later they graduate. The drama is inherent in the transformation of these pimply-faced, long-haired louts at the beginning to the few, the proud and the converted at the end. It really was a piece of cake. The hardest part was having to cry over footage that couldn't be included, because we easily had enough material for a two-hour film.

I would have preferred if Gwynne [Dyer, the narrator/host] were not in the film and, much to his credit, he agreed with me. I thought he did a really good job; but in terms of cinema, it was a stronger film without him because for every minute of screen time Gwynne took up, we had to throw

out really compelling footage. But the film was part of a series for television and the series format included a commentator/host. So it was necessary that he be there and I absolutely agreed with that.

I've heard that some people are uncomfortable with the narration because they feel that, whether it was intentional or not, Gwynne sounded as though he was putting down kids who didn't have many other choices. I would say that's probably true. There was a certain condescension in the commentary which is partly Gwynne's style. He has a rather acerbic, wry way of writing and speaking and I thought in some cases it did those kids a disservice, but not really very much.

point of view

One brings a lot of one's own filters to this film. Some people see it as a condemnation of the Marines and other people see it as a recruiting film for the Marines. And times change those filters, too. If you screened *Anybody's Son* right after the Gulf War, you'd probably get a different reaction from the audience than you would have if you had showed it eight months before. In late 1990 you would be more likely to have people cheering in the aisles, while another time they might have been quite horrified by it.

I have to say that, personally, I liked those kids and officers. I thought they were honest, honorable people who were doing something that nobody else wanted to do. After all, basically the middle class majority gets the underclass to fight their wars for them. And you can't blame the underclass for that.

The thesis of the film is that you can take 18-year-old males — probably in some kind of difficulty with the law or unable to make it in society for a number of reasons — you can take those kids and you can make them anything you want in 11 weeks, if you totally control their environment. Given that, we as a society get those kids to do our killing and our dying for us. If one sees a problem, those kids are not the problem.

I sometimes think it's unfortunate that they couldn't take the energy that they put into making these guys a fighting force and make them into a force to clean up the environment, for example. You can motivate people to do a lot of things which are positive too. Maybe it's true you couldn't find the buttons to push. Maybe if the womenfolk weren't threatened by the barbarian hordes, you couldn't motivate these guys. Maybe the fact that we're losing the forests wouldn't turn people on. But I'm not convinced of that.

—MONTREAL, 1991

quotes from the film

Narrator:
"The secret of basic training is that it's not really about teaching people things at all. It's about changing people so that they can do things they wouldn't have dreamt of otherwise."

Drill Instructor:
"I can motivate a recruit, and in third phase if I tell him to jump off the third deck, he'll jump off the third deck. I can do anything I want to do because I guess you could say, in a way, we brainwash them a little bit. But you know, they're good people."

Recruit:
"I had a little two-bit job as a maid and one day I just said to myself, you know, you're a maid — what are you doing here? You've got to get your act together."

Drill Instructor:
"We say in the Marine Corps that we build men."

Narrator:
"Women lack a lot of the traditional male notions that make men recruits easy to mold into soldiers ... The basic combat unit, a small group of men

bound together by strong male ties of loyalty and solidarity, is a time-tested system that works. If you let women in, then who are the men protecting and who can they feel superior to?"

Narrator:

"It doesn't really matter who the enemy is, it's the idea of the enemy that's important."

Drill Instructor:

"If that's what you get paid to do is bag groceries, you bag groceries. If you get paid to look down your sights and pull the trigger and kill a man, that's what you do."

Narrator:

"If you're young enough, all the ideas about heroism and military glory that you picked up in childhood are still there, unadulterated by adult experience, like buttons waiting to be pushed."

Narrator:

"Governments acting on our behalf are the cause of wars. We simply employ soldiers to do the dying for us."

students' comments

"This film is so interesting that it's almost like a real movie!"
17-YEAR-OLD STUDENT

"The fact that a shy teenager can be turned into a killing machine completely devoted to his country is quite a terrifying topic."
15-YEAR-OLD STUDENT

"This is a very powerful and inspirational film. It almost justifies the money our government spends on defence."
16-YEAR-OLD STUDENT

"The film hit me quite hard in both directions — I felt both hatred and admiration for the soldiers at different points in the film."
16-YEAR-OLD STUDENT

"I was interested because it showed us what life was really like in the Marines, not the way it's shown in the movies."
16-YEAR-OLD STUDENT

IDEAS *for* DISCUSSION

In addition to using "Quotes from the Film" as a basis for discussion, you may want to try out some of the following suggestions:

1

I'm sick and tired of begging for a measly dime or a quarter. I'm fed up with looking for a job all over town. The army's the right place for a fellow like me. I have no trade, no education. I'll be better off there.

GABRIELLE ROY, *THE TIN FLUTE*

Discuss the issue of class and how it conditions the young men's choices in **Anybody's Son Will Do,** *particularly in the light of Paul Cowan's comment that the middle-class majority gets the underclass to fight its wars.*

2

Screen the excerpt from **Docudrama: Fact and Fiction** *that includes clips from the documentary* **The Kid Who Couldn't Miss** (*THE POLITICS OF TRUTH,* *video location 25). Then discuss the issues of patriotism and heroism raised by that film and* **Anybody's Son Will Do.** *Consider Gwynne Dyer's statement, "If you're young enough, all the ideas about heroism and military glory that you picked up in childhood are still there, unadulterated by adult experience, like buttons waiting to be pushed."*

ACTIVITIES

1

The question of the film's point of view — what it is, how it has been constructed, its possible ambiguity — is one of the central issues in any discussion of *Anybody's Son Will Do.*

The following activity was devised by Trish Skrzypczyk of Emery Collegiate Institute in Toronto, Ontario, to be used with her grade 11 English students when viewing the film for a second time. With the second screening, students were assigned to groups to take notes.

Part A
Guided Viewing - group assignment: point of view

GROUP 1: Recruits — Identify specific feelings the recruits have and the events that cause them. What message is the filmmaker presenting through these feelings?

GROUP 2: Veteran Marines — Identify specific attitudes they express about war, the Marines and the United States. What message is the filmmaker presenting through these attitudes?

GROUP 3: Narrator — What comments does the narrator make about soldiers and war? What message is the filmmaker presenting through these comments?

GROUP 4: Military Life — What picture does the film present of life in the Marines? Look at the drill instructors, the environment, the uniforms, the activities.

At the next session, students in groups compared their notes to try to reach some conclusions about the film. Then, either as a whole class or in groups re-formed jigsaw style, a discussion was held to see if the conclusions reached were compatible or conflicting and to figure out why.

Part B:

Written Assignment
In one page, explain what you think the film is trying to say about soldiers and war. Offer specific details from the film to support your points.

2
Besides building soldiers, the Marines build "men". Screen the film to see what values and assumptions about masculinity are being imparted. You may want to focus on the scene where the recruit insists that he wants to go home, or the scene with the drill sergeant talking to his men about Susie Rotten Crotch.

3
Access — being given permission to film particular people in particular locations — is crucial to the making of any documentary. In pairs or groups, brainstorm the following problem: You have decided to make a documentary about a company that is dumping waste into a local river. You want to get access in order to film inside the plant. Who would you talk to? What would you say? What would the company's concerns be about what's presented? Is the company likely to give you permission to film? Would you give it any editorial control? Role play the situation. (For further information about access, see Paul Cowan's interview, p. 168.)

4
Compare *Anybody's Son Will Do* with a feature-length fiction film about soldiers, such as *A Few Good Men* or *Full Metal Jacket*, the first portion of which was also shot on Parris Island. Do the portrayals differ? If so, how? Which do you prefer and why?

5

See the excerpt from *Anybody's Son* in the STUDY EXTRACTS (SHAPING REALITY, video location 66). Suggestions for related activities appear on p. 110.

FURTHER RESOURCES

film/video

To see soldiers from the "enemy's" point of view, screen *Of Lives Uprooted* (VOICES OF EXPERIENCE, VOICES FOR CHANGE, PART 1, video location 71) or *Children of War* (VOICES OF EXPERIENCE, VOICES FOR CHANGE, PART 2, video location 00).

Return to Dresden is a beautifully constructed documentary about a veteran returning after 40 years to the city he firebombed as an 18-year-old who was "following orders". There, he comes face to face with his former "enemies" with whom he discovers a joint longing for peace. Available from the NFB.

print

The essay "Faces of the Enemy" in *Thought and Style,* edited by Kellow and Krisak (Toronto: Prentice Hall, 1987), seeks to describe and categorize images used to dehumanize the enemy.

voices of experience, voices for change

You may say, how can a voice be invisible? A voice not heard and a vision not seen, a reality not shown and a reality not revealed, is a reality that's invisible.

LAURA SKY, FILMMAKER

Whose voices get to be heard in the media? Whose stories are most often told in movies and TV shows? Whose stories are ignored? From whose perspective are events framed? What role has documentary filmmaking played in the struggles of people on the margins to have a say in their society?

This selection of films and interviews examines documentary as a vehicle for reclaiming and celebrating cultural and social histories, identities and voices. It is, in part, a challenge to the "whiteness" and "middle classness" of mainstream media production. It is also an affirmation that the cultural and class diversity of student and other viewers be acknowledged and represented.

Who gets to speak? Who doesn't? Who gets heard? Who's a witness? Who's an expert? Who's behind the camera? Who's not? Who sets the agenda? Who chooses the frame?

Like so many films in this package, the following material connects with issues raised in other sections: point of view; interpretation of reality (personal, cultural, historical, political); the filmmaker as social and political advocate; strategies and approaches related to form.

Traditionally, documentary film has been linked with social and political issues, although as we have demonstrated, there are many other aspects to this genre as well. Whether a documentary is a mirror that reflects its society or a hammer that actively changes it (Bertolt Brecht, p. 56) — or perhaps both — depends partly on the commitment, vision, and orientation of the filmmaker, and partly on the social/cultural/political context in which she works. What is, perhaps, most notable is that some of these films tend to be "inside stories". *The Ballad of Crowfoot* is a poetic re-interpretation of Canadian history from an Aboriginal point of view. *Richard Cardinal: Cry from a Diary of a Métis Child,* about the suicide of a Métis boy who had been shuffled through 17 foster homes, is a powerful example of documentary advocacy. Excerpts from *Foster Child,* in which the filmmaker sets out to uncover his own past, are offered as a follow-up to issues raised in *Richard Cardinal.*

Michèle Lalonde's poem about power and oppression is translated into a concise and compelling film, *Speak White. Of Lives Uprooted* features the drawings and voices of Central American refugee children who describe their flight from their war-torn homelands. *Children of War,* about the experiences of youth from ravaged countries, illustrates the power of film to convey the realities of life in other parts of the world, and to stir social and political awareness. Finally, *Black Mother, Black Daughter* is a celebration of women's contributions to Black culture in Nova Scotia. It is an example of the increasing use of documentary as a means of disseminating unwritten chapters of social history.

For further information about voice in filmmaking and the choices available to the filmmaker (narration in the first and third person; the voice of the interview subject; the voice of the director), see WAYS OF STORYTELLING, p. 5.

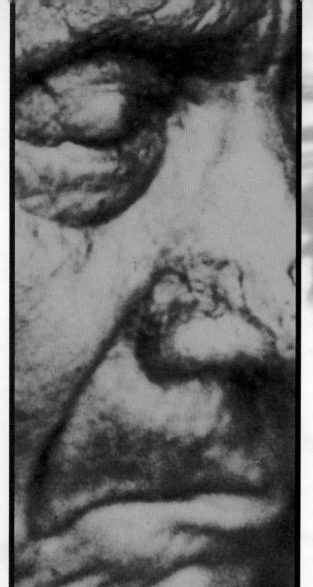

the ballad of Crowfoot

VIDEO LOCATION **00** IN *VOICES OF EXPERIENCE,*
VOICES FOR CHANGE, PART 1

11 MINUTES

BLACK & WHITE

1968

DIRECTOR: *WILLIE DUNN*

PRODUCER: *BARRIE HOWELLS*

DISTRIBUTOR: *NFB*

SUGGESTIONS *for* USE

- *For the first screening, show a portion of the film with no soundtrack. (For more information, see "Before Viewing" Activity 2, p. 187.)*

- *The words of the song have been included here, pp. 182 - 183.*

- *For discussion ideas, see "Before Viewing" Activity 1, p. 187.*

The Ballad of Crowfoot is a bitter, haunting, and impressionistic film that examines the situation of Aboriginal people in North America through the figure of Crowfoot, the legendary 19th-century Blackfoot leader of the Plains. A rapid montage of archival photos, etchings and contemporary newspaper clippings is married to the words and music of an impassioned ballad written by Micmac singer and songwriter Willie Dunn.

Dunn directed the film as a member of the Indian Film Crew, seven Native people recruited from across the country for a two-year program in filmmaking, co-sponsored by the Company of Young Canadians and the National Film Board. *The Ballad of Crowfoot,* produced in 1968, was one of the very first films made by members of the group; its form is a precursor to that of contemporary music videos. Fueled by historic anger, *Ballad of Crowfoot* was created during a decade marked by political activism and protest — AIM (the American Indian Movement), the rise of the FLQ (Front de libération du Québec), protests against the Vietnam war, the civil rights movement — and makes no attempt to hide its point of view. It speaks with an insider's voice about the cultural and social consequences for Aboriginal people of the opening of the Canadian West.

the ballad of Crowfoot

chorus:

Crowfoot, Crowfoot, why the tears?
You've been a brave man for many years,
Why the sadness, why the sorrow?
Maybe there will be a better tomorrow.

Comes the spring and its warm thaw,
Around your neck the eagle claw,
Upon your head the buffalo horn,
Today a great new chief is born.
So raise him now toward the sun,
A heart now beats, a life comes forth,
It's eighteen hundred twenty-one,
Today a Blackfoot soul's begun,

chorus . . .

Your youth is gone, the years have past,
Your heart is set, your soul is cast,
You stand before the council fire,
You have the mind and the desire,
Of notions wise you speak so well,
And in brave deeds you do excel,
It's eighteen hundred fifty-three,
And you stand the chief of confederacy,
You are the leader, you are the chief,

You stand against both the liar and thief,
They trade braves, whisky, steal your land,
And they're coming in swift like the wind-blown
    sand,
They shoot the buffalo, kill the game,
And send their preachers in to shame,
Its eighteen hundred sixty-four and you think of
    peace
And you think of war.

chorus . . .

You see the settlers in more numbers,
He takes whatever he encounters,
You've seen the Sioux all battered, beaten,
They're all in rags, they haven't eaten,
The Nez Percé were much the same,
It seems like such a heartless game,
And it's eighteen hundred seventy-six,
And the enemy's full of those death-dealing tricks.

Today the treaty stands on the table,
Will you sign it, are you able?
It offers food and protection too,
Do you really think they'll hold it true,
It offers a reserve, now isn't that grand?
And in return you cede all your land,
And it's eighteen hundred seventy-seven
And you know the scales are so uneven.

chorus . . .

Well the buffalo are slaughtered,

There's nothing to eat,

The government's late again with the meat,

Your people are riddled with the white man's
    disease,

And in the summer you're sick,

And in the winter you freeze,

And sometimes you wonder why you signed that
    day,

But they broke the treaty themselves anyway,

And it's eighteen hundred eighty-nine,

And your death star explodes and then it falls.

chorus . . .

The years have past, the years have flown,

The nation since has swiftly grown,

And yet for the Indian it's all the same,

There's still the hardship,

There's still the pain,

There's still the strife,

Its bitterness shines like a whetted knife,

There's still the hypocrisy,

There's still the hate,

Was that in the treaties, is that our fate?

We're all unhappy pawns in the government's game,

And it's always the Indian who gets the blame,

It's a problem which money can never lessen,

And it's nineteen hundred and sixty-seven.

chorus . . .

Maybe one day you'll find honesty,

Instead of the usual treachery,

Perhaps one day the truth shall prevail,

And the warmth of love which it does entail.

chorus . . .

a biographical note on Crowfoot

A renowned hunter, brave warrior and eloquent spokesman for his people, Crowfoot was born in 1821 near Blackfoot Crossing on the Bow River, now part of Alberta. Born a Blood, he grew up among the Blackfoot and quickly became known as a compelling orator for the Blackfoot Confederacy.

Crowfoot was a perceptive, farseeing and diplomatic leader who established good relations with the fur traders and sued for peace with the Cree. In September 1877, he unwillingly signed Treaty No. 7 on behalf of his Nation, which ceded 50,000 square miles of prairie land to the Canadian government. This treaty led to the rapid disappearance of the buffalo and the near-starvation of the Blackfoot people.

After the Blackfoot settled on their reserve in 1881, Crowfoot became increasingly disenchanted with the Canadian government; but he refused to allow his followers to join the 1885 Northwest Rebellion, which he saw as a losing fight. Crowfoot died in April 1890. (Reference: *The Canadian Encyclopedia*, 1st ed., vol. 1, p.545.)

A different perspective: Morris Wolfe argues for the voices of change

In the late 1960s, members of the Indian Film Crew (as it was then known) were given an opportunity to develop skills so they could tell the stories of their people in their own voices. On November 12, 1991, this article by Morris Wolfe about the need for employment equity in the media appeared in the Globe and Mail.

The Ontario government has announced it will introduce employment equity legislation in the next few months. The groups to be covered by the legislation are women, racial minorities, people with disabilities, and aboriginal people. Nowhere is the lack of employment equity so apparent as in the media. Although one in four people in Metropolitan Toronto is non-white, this city's mainstream newspapers, magazines, radio and television stations remain largely white. Nothing close to one in four of Toronto's reviewers, columnists and reporters is non-white. Among senior decision-makers in the media, the proportions are much worse. An invitation to a symposium on the future of Canada's newspapers lists 82 participants, 14 of whom are women. I'd be surprised if more than a few are non-white. A 1986 study of 20 Canadian newspapers revealed that only 1.7 per cent of newsroom employees were either members of visible minorities or disabled.

Would employment equity make a difference to consumers of the mainstream media? I think so. If I were non-white, I'd be enraged by most of the reviews of films that touch on the Third World, such films as *A Passage to India, Out of Africa,* and *The Gods Must Be Crazy.* Mainstream reviewers, almost all of whom are white, frequently seem insensitive when they write about such films. One has to turn to small-circulation, alternative magazines such as the excellent Canadian quarterly *Tiger Lily: Journal by Women of Colour,* for a different perspective.

"The white man," says English professor Arun Mukherjee in Issue No. 7, "wants the Third World native to tell him that it was all right...to have taken away the victim's birthright, that it was indeed good...that the white man came to this country and 'civilized' him." Mukherjee shows us how filmmaker David Lean deliberately muted E.M. Forster's novel, *A Passage to India.* Lean's Dr. Aziz is

a wimp rather than someone who, like all the Indians in the Forster novel, is "skillful in the slighter impertinences." *Out of Africa,* by focusing on a romantic couple in a beautiful setting, reduces black history to a mere footnote.

Mukherjee's angriest comments are reserved for *The Gods Must Be Crazy.* She quotes anthropologists Richard Lee and Toby Volkman, who debunk the film's myth of the Bushman as a noble savage. "There is ...little to laugh about in Bushmanland," they write, "1,000 demoralized, formerly independent foragers crowd into a squalid, tubercular homeland, getting by on handouts of cornmeal and sugar, drinking Johnnie Walker or home brew, fighting with one another and joining the South African army." What could be neater, writes Mukherjee, than portraying the natives as rejecting such gifts of civilization as a Coke bottle. "The white man can enjoy his consumerism and standard of life without worrying about the native's poverty because not only does he like his poverty, but also because he rejects material goods since they destroy his harmonious life style. What could be a better salve for the white man's conscience?" Even if one disagrees with these comments, it would have been useful if they have had appeared in the mainstream press.

Or consider *Paris is Burning,* a documentary about the poor, black gays who imitate white women at drag balls in Harlem, in the heart of America's Third World. Reviewers in the mainstream media focussed almost entirely on the film as spectacle. *Sassy Magazine* was typical. It declared that *Paris is Burning* is "about pretending your way out of poverty and oppression because for as long as you're dancing, you really are a superstar." Attempts at analysis were, at best, cursory. Vincent Canby of the *New York Times,* for example, concluded a lenghty discussion of the film as spectacle by saying, "yet there is a terrible sadness in the testimony. The queens knock themselves out to imitate the members of a society that will not have them." End of review.

The only piece I've read about *Paris is Burning* that goes beyond spectacle to real analysis is by the black lesbian critic, Bell Hooks, in the left-wing American magazine *Z.* She sees the film as a portrait of the way "colonized black people...worship at the throne of whiteness, even when such worship demands that (they) live in perpetual self-hate." She criticizes the film for its failure to tell us about the men's friends, families and lives apart from the balls. Hooks concludes with a passionate reminder. All of us need to rid ourselves, she says, of the "longing for an illusory

star identity, so that we can confront and accept ourselves as we really are—only then can fantasy... be a site of seduction, passion and play where the self is truly recognized, loved and never abandoned or betrayed."

In addition to confronting and accepting ourselves, we need to hear a much broader range of others' voices and opinions in the mainstream media. Employment equity may help us do so.

IDEAS *for* DISCUSSION

1

What is your response to this film? To the images? To the music? What kind of mood is created?

2

From whose point of view is the ballad sung?

3

Does this view of Native history differ from the images and stories about Aboriginal people presented in other films, videos or television programs you have seen? If so, how? (For suggestions about other films and videos, see "Further Resources", p. 188. Additional material about cinematic re-interpretations of history can be found in the chapter "Docudrama: Fact and Fiction", p. 124)

ACTIVITIES

Before Viewing

1

Since *The Ballad of Crowfoot* was produced in 1968, the language used to refer to this country's original inhabitants has changed: from "Indian" to "Native" to "Aboriginal" to "First Nations". (In most Native languages, the term used translates as "the people".) What are the denotations and connotations associated with each of these words? What are the possible causes for such changes in terminology? Examine the language used to refer to First Nations people in history texts from the 1950s to the present. Which terms are used? By whom? How was Aboriginal people's part in Canadian history represented?

2

Screen a portion of this film without the soundtrack. What mood do the visuals suggest? Does the rhythm with which they are presented create a mood? If so, what is it? What do you imagine the soundtrack would be like for these visuals? Would there be a narrator? First or third person? Man or woman? Young or old? Aboriginal or non-Aboriginal? Would there be music? What kind?

After Viewing

1

Screen *Speak White* (VOICES OF EXPERIENCE, VOICES FOR CHANGE, PART 1, video location 64), which also uses stills and a poetic soundtrack to re-vision history from the point of view of a particular cultural group. What differences and similarities do you see between these two films? Why is it important for these voices to be heard?

2

Write or find a protest song (on a social, political, or environmental issue, perhaps) and find visuals to complement the words and music. Present the visuals either as slides or on video.

3

Examine a current newspaper article or television news item or documentary about Aboriginal people. From whose point of view is the material presented? Are there significant similarities with the conditions detailed in *The Ballad of Crowfoot?* Or collect recent newspaper headlines about First Nations issues and collage them. Does their content differ from the collages in the film? If so, how?

4

See *"City of Gold"* (p. 8) for activities involving stills (including a model for a mat that can be used to frame portions of photos in different ways.)

FURTHER RESOURCES

film/video

The feature films *Dances with Wolves, Black Robe* and *The Last of the Mohicans* may provide viewers with some interesting similarities and contrasts between those films and Crowfoot.

The "Westerns" section of most video stores is well stocked with examples of the kinds of images of "Indians" and of the versions of history against which the makers of *The Ballad of Crowfoot* were reacting. Some titles that might reward investigation include *Broken Arrow, Buffalo Bill's Wild West Show, Tell Them Willy Boy Was Here* and *Little Big Man.*

First Nations: The Circle Unbroken is a series of thirteen 20-minute programs about current issues, cultural identity, and relations between First Nations and Canada. Available with a teacher's guide from the NFB.

Incident at Oglaga is a documentary investigation of the case of Leonard Peltier, a leader of AIM (the American Indian Movement). Charged with murder in the 1975 shooting of two FBI agents at Pine Ridge Reservation, he was sentenced to life imprisonment, a verdict many consider a grave miscarriage of justice.

print

A useful annotated catalogue available from NFB
offices is *Our Home and Native Land: A Film and
Video Resource Guide for Aboriginal Canadians.*
Hugh Dempsey's biography *Crowfoot: Chief to the
Blackfeet* (Halifax: Goodread Biographies, 1988)
examines the life and times of the leader of the
Blackfoot Confederacy.

In the Spirit of Crazy Horse by Peter Mathiessen
(New York: Viking, 1991) deals with Leonard
Peltier, his involvement in AIM, the shootout at
Oglala, and the sorry state of Aboriginal American-
U.S. relations.

For a re-visioning of history, see Dee Brown's *Bury
My Heart at Wounded Knee: An Indian History of
the American West* (New York: Holt, 1970, 1991).

For a glimpse into another aspect of Native history,
tradition, and heritage see Paula Gunn Allen's
collection *Grandmothers of the Light: A Medicine
Woman's Sourcebook* (Boston: Beacon Press, 1991).

Touch the Earth: A Self-Portrait of Indian Experience
(ed. T.C. McLuhan, New York: Pocket Books,
1972) contains passages taken from the speeches
and writings of North American Aboriginal peoples
from the 16th to the 20th centuries.

Richard Cardinal: cry from a diary of a Métis child

VIDEO LOCATION **11** IN *VOICES OF EXPERIENCE,*
VOICES FOR CHANGE, PART **1**

30 MINUTES

1986

DIRECTOR: *ALANIS OBOMSAWIN*

PRODUCERS: *A. OBOMSAWIN, M. CANELL, R. VERRALL*

SUGGESTIONS *for* USE

- *This film must be previewed by the teacher. Also, we suggest that students be told briefly the gist of the film before it is screened, in case there is anyone who does not want to view it.*

- *See other suggestions that follow on page 192.*

Richard Cardinal: Cry From a Diary of a Métis Child is an emotionally powerful film about a 17-year-old Métis boy from Alberta. Cardinal committed suicide after a childhood and youth spent in 28 foster homes, group homes and lock-up facilities, far from his original home community. Following his death, a poignant diary of his anguished years was discovered by his last foster family. Extracts from this diary, dramatic re-creations of events from his childhood, and interviews with his brother and various foster parents have been woven into a haunting blend of testimony and tribute.

The director, Alanis Obomsawin, above, an Abenaki from the Odanak reserve northeast of Montreal, has been working in documentary production for more than 15 years. A storyteller and singer, she was attracted to film's potential to communicate the experiences, history, and injustices of her people, and to further the struggle for social change. As she commented in a 1987 interview in *Cinema Canada:*

One reason I make the films I do is to fight injustice, to find a way to make people change their attitudes towards other human beings who are different from them. For me, for our own people, it's a place to speak directly to the world. To see the real people — all their lives nobody's listened to them, nobody's interested and all of a sudden, they have a chance to speak to millions of people and say exactly what it's like. That's why I think it's so important to do documentaries.

Richard Cardinal is an example of advocacy filmmaking from a strong and committed point of view. Like Sylvia Hamilton in *Black Mother, Black Daughter,* Alanis Obomsawin speaks from within her culture about the stories and issues that are critical to her community.

The film is followed by an interview with its director in which Alanis Obomsawin talks about *Richard Cardinal,* her commitment to fight social injustice, the value of documentary in that struggle, and her belief in maintaining a passionate point of view in her films.

The Alberta government bought multiple copies of the film. It became compulsory viewing for all social-work students in the province. As a result of the inquest into Richard's death, sweeping changes were instituted to the Child Welfare Act in Alberta, and Aboriginal people were given the right to run their own social service agencies.

To make the film, Alanis Obomsawin had to solve a problem. How, as a filmmaker, does one pay tribute to someone no longer alive — and someone whose story transcends the personal? In this case, the director chose not to take a "journalistic" approach, in which welfare administrators and government policy makers could present the "other side" of the story. The film belongs to Richard Cardinal who finally got to say all the things that no one heard him utter in his short, tragic life.

> I think that Richard speaks very well for himself. Nobody has to be told "It's your fault" or "It's not your fault". His gesture is strong enough. For me, the film is for all people concerned with children — any children. I want people who look at the film to have a different attitude next time they meet what is called a problem child, and develop some love and some relationship to the child — instead of alienating him. I want even the worst person, who makes problems for children, to go home and change his rules and attitudes.

ALANIS OBOMSAWIN, *CINEMA CANADA*, #142, JUNE 1987

SUGGESTIONS *for* USE

- *We found that students reacted strongly and emotionally to Richard's story; they felt it was important that what had happened to him be widely known. Our teacher consultants considered the film particularly valuable for the issues it raised and the response it evoked. However, they urged us to tell other educators to show the film at the beginning rather than the end of a week, in case some students had a delayed reaction to the material and might want someone (a teacher, a school counsellor or social worker) to talk to over the next few days.*

- *Students will need time to process and discuss/work with their feelings about this film, so it is especially important to give them opportunities to talk or write about their responses. See the "Before Viewing" activity, p. 202, which involves working with Richard's diary.*

- *We noticed during test screenings that while some students were quite aware of the social and cultural dimensions of Richard's plight, there were others who tended to see the events of his life in purely psychological terms. We have therefore provided some further context for viewers by juxtaposing two other films with this documentary.* **The Ballad of Crowfoot** *(VOICES OF EXPERIENCE, VOICES FOR CHANGE, PART 1, video location 00) sketches some of the historical background pertinent to Richard's situation.* **Foster Child** *(VOICES OF EXPERIENCE, VOICES FOR CHANGE, PART 1, video location 49), which should be screened as a follow-up, provides further information about the child-welfare system. It also offers viewers a chance to examine the situation of another dislocated Métis "foster child", more fortunate than Richard, who at the age of 35 sets out to discover his "real" family.*

I Was a Victim of Child Neglect
by Richard S. Cardinal

The text of Richard's journal, exactly as he wrote it, has been reprinted here. It is this text that Alanis Obomsawin used as the basis of her dramatic re-creations of parts of Richard's life.

Special thanks to my brother Charlie Cardinal who inspired me to wright this book.

I was born in Ft. Chipewyan that much I know for certain because it's on my birth-certificate.

I have no memories or certain knowledge of what transpired over the next few years. I was once told by a Social Worker that my parents were alcoholic's and that all of us kids were removed for this reason. I was separated from the rest of the family and placed in a foster home somewere in fort MacMurry.

> GOD
> Grant me the serenity
> to accept the
> things I cannot change...
> Courage to change
> the things I can, and
> the wisdom to know
> the difference.

My earlyiest memories are from when I was liveing with a family (DUPRUIG'S) in Wandering-River. I have little memory of this home but I do remember that I was playing with some wooden match'es and I guess when I left one was still going and the outcome was desastrous, the shed in which I had been playing had caught on fire, which spread and caught onto the hay stack. When they had finally put the fire out and managed to save 3/4 of the stack I was given the wipping of my life, and was made clear that if I ever played with matches again it would be worse the next time, I was often tested on this, however, I had learnd my lesson and never touched a match while I lived there. I was also reunited with my brother at this home so I did not feel so alone any more. We were moved after about a year.

Our next home was in the same town just a few miles away form DUPRUIS. This home was good in one way but bad in alot of ways. It seemed that for every good happenings there were two bad ones. I remember one night we were not fed and there was a bag of raw turnips by our bedroom door so we ate about three apiece. Their was another time when we were hauling gravel from the driveway to the garage that the HEBERTS were building and then we had to tamp all bumps and big rocks out so that the floor was level. Well we worked on this for about a week and when we finished we were both paid one dollar apiece. When I got my dollar I felt as though I owened the world because a dollar was worth quite a bit back then. Well me and Charlie both went running as fast as our little legs (mine were smaller so I had to run twice as fast) would carry us, down to the general store which by the way was the only-one in town. When we were finished purcaseing all we wanted, we had close to a grocery bag full of candy. about three months later my sister Linda (who is the oldest of the girls in our family) was moved into our foster home. Charlie and linda were always playing together and seeing as I was still pretty small I was always left-out so I began to spend alot of time alone. There was a time all of us kids (includeing the neighbours kids) were all caught smokeing and I was punished by having to smoke a cigar and one package of cigarettes one after another and I had to inhale every drag I took too. I was pretty sick for a couple of days after this too. There was another time when one of their girls had a birthday and we celebrated by each getting a 1/2 cup of wine, well everything was great until I finished my cup and asked if I could have another, well I got one more but it sure was'nt wine because after I was finish I felt as though I was standing in a canoe in the middle of a storm on the high seas. I can't remember anymore of that night.

Our next move was a few month's later, we were moved to live _____ we lived with a elderly couple by the name of_____. I enjoyed this home for the first two days then everything went wrong when we had to go back to school. The first day I was sent to the office three time's in the same day for fighting. It was at this home that I took up the habit of smokeing also. We (chuck, linda and I) would steal Mr._____ cigarettes from the fridge where he would keep them so they would stay fresh. When we got a pack we would go behind the barn and smoke a few, then linda would hide them in her room. I began to get into a lot of trouble for neglecting my chores and was hit several time's with a stick and sent to bed. I could hear Mr. &

Mrs._____ arguing late into the night, About them hitting me. In school it was worse than ever I was constantly in trouble with the principle for fighting and not doing my work in class. I was also considered an out-cast among students, while my brother and sister were always popular however they both stuck up for me when I needed it. Which is probably the reason were in the office as much or more as I was. In the barn-yard at home we had a small, fast-running creek which we enjoyed tire tubeing down and one day I could not stop so charlie and linda were forced to follow me away's

down the creek until they could stop me. There was a hill across the creek about five hundred or six hundred yards away from the yard, which was constantly covered in gophers so if I wasn't out romping with rex (The family dog) we were found up on the hill hunting gopher's. One day we saw one and went to his hole and began to dig and after about two hour's digging we reached his nest and I went to grab him and he sunk his teeth into my hand and would not let go so me and Rex began to beat on his head and when he finally let go, Rex bit him to ribbons for makeing my hand into minced meat. When fall returned it was back to school for us kids. I can remember _____ trying to get us ready before the bus arrived but we were so excited that we were hopping around like grasshoppers on a hot summerday. I would be returning to grade two this year. I was not considered an outcast this year and got my first tast of puppy love with a girl named Heather. I was half-way through the school year when a Social Worker came to our home and I was to be moved and asked me how soon I would be ready to move and I answerd, 1 week, I should have answered never. When I would move alone Charlie and linda would stay.

I had 4 hours before I would leave my family and friends behind and since linda and charlie were at school, I went into the bedroom and dug-out my old harmonica and went down to the barn yard and sat on the fence and began to lay to the cows. I did'nt know how to play at all but I played real slow and sad like for the occation, but before halfway through the song my lower lip began to quiver and I knew I was going to cry and I was glad so I didn't even try to stop myself. I guess that

_____ heard me and must have come down to comfort me, when she put her arm around me and I pulled away and ran up the road aways. I did'nt want no one's love any more I had been hurt to many times so I began to learn the art of blocking out all emotions and I shut out the rest of the world out and the door would open to no one.

The Social Worker arived to take me away to my new home. On the way their he tryed to talk to me but I was'nt hearing or trying to hear. When we arrived the Social Worker wanted to talk to the parents alone so I remained in the car. About half an hour later, he came out and called me but I would not move and when he came to the car I locked the doors, I did not want him to leave me hear. Hear I was friendless, alone and very scared. finally thy coaxed me out of the car and I began to cry. The Social Worker told them___that I would get over it soon and left, But I would'nt get over it, not now, not ever! I told myself. I was taken into

their house and _____ showed me were I would sleep. The room was in the basement of the house. When I walked into the room I could not believe my eye's. The floor was covered with water (about an inch and half) and there were boards on the floor to keep your feet from getting wet. The walls had been painted red but had long before began to peel off, the window which was no bigger than a atlas had a gape between the foundation and the bottom which let in the cold winter wind and the beds were no wider than two feet across and about a foot off the floor. There was a 40 watt light that was in the ceiling (which was not completely finished) and you had to pull a string to turn it on. It looked like something that you would see in a horror movie! "You'll be sharing this room with another boy" he said and with that he returned upstairs. The night was a night mare in it self, The wind constantly blew through the crack and it was like sleeping in a cool room I had a spider crawl across my face twice before I finally killed the dumb thing. and I was constantly cold. In the morning I was assigned chores to do and I would be fed after they were done. When I was finished I was returning to the house to eat and found a lunch bag in the door way, this was my breakfast. I was not allowed to eat with the family in the house, and the same with lunch and supper. The next few days were like living in a jail, I was set boundries in which to stay in and I was to come running "when I was called." I kept telling myself that this was all a bad dream and that I would wake up soon with charlie and linda and the rest of the family in our home back in Ft. Chipewyan, but in reality I knew that I would'nt wake up and that this was real, and not just some bad dream. The first month's rolled by slowly and then bang! it was my birthday, I was now nine however it seemed that everybody could careless. I remaind "locked in my own little world and would not let anything in or out." I was enrolled into Westlock Elementy School, I was better hear I was away from the farm and the family that lived their. Here I began to fall into bad company and got into alot of trouble. We were let out of school for two weeks for Christmas holadays. I figure things would eased-up abit between The Family and I during this period however I was wrong. Things got worse. I was beginning to feel rejected and unwanted. Christmas morning I was sent outside and not allowed back in till dinner and even then I had to eat in the basement. This was it I could'nt take anymore of this I had to leave, go somewere were nobody would find me. I pack my belongings into my back-pack and I had stoled a bottle of rye so I packed that to I snuck out of the house and went over to the garage and rolled up the old tent and secured this onto my pack I was almost ready. I went back into the house and got a

box of wooden matches and stuffed it into my pocket's. as I was comeing back-up the stairs and noticed for the first time the guns hung on the wall there was a box below the gun rack and I opened It up. "Beautiful I told myself, the box had pagages of shells for the guns. Each pack contained 3 boxes of fifty shells. I took two packs and stuffed them into my jacket. When I had got the gun out of the house to the garage I slipped on my pack picked up the gun and head away from the house. I had been gone 4 days before I was caught and brought back to the farm however I felt as though I had done darned good since I was only 9 years old. I spent the rest of the winter here feeling lonly and very depressed. And I began to seriously think about suicide. The first time I attempted it I used a rasor blade to cut my arms but it hurt to much so I did'nt try that agian. When school started up once more I began to skip classes and the _____ were informed. When I return to the farm that evening _____ was waiting for me and he began to yell and sceam at me. I was'nt listening and did not care. finaly he blew his stack and hit me. It was the first time I was hit by him and I guess he exspected me to start in bawling but I did'nt I just stood there and stared blankly at him. This must have scared him because he backhanded me. My lip began to bleed quite badly. When I tasted the blood I spit it beside his shoe's and told him to "GO TO HELL," and with that I walked away while I left him standing there looking rather stupid. After school I would do my chores and sit in the barn and think and one day I was in there thinking, and it struck me I could kill myself now and no one would know until it was to late, and it just so happens that the bail I was sitting on still had a bailer twine on it so I slipped it off and climbed up into the rafters. After I had secured the rope I climbed down and placed some straw underneath the rope I climed on and stood up determind to go through with it. I said a short Prayer for god to take care of my family. I placed the rope around my neck and kicked. my lungs felt like they were about to burst and my ear's felt like they wer melting right off my head. Finaly I blacked out and was engulfed in a blanket of black...

Unfortunately I woke up. I could see alot of people above me, all of a sudden thay all began to talk to me at the same time. I could not make out what they were saying all the words were echoing in my head and my eye's would not focus in on the peaple above me then I was swept back into a sea of blackness.

When I woke-up next I tryed to sit up but my arms were straped down and a sudden burst of pain shot through my neck, it was so suddun and hurt so much I ended up yelling in pain and then I burst-out crying and to this day I still have'nt figured out why. Well anyways about two or three nurses came running into my room and one nurse unstraped my arms. One nurse held me in her arms and repetidly told me everything was OK now. It felt strange to be held and yet it also felt soothing and warm inside. I can't remember how long it had been since I had been held by anyone and I knew that I missed it vary much. Later on I ask one nurse how I ended up in the hospital, and she explained how _____ had notice that my supper had not been touched so he came out to see what I was doing and where I was. she said when he walked into the barn and seen me he wasted no time in cutting the rope and getting me to the car. She also said when I was emited to the hospital my face was still a dark blue and purple coulor, and that my neck was seaping out blood. I then asked her how long I had been out and she replyed 3 days, since the first time I woke up. I had been in a coma and was suffering from shock. I remained in the hospital for anouther week in which I was kept company by a few different nurses. I enjoyed the company and I also enjoyed sleeping in a real bed.

_____ had come to see me and kept talking to me about what happened thay told me thay knew things were rough for me now but things would get better. But I didn't listen to them. How could thay possibly know how things were for me. Thay had their family's, I did'nt and for that matter I didn't even have any friends.

I was released from the hospital after about a week. I was returned to the _____family my social worker was there. We sat and talked for about two hours about how things were going. I exsplained to him that I wanted to be with Charlie and Linda, however he tryed to exsplaine to me how that was impossible for me to go back because (The original of Richard's journal ends here. But the copy of the original made by the police soon after Richard's death carries on for two more pages. These pages have since gone missing.)

_____was not feeling very good and that she was getting too old for so many young kids to take care of an eventually the JONES's would get another boy my age and just before he left I was informed that I would be seeing a phychologist every three days, then he left.

On the first day that I went to see this phychologist, we just sat there and talked about each other, generally just getting to know each other. He kept caling me "my friend" I did not consider him my friend I thought of him as an enemy. He was trying to make me remember, I didn't want to, I just sat and stared at him blankly.

I'm skipping the rest of the years, because it just continued to be the same. However, I would like to say thanks to a special person who made the world a little better for me.

Cheryl MILLER, I still care for you and I want to thank you for making my world a lot brighter for the months when we were going out with each other and I want to say that I still love you! GOOD-BY!

I want to say to the people involved in my life, don't take this personal it's not your fault. I just can't take anymore! and Mrs. KESLER thank you also. Charlie please for once in your life try to understand me. I LOVE YOU!
Lord, Jesus Christ, I'm upset & disturbed, and I pray that you will grant me the grace of inner peace. As you comanded the storm winds at sea to be calmed. Give me the patience I need to cope with the burdens and the anxieties of my life. Grant me the strength to better deal with my problems, and the understanding to be more tolerant and kind to outers. Teach me to seek after your will which alone brings peace of mind and peace of hart.

Amen.

LOVE

Love can be gentle as a lamb
or ferocise as a lion.
it is something to be welcomed
yet it is something to be afraid of
it is good and bad, yet peaple
live fight, and die for this.
somehow people can cope with
it I don't know, I think I would
not be happy with it yet
I am depressed and sad without
it, love is very strang.

RICK CARDINAL

I D E A S *for* D I S C U S S I O N

1

What response do you have to this film? What aspects of Richard's story affected you strongly as you watched? Why do you think you were so moved?

2

What was the difference — in feeling, tone, voice, point of view, effect — between the TV news report about Richard's death included in the documentary, and the documentary as a whole? Were you moved by the news report? Why or why not? Did you feel that it was a strength or a weakness that this film was not "objective"?

3

Mr. Carrothers, Richard's last foster father, says that if he had not photographed Richard hanging in a tree and sent out copies of that photograph, Richard would have been "just another dead Indian." What difference did that photograph make? Why?

What documents/documentation of Richard's life were there in the film? What was the value in documenting Richard's story? Is this story about more than Richard's painful life?

4

After screening Alanis Obomsawin's interview (VOICES OF EXPERIENCE, VOICES FOR CHANGE, PART 1, video location 41) : Do you think it made a difference that this film about a Métis boy was made by an Aboriginal filmmaker? If so, in what ways?

5

If you were going to tell the story of Richard's life, how would you do it? Would you choose to make a documentary or a fiction film? From whose point of view would the story be told? Discuss the reasons for your choices.

What do you feel the dramatic re-enactments of parts of Richard's life add to the film? (For further information about re-enactments and docudrama, see "Docudrama: Fact and Fiction", p. 124.)

6

Is it important that films like this get made, that stories like this get told? Why? Can you think of other films or books that gave you a sense of a person or situation you might never experience in your daily life? Did any affect you strongly? Why?

7

In her interview (video location 41), Alanis Obomsawin vigorously defends her approach to filmmaking — speaking as an advocate for her people rather than an "objective" reporter. Discuss her arguments. Did you find them convincing? (For further background material on the question of objectivity in filmmaking, see video selection WHAT IS A DOCUMENTARY?)

ACTIVITIES

Before Viewing

Have students read Richard's diary. Ask them to discuss how they would go about making a film about this person's life, based on what they had read: Would they work with actors? Would they do interviews? With whom? From whose point of view would the story be told? After they've shared their proposals, screen the film.

After Viewing

1

After watching *Richard Cardinal,* write a letter to one of the film's characters or to the director, sharing your thoughts and feelings. (This activity was suggested by Heinz Senger, educator, Earl Marriott Secondary School, Surrey, B.C.)

2

Screen the excerpt from *Foster Child.* (VOICES OF EXPERIENCE, VOICES FOR CHANGE, PART 1, video location 49). Does it add anything to your understanding of Richard's situation?

3

This documentary was made not only to pay tribute to Richard Cardinal but to agitate for change in the way the Alberta child-welfare system dealt with Aboriginal and Métis children. Research how the child-welfare system works in your province. Why are children taken into foster care? What happens to them? What guidelines are used to place them in various homes? Are there provisions made to respect racial and cultural heritage? Invite a speaker knowledgable about such matters into class.

4

Tell the story of someone who is no longer here, perhaps a family member. What documentation do you have — photos, letters, a journal, interviews with those who knew that person? From whose point of view will the story be told? What scenes will you show? What music and/or sounds would you use to suggest something about that person? (It could be a collection of photocopies and written memories, or slides and a soundtrack, or a video production.)

5

Choose a situation about which you feel strongly. Decide how you would present it on film. Is there a person you know whom you could focus on, in order to get your point across?

FURTHER RESOURCES

film/video

Dreamspeaker, directed by Claude Jutra, is the moving tale of a native elder's attempt, through patient and generous applications of love and wisdom, to heal a psychically wounded white boy who has been failed by mainstream institutions. To borrow, check your local media resource centre or public library. Available for purchase from CBC Educational Sales, Box 500, Station A, Toronto, Ontario M5W 1E6. Fax: (416) 205-3482

print

Our Home and Native Land: A Film and Video Resource Guide for Aboriginal Canadians is an annotated list of productions which have been grouped into thematic sections. Available from the NFB.

In Search of April Raintree by Beatrice Culleton (Winnipeg: Pemmican Publications, 1984) focusses on a young Métis girl and her sister who are raised in a variety of foster homes. April finally turns her back on the white culture in which she was raised and learns to accept her Métis heritage.

Cam Hubert's book *Dreamspeaker* (Toronto: General, 1989) was the inspiration for the Jutra film described above.

Blood Red Ochre by Kevin Major (New York: Dell, 1990) is the story of a young woman who believes that she is the last of the Beothuks.

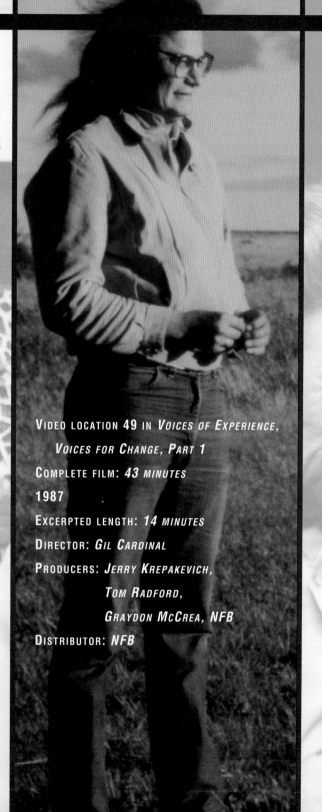

foster child

VIDEO LOCATION **49** IN *VOICES OF EXPERIENCE,*
VOICES FOR CHANGE, PART 1
COMPLETE FILM: *43 MINUTES*
1987
EXCERPTED LENGTH: *14 MINUTES*
DIRECTOR: *GIL CARDINAL*
PRODUCERS: *JERRY KREPAKEVICH,*
            TOM RADFORD,
            GRAYDON McCREA, NFB
DISTRIBUTOR: *NFB*

SUGGESTIONS *for* USE

- *We suggest that this film be used as a follow-up to* Richard Cardinal: Cry from a Diary of a Métis Child *(VOICES OF EXPERIENCE, VOICES FOR CHANGE, PART 1, video location 11).*

- *Before giving students copies of the interview with Gil Cardinal to read, ask them to brainstorm what questions they might put to the filmmaker, were he to be present. After reading the interview, notice which questions remain unanswered; see whether they can be dealt with in small-group or class discussion.*

- *After viewing this excerpt, you may want to screen the entire film, which is available from the NFB.*

Métis filmmaker Gil Cardinal became a foster child at the age of two, and spent the rest of his childhood and adolescence with the same loving family. Now, at the age of 35, driven by the desire to learn about his birth family and the culture from which he came, he sets out to trace who he is and to unravel the circumstances that led to his being taken into foster care. This unrehearsed cinéma vérité film documents the process of search and discovery.

Foster Child is an autobiographical documentary; the director uses his own story to throw light on the experiences of many Aboriginal people with the child-welfare system. Cardinal does so, as he mentions in the interview on p. 206, in order to assure other foster children that they, too, can take control of their own lives by reclaiming their past.

After screening *Richard Cardinal: Cry from a Diary of a Métis Child,* we realized that some students had very little sense of the historical and sociological dimensions of Richard's situation, and little awareness of how the child-welfare system worked. We selected excerpts from *Foster Child* to provide some of that background, as well as to give viewers an example of a Métis foster child who had had a different experience from that which scarred Richard so deeply. Finally, we felt that *Foster Child* was a striking instance of an autobiographical documentary, in which the filmmaker movingly recounts a tale from the inside, in a way that illuminates lives beyond the filmmaker's own.

excerpts from an interview with Gil Cardinal, director

The following interview with Gil Cardinal took place in Edmonton, Alberta, shortly after the release of Foster Child *in 1987.*

What made you decide to make a film of your search?

I had wanted for some time to do a comprehensive film about the experience of Native people with the child-welfare system — it's been such a common and devastating history among our people. And I thought, along with the other stories we would tell, I would tell some of my own, to give that wide-ranging film a personal chapter. Gradually, it became clear that the best story I could tell was the one I knew best — my own. The NFB style is to tell a larger story by telling one personal story. Also, it is important that we Native people look at our own history and tell our own stories! We can't just sit back and complain about our stories being told and ripped-off by non-Natives. We've got to do it

ourselves. We've got to be willing to look at our own history, what's happened to us and what we've let happen, because we have to heal ourselves.

I didn't feel my personal story was important in and of itself. In fact, it's a rather tame story, considering the horrific experiences Native children have had in foster and adoptive homes. But I felt it was important for other foster and adoptive children who are now adults to see we can take control of our lives, we can reclaim what was lost and denied; we don't have to keep feeling and functioning like we are still wards. We have a right to know and, further, I think we have a deep need to know, however long it takes us to recognize that and accept it. And all of those reasons are especially true and important for Native foster and adoptive children and adults.

Wasn't it difficult to be orchestrating a film at the same time as this very personal and dramatic experience was unfolding?

The most difficult part for me overall was the sort of schizoid feeling of confusion: Am I making a film or am I having a personal experience? But once an encounter was set up and we were shooting a scene, I almost forgot about the camera and was fully engaged in what I was doing or who I was talking to. A lot of the credit has to go to the crew — the producer, Jerry Krepakevich, cinematographer Jim Jeffrey, and soundman Alan Bibby. I knew they were taking care of the filmmaking, especially Alan and

Jim, who were with me every step of the way and gave me a lot of support. So there was a lot of trust. Also, I knew I was the director of the film and I didn't have to turn over my heart and soul and guts to somebody else; I would be involved in shaping the film right to the very end.

One specific incident that crystallized the filmmaker-personal conflict had to do with my mother's grave. After finding out that there was no headstone, I was glad, even relieved, that the sequence of my response was first that I wanted to give her a marker — I felt that immediately and unconditionally — then, second, that that would be important and relevant to the film.

When you began, what kind of plan did you have?
Actually, the film was precipitated by my initial request to Social Services for background information on my family. I received a two-page summary drawn from my Child Welfare records in July of 1985. I read the covering letter but couldn't go any further. I knew my discovery of what was on those next two pages had to be filmed.

Is the film a fairly straightforward portrayal of what happened, or did you have to "stage" some scenes?
Nothing in the film was staged or recreated. It is documentary filmmaking at its most basic, raw level. It's cinéma vérité, direct film. Whatever happens, happens. Everything that happened was spontaneous

— the only opportunity we would have to shape and focus the events would be in the editing.

Did making the film at the same time hinder your search at all?
It did, but thanks to the willingness and openness of the people involved, not as much as it could have. I mean, from their perspective, here was this guy calling up out of the blue and saying, "I'm part of your family and I'd like to meet you and oh, by the way, can I bring a film crew along?" In some ways the filmmaking aspect both prolonged and sped up the process.

And when I went to Calling Lake to follow up information on my father, it was apparent this was a touchy situation and I just couldn't walk in on people with a film camera rolling and then just disappear. So we took that slow and easy, spent a couple of days and took still pictures instead, which was all right with the people involved — they could understand that.

How do you think *Foster Child* will affect others who want to begin their own search?
I would hope they would see knowledge matters. When we don't know anything we make up the worst possible scenarios. Nothing we could find out is worse than the powerlessness of not knowing, of dealing with fantasies. We don't have to be foster children and wards all our lives. We can be pro-active.

We tend to have a negative attitude — they must have been bad people, otherwise why couldn't they keep me? — we're prisoners of that. They had their stories, too, and whether you accept or understand the reasons, it feels good knowing you probably weren't thoughtlessly abandoned.

What was the most memorable moment in making the search/film?

Seeing my mother's face for the first time, seeing absolutely clearly me in her, my face in her face. Seeing the woman who gave birth to me and held me in her arms, at least for some short period of time, before giving me up or losing me. She is real ... and now, somehow, I am more real. Also, meeting my uncle, seeing that Métis face.

There are an estimated 5,000 children in foster care in Alberta. If you were put in charge of social services, what would your first action be?

To make it easier for information to be made available, at least regarding foster children. (Recognizing the situation with adopted children is a trickier matter.) More effort needs to be made to compile a comprehensive history of the child's circumstances in coming into care, information about the natural family; an effort made to place the child with extended family.

Do you have regrets about what had to be left out?

There is still a big gap in my understanding of what happened to me before I got to the Wilsons and if I was kept locked up in a room. I still do not believe that Social Services doesn't have this information.

The ultimate question or dilemma is: for the sake of the child, what's best? It's not black and white. I can't say what happened to me was all good or all bad — it's unresolvable. I lost my heritage and culture and grew up full of denial, feeling I didn't fit or belong. But what was the alterNative? Someone, some force, had to act on our behalf, and I was lucky I survived. I'll probably never really know at what cost; it's still a dilemma. I wish we could have explored that more in the film.

Something I learned when I did a film on children of alcoholics is that they tend to feel guilty for the alcoholic's action. I think maybe that was also buried deep inside me. I was hard on myself. Now I'm not a freak, not a mistake. I've been set free a little. And I have a new, neat uncle; a loving and accepting sister-in-law and nephew and niece; a brother who was a warm and talented man much loved by his family of friends on his Métis squatters' island; a strong and proud man who I would be proud to call my father; a whole batch of aunts, cousins and Métis *kokhums* and *moshums* [grandmothers and grandfathers] who accept me; and a mother who wanted more for me and never forgot me. I'm glad I did it.

—EDMONTON, 1987

IDEAS *for* DISCUSSION

1

What was your reaction to this film? What was the most striking aspect of the film for you?

2

*Is what you felt different from what you felt when you saw **Richard Cardinal**? If so, in what way? Has this excerpt added to or changed your understanding of what happened to Richard and why?*

3

Did you notice anything particular about the soundtrack? (There is no music.) Why might the director have made that decision? How would music have changed the feel and flavour of the film?

ACTIVITIES

1

Document a personal experience. How would you treat the subject (with photos, slides, video, words)? Would it be a past event or something happening in the present? If it were a past event, you would be able to see its shape as a whole. If you didn't have material documenting that event or time in your life, would you re-create it? (See "Docudrama: Fact and Fiction", p. 124, for information about re-creations.) If you are documenting a process happening in the present, you must trust to the unfolding of the event, as you don't know where it will take you.

FURTHER RESOURCES

film/video

Tikinagan by Gil Cardinal is an honest and uncompromising look at difficulties encountered by workers in a revolutionary, Native child-care agency operating out of Sioux Lookout, Ontario.

print

See "Further Resources" in "Richard Cardinal: Cry from a Diary of a Métis Child", p. 203.

speak white

VIDEO LOCATION 64 IN *VOICES OF EXPERIENCE,*
VOICES FOR CHANGE, PART 1

6 MINUTES

BLACK & WHITE

1980

DIRECTORS: *PIERRE FALARDEAU, JULIEN POULIN*

PRODUCER: *ROBERT FORGET, NFB*

DISTRIBUTOR: *NFB*

The poem *Speak White* was written by québécoise poet Michèle Lalonde; she read it at the Montreal *Nuit de la Poésie* (Poetry Night) which took place in 1970, at a time of heightened political awareness. Ten years later, filmmakers Pierre Falardeau and Julien Poulin felt it was still pertinent enough to merit being translated into images.

As we hear Marie Eykel's rendition of the poem, backed by an evocative soundtrack, a rapid montage of still images confronts us: portraits of an elite juxtaposed with photos of marginalized minorities become a relentless stream of current and archival images of work, struggle, resistance and repression. Though the poem (and the film) begin in a québécois context, the defiance hurled in the face of imperialist and colonial regimes widens to include all the exploited peoples of the world.

Like *The Ballad of Crowfoot, Speak White* uses a poetic text and archival black-and-white stills to re-vision history, to present past and present events from the point of view of the oppressed, whose voices are rarely heard. Created in an era of social activism, the poem's perspective is unambiguous.

SUGGESTIONS *for* USE

- *Students' comments have been included as a jumping-off point for discussion.*

- *There are a number of ways to use this film. You may want to screen the film first without the soundtrack or have students look at the film without having read the poem, so they can respond solely to the power of the visuals. (See "Activities", p. 217, for further ideas about how to do this.) We suggest telling students without much working knowledge of French that an English translation will be supplied after the screening, so they need not be concerned if they cannot understand some of the language at first hearing.*

- *The film is so short that it can easily be screened more than once. After working their way through the poem, students may then want to look again at how the filmmakers have rendered its meaning through images.*

- *When working with the poem, you may want to address the use of irony and the use of sarcasm in literature.*

students' comments

The combination of the provocative poem, the forceful reading, the black-and-white images and supporting soundtrack produced an interesting, moving film.
16-YEAR-OLD VIEWER

She got too excited, I really didn't like how she came on as criticizing me.
15-YEAR-OLD VIEWER

I thought it was interesting the way the narrator switched languages while talking about languages.
16-YEAR-OLD VIEWER

The film portrayed a side of the world which many try not to admit. It talked about the prejudices of a society.
16-YEAR-OLD VIEWER

It shows us the opinion of other people and how they feel. It's good to see what other people think, compared to what you think yourself.
16-YEAR-OLD VIEWER

This is a very emotional and powerful film. But why "speak white"? Why not "speak black"?
16-YEAR-OLD VIEWER

speak white

by Michèle Lalonde

Speak white
It's so lovely to hear you
talk about *Paradise Lost*
and the charming but nameless figure moving
through Shakespeare's sonnets

We are an uncultured stammering people
yet we are not deaf to the uniqueness of a tongue
speak with the accent of Milton and Byron and
Shelley and Keats
speak white
and forgive us if we reply
only in the harsh songs of our ancestors
and the deep pain of Nelligan

speak white
speak of this and that
tell us about the Magna Carta
or about Lincoln's monument
or about the grey charm of the Thames

or about the pink waters of the Potomac
tell us about your traditions
We are a people of little brilliance
yet we are quite able to appreciate
the full import of crumpets
or the Boston Tea Party

But you *really speak white*
when you *get down to brass tacks*

To speak of *gracious living*
and of the standard of living
and the Great Society

speak white a little louder
raise your foremen's voices
we are a little hard of hearing
we live too close to the machines
and hear only our sighs above the tools.

speak white and loud
let yourselves be heard
from Saint-Henri to Santo Domingo
yes what a splendid tongue
for hiring
giving orders
deciding the hour death joins the job
and the pause that refreshes

and the dollar that effervesces
Speak white
tell us that God is a great big shot
and that we're paid to trust him
speak white
talk production profits and percentages
speak white
yours is a rich tongue
for buying
but as for selling oneself
but as for selling one's life blood
but as for selling oneself

Ah!
speak white
big deal
but as for explaining to you
the eternity of a day on strike
recounting
the life of a janitor-people
but as for going home at night
when the sun comes bursting above our alleyways
but as for telling you that yes the sun sets yes
each day of our lives in the east of your empires
Nothing can match a language of curses
our somewhat unkempt jargon
spattered with axle-grease and oil.

Speak white
enjoy what you say
We are a rancorous people
yet reproach no one
for having a monopoly
on speech correction

In the sweet tongue of Shakespeare
with the accent of Longfellow
speak a pure and gruesome white French
as in Vietnam, in the Congo
speak an impeccable German
gnashing a Star of David in your teeth
speak Russian speak order speak repression
speak white
it's a universal language
we were born to understand it
with its tear-gas words
with its black-jack words

Speak white
tell us again about Freedom and Democracy
We know that liberty is a black word
just as misery is Negroid
and as blood mingles with dust in the streets of
Algiers or Little Rock

Speak white
take turns from Westminster to Washington
speak white as they do on Wall Street
white as in Watts
Be civilized
and in the circumstances understand our speech
when you politely ask us
how do you do
and you hear us reply
we're doing all right
we're doing fine
we
are not alone
We know
that we are not alone.

Translation from French by BEN Z. SHEK

IDEAS *for* DISCUSSION

1

What is your response to this film? To its images? To its words? To its tone of voice?

2

What does "speak white" mean in this poem? Who are the power holders? What kind of power do they wield? Which images in the film reinforce that meaning for you? What relevance does it have for our personal lives? For our society? For others?

3

From whose point of view is this poem written? Who's speaking? To whom is the poem addressed? Is there a value in making one's point of view clear and unambiguous? (For further discussion on this issue, see the discussion of objectivity and bias in THE POLITICS OF TRUTH, pp. 137. For more questions related to the film itself, see "Activities" below.)

4

Both Speak White *and* The Ballad of Crowfoot, *created during an era of political activism, are fueled by a strong sense of anger and social protest. Marie Hamilton in* Black Mother, Black Daughter *talks about the possible negative consequences of giving in to anger. In what ways might it be destructive? Are there times when anger — on a personal, social or historical level — can be justifiable and useful? If so, when, and how?*

ACTIVITIES

1

Screen the film without the soundtrack. As you watch, jot down words to help you remember the images. What do you remember? What do you think the film is about? What do you think might be on the soundtrack? A voice? Whose? Saying what? Is there music and/or sound effects? If so, what kind?

2

Screen the film again, with sound. (Mention to students that part of the poem they will hear is in French and that they will receive the English translation later.) Jot down the sounds you are conscious of as you listen. Was the soundtrack what you expected? Now what do you think the film is about? How do the sound effects and the narrator's style of delivery add to the impact of the poem? Would the film have the same effect if the images were in colour? If not, how might it be different?

Work with the poem and then look at the film again.

3

Screen *The Ballad of Crowfoot* (in VOICES OF EXPERIENCE, VOICES FOR CHANGE, PART 1, video location 00) which also presents a "view from the inside". As in *Speak White, Crowfoot* comprises black-and-white still images that have been animated and combined with a poetic soundtrack. What other similarities and differences do you see between these two films? Is it important for these voices to be heard? If so, why? Do these films fit your notion of a documentary?

4

See material for *The Edit,* p. 74, and *City of Gold,* p. 8, for other suggestions related to working with stills.

# of lives uprooted

VIDEO LOCATION 71 *IN VOICES OF EXPERIENCE,*
VOICES FOR CHANGE, PART 1

10 MINUTES

1987

DIRECTOR: *PIERRE MARIER*

PRODUCER: *ROBERT FORGET, NFB/ONF*

SUGGESTIONS *for* USE

- *It is advisable to preview this film before showing to students.*

- *Students' comments about the film have been included, page 223, to spark discussion.*

- *Before giving students copies of the interview with Pierre Marier to read, ask them to brainstorm what questions they might put to the filmmaker, were he present. After reading the interview, tackle unanswered questions in small-group or class discussion.*

*We don't see bodies talking in front of the camera
but it's still a documentary.*

PIERRE MARIER

Of Lives Uprooted is another "telling of history", an
insider's look at war, as experienced by children of
Central America. Composed almost entirely of young
refugees' drawings and texts about their experiences,
the film presents the voices and points of view of those
who rarely get to speak for themselves — the victims
of war, and, especially, the youngest among them. Like
Memorandum or *Richard Cardinal: Cry from a Diary of
a Métis Child, Of Lives Uprooted* is a striking example
of the power of documentary to "bear witness", to
present the testimony of those whose stories might
otherwise go unheard. This tradition of *testimony* has
been particularly important in political documentary,
and nowhere more so than in Latin America during the
1970s and 1980s.

In its style and approach, *Of Lives Uprooted* also raises
interesting questions: What constitutes a documentary?
Must it have actual people and live action footage? Are
on-camera interviews always the most powerful and
expressive means of presenting testimony? What are
our reactions to images of violence? What is the role of
sound in guiding our emotional responses?

Interview with Pierre Marier, director

In the following interview, Pierre Marier discusses some of the decisions he made in the process of turning a pile of drawings and written texts into a film.

In Montreal in 1986, I went to an exhibition [called *Disrupted Lives*] of 64 drawings and accompanying texts done by children in the refugee camps of Central America. I found their testimonies more eloquent and more powerful than any documentary that I had seen about the war in that part of the world. We are used to looking at news reports about war; but they do not necessarily make us *feel* what that experience means for ordinary people, especially for the children who don't understand the reasons for war, the reasons for the loss of their parents and their homes. But those little drawings and those little texts contained

the information and emotion to make us understand. Even though I had been in Central America myself a few months before, it was in Montreal, looking at the children's work, that I really experienced what that war had meant. So I decided to make a film, using their words and pictures to show what was happening.

I asked Linda Dale, the organizer of the exhibition, for permission to use the drawings and she gave me the whole box. There were between 900 and 1000 pictures. Many of the children began to attend schools only in the camps, so they were very proud to be literate and they loved to add words, sometimes on the back of the drawing, sometimes in the drawing itself to explain what their picture was about. I selected drawings that I liked, that seemed to show the least adult influence.

I chose the texts separately. I then organized the texts into four stories to give the impression that four children were giving testimony. I invented the characters: a young girl 7-8 years old; a 12-year-old girl; and two boys. They introduce themselves at the beginning of the film and after that, I interwove their four stories.

Technically, the most challenging problem I faced was what to do about the sound track. At first I had thought of doing interviews with children living in the camps in Honduras or Mexico. After looking at a few interviews that had already been done by some friends of mine, I realized that in many cases the children were not able to put into words for the camera what they were able to put into their drawings. Most of the time they were looking at the ground. I think that the emotions were too powerful when they tried to speak about their parents or their uncles that had been shot in front of them. I felt that the testimonies were actually stronger and more expressive on paper than on film. So I decided to use chldren living in Canada who were refugees from Guatemala and El Salvador to read those original texts.

We did a French and Spanish version in Montreal. I sent the Spanish version to Honduras and El Salvador. It has been used a lot with Honduran children to explain to them what these Salvadorean young people were doing in their country. Then I came to Toronto and we did the English version with children we found there. We looked for children who could read well in English but who still had a Spanish intonation when they spoke and were also able to convey the emotions of what they were reading. One of the girls we used is the daughter of a man in charge of the Human Rights Committee in El Salvador who had been shot a few

months before. She had been living in Toronto for only six months when we recorded the sound.

When we began the recording, I realized that the children sounded as if they were reading rather than acting. It all seemed very stilted and artificial, so I asked them to handle the words as if they were reading a letter sent to them by a cousin from Central America. After the texts had been taped, I asked them a few personal questions, so the testimonies you hear during the credits are their own actual stories.

The photos of the children at the end were pictures of children in the refugee camp. I used them to give a sense of who the kids in my film might be.

Of Lives Uprooted was the first time that I had worked with an animation camera. Before filming under that camera, I did some tests with a video camera to explore the different movements that could be made. A few people advised me to perhaps cut the drawings and rearrange them through animation but I decided to manipulate them only through the movement of the camera.

For my audience, I was originally thinking about Canadian children in the same age range as those who made the drawings, that is between 8 to 14 years. When the film was tested with young children in some elementary schools, it was a little frightening for them. They all remembered the comments about the pregnant woman. While I was doing the film, I read many testimonies that were stronger than that one, much more horrible, and I eliminated them because it was too much.

I gave a minimum of contextual information — this is Central America, there was a war there, and a lot of refugees — because I wanted to make young children feel what civil war is anywhere in the world. Also the NFB asked me to make a film that could be used for the next 20 years, so the references couldn't be too specific and contemporary. I think they were right because everything has changed since I made the film. The camps are closed, most of the Salvadoran refugees have gone back to their country, and the war there is basically finished, although the situation in Guatemala hasn't really changed. But now there are new civil wars in other parts of the world.

I think some of this material can be traumatizing for young children, that is between the ages of 8 to 14; but personally I think that we must traumatize them sometimes with the realities. They are watching very violent films and programs on television every day. In discussions I've had with kids about my film, they've said, "We know that this is real. And when we're looking at television, we know that that is all a set-up, it's not real."

There are a lot of children in the world living through some very tragic events, so maybe we have to shock young people in Canada a little bit about these kinds of experiences. One thing I asked myself when I was working on this film was, "What will these children be like, given their experiences, when they become adults? Will they continue to fight, to use guns, or will they choose another way?"

—MONTREAL, 1992

students' comments

The use of kids was very effective. They portrayed the honesty of the situation, unlike adults who tend to cloud the reality or fabricate.

17-YEAR-OLD VIEWER

It was inappropriate to use children's descriptions. Adult input would have been more effective than innocence.

19-YEAR-OLD VIEWER

I really like the way the pictures and sound effects blended together.

19-YEAR-OLD VIEWER

I see it every day in the news, read it every day in the papers. It's not that I'm used to it or like it's OK or normal, I just want to hear something good for a change, some happy news and not so depressing.

19-YEAR-OLD VIEWER

I wish there had been some explanation about the situation and not just the children's narration. I'm not sure that I got the film's message.

20-YEAR-OLD VIEWER

IDEAS *for* DISCUSSION

1

What was your emotional reaction to this film? What do you remember, when you think about it? Was there anything that particularly impressed you?

2

From whose point of view is the story told? (See "Activities", below, for further exploration of this aspect of the film.)

3

What elements of the soundtrack were you aware of?

4

We don't see bodies talking in front of the camera but it's still a documentary.

PIERRE MARIER

Do you agree or disagree with this comment? Why?

5

Was there anything missing for you in this film?

ACTIVITIES

1

When have you heard voices of children in film or on television? Watch a few TV programs with kids in them. Do the children seem realistic/authentic to you? Why or why not? How do they differ from the "voices" of children in *Of Lives Uprooted?* Are there other groups of people whose voices you rarely hear in film or television programs?

2

Screen *Of Lives Uprooted* and a news report about a war. What are the differences between the two — in the material presented and the ways in which the material is presented? Who gets to speak? Who doesn't speak? Which do you respond to more strongly? Why?

In his interview, Pierre Marier comments on young people's response to the violence in his film and the violence to which they are daily exposed in their television viewing. Do you agree with what he has to say? Give reasons for your position.

3

Compare the points of view about war in *Anybody's Son Will Do* (in THE CANDID EYE?, video location 52) — particularly the section where the drill sergeant talks to the recruits about the "enemy" — and in *Of Lives Uprooted* (VOICES OF EXPERIENCE, VOICES FOR CHANGE, PART 1, video location 71) and *Children of War* (VOICES OF EXPERIENCE, VOICES FOR CHANGE, PART 2, video location 00). Also see the excerpt from *The Kid Who Couldn't Miss* in the selection *Docudrama: Fact and Fiction* (THE POLITICS OF TRUTH, video location 25).

4

There are a number of films in this collection that use still photos to tell their story, including *The Ballad of Crowfoot, Speak White* and *City of Gold.* Compare one or more of these films with *Of Lives Uprooted.* How does the use of still images add to each film?

5

Take a series of stills — either as slides or shot on video — and create a soundtrack to go with them.

FURTHER RESOURCES

film/video

For other films in this collection that also "bear witness", see *Memorandum* (WAYS OF STORYTELLING, video location 55); *Richard Cardinal: Cry from a Diary of a Métis Child*; and *Children of War* (VOICES OF EXPERIENCE, VOICES FOR CHANGE, PART 2, video location 00).

To furnish some context for the situation the children speak about in *Of Lives Uprooted*, see *The World is Watching*, about the way North American news media covered (or didn't cover) events in Central America. Available from the NFB. Also available in a shorter version, *Only the News that Fits.* The latter film is included in *Media & Society* and can also be borrowed as an individual film from the NFB.

print

For a moving personal testimony see *I, Rigoberta Menchu: An Indian Woman in Guatemala* (London: Verso, 1984) by the 1992 winner of the Nobel Peace Prize.

children of war

VIDEO LOCATION **00** IN *VOICES OF EXPERIENCE,*
VOICES FOR CHANGE, PART 2
25 MINUTES
1987
DIRECTOR: *PREMIKA RATNAM*
PRODUCER: *MICHELINE LE GUILLOU, NFB*
DISTRIBUTOR: *NFB*

In *Children of War*, six teenagers from conflict-torn lands talk to their Canadian peers (in grades 8 and 11) about what life is like in the absence of basic human rights. All were participants in the 1985-1986 International Youth for Peace and Justice tour, organized by community groups and school boards across Canada and supported by the government.

In this film, the young speak directly about the costs of living under military and political repression. Their testimony, unmediated by the comments of adult "experts", puts a human face on stories we hear and see in the media. For a change, teenagers, many of them from Third World countries, are recognized to be the ones with knowledge to impart and share — not only of the horrors and brutality they and their fellow citizens have suffered but also of the examples of courage and resistance that inspire and sustain them.

The director of the film, Premika Ratnam, was herself in her early twenties when she started working on *Children of War*. As the documentary was to be part of a training program for International Youth Year, she was given a limited amount of film stock. In the following interview she talks about how the technical constraints and her ethical concerns influenced what she shot and how she shot it.

SUGGESTIONS *for* USE

- *It is advisable to allow students to share their own responses to the film and raise their own questions before reading the interview with the filmmaker.*

interview with Premika Ratnam, director

How did you come to make this film?

I am originally from India and I have always been concerned about war, having lived through two of them in my own country. When I came to Canada, I made a film, *I Hope Not*, which looked at children's reactions to the threat of a nuclear holocaust. When I finished that film, I decided that I wanted to make another one in which children could speak directly to other kids about their feelings and experiences during wartime.

Originally I imagined an audience for the film of kids from 10 to 14, but actually *Children of War* has been used by a much wider age range that that. It's also been used a lot by English as a Second Language students, many of whom come from the countries discussed in the film. It's been a good catalyst for them to talk about their own experiences.

I made the film as part of the International Youth Year Training Programs for women under the age of 25. Twenty-five of us from across Canada came together at the NFB to work on one another's projects. We were each given 10 to 12 rolls of film and were told to make 10-minute movies.

Twelve rolls of film is just a little bit over two hours. I made a half-hour film, so the shooting ratio [the ratio of film shot to the footage used in the finished film] was approximately 4:1. [Most NFB documentaries have a shooting ratio of about 20:1.]

How did those constraints influence the way in which the film was made?

I didn't actually begin with a certain length in mind, like you often do when you're making something for television. I wanted to make an interesting film, and it could have been 10 minutes or half an hour. But I did have very little film stock to work with. Also, I don't really like to do too many set-ups or re-creations. I like to be able to shoot things more or less on the fly. Some directors will say, "Okay, we'll have you walk from space A, you pick up your bag, go through your school and then into your classroom, you drink a glass of water and then the camera will go like this, and remember to hit these marks" and so on. And then they'll have endless voice-over over the film footage, particularly in low-budget productions with low shooting ratios. I didn't want to do that.

Instead, I thought it was important to have direct interviews where the audience gets to see who's talking and the expression on their faces as they talk. So I knew I was going to make a talking-head movie, given the kind of shooting ratio I had.

Also, I chose to film the International Peace Tour of Youth and Justice: 25 students, refugees from war-torn countries, who were touring with a group of Canadian students. I didn't really have a chance to get to know them and I was constantly having to make decisions. I'd meet someone in the evening and decide to shoot the next morning. Everything had to be done on the spur of the moment; and, basically, I structured the film on location. I knew what I was going after in terms of content, but I didn't know the best way way to capture that.

There were also lots of ethical questions. Some of the kids had travelled from far-off places and were already pretty stressed out. I didn't want to tax them too much because they hadn't really come here for the film. Also I wasn't sure they really understood what it meant to be in a movie. Besides, I had to think about whether they would be in any political danger by being in the film.

We shot for four days. Half was at a weekend retreat where the visitor students and the Canadian students got together to workshop their presentations. The other two days we shot in schools.

So I had interviews but no context for them. I certainly didn't have the time or money to go shoot in six different countries and show their homes and their families. I got maps of the different countries and also stock footage though there wasn't any money to buy that footage [sequences available from stock footage libraries]. I had to call up everyone and convince them that this was a wonderful cause and they should give us the stock footage for free. CBC donated 60 seconds worth which was a generous donation; otherwise, it probably would have cost me about $50 a second.

Some people felt that the footage should show very violent scenes but I really resisted that. You get to see so much of those kind of images on television that they tend to lose their meaning. It all becomes somehow dehumanizing. Instead I wanted to establish the insidious presence of the military and the feeling of what it means to be constantly living under fear and to have that potential threat hanging over you on a day-to-day basis.

I can't help feeling that if we respected and cared for people from other countries as much as we respect and care for people from our own country, we'd react differently to events like the Gulf War, for instance. So I wanted these teenagers from other nations to be the focus of the film. I wanted them to have the power to talk directly about what had happened to them. I didn't want to concentrate on how those in power had taken over these people's lives and portray them as passive and silent victims.

Because I wanted the film to centre on young people, I decided to use one of the Canadian students as the narrator, instead of looking for an adult to do the voice-over. I wrote the text of the commentary with a 17-year old girl, Pat Dillon, who was working on the documentary with me.

Do you know what has happened to the film since its release?

Through the Film Board, the tour organizers got a grant and made 200 copies. Some of the participants use the film in their own countries and it's also being screened through whatever networks the organizers here and abroad have.

I had hoped the film would be used as an ice breaker so that students who were immigrants or refugees in Canada would have a way to begin talking about their experiences to other people in their classes. From that point of view, I think it's been really successful.

—TORONTO, 1992

IDEAS *for* DISCUSSION

1

What are some of your thoughts and feelings after viewing the film? Are there details you find surprising? Which teenager impresses you the most? Why? Does it make a difference to you that these are young people telling the stories? Why?

2

Does this documentary seem to be different from reports you hear on the news? How?

3

What aspect of Premika Ratnam's interview was the most interesting to you? Why?

ACTIVITIES

1

In her interview, Premika Ratnam talks about the ethical concerns she had while making the film. Pick a topic about which you would like to make a film: it could be about a political or social issue or someone in your family or community. What would you want to film? What questions would you want to ask? How would you approach the person? What ethical concerns might you have to consider, while making the film?

2

Of Lives Uprooted (in VOICES OF EXPERIENCE, VOICES FOR CHANGE, PART 1, video location 71) also uses testimony from children who have experienced civil war, but the film is put together in a very different way. Compare the two documentaries in terms of style, content, audience, and their effect on you.

3

Screen *Anybody's Son will Do* (in THE CANDID EYE?, video location 52), which shows how young recruits are turned into soldiers who kill. You might want to focus on the sequence in which the drill instructor is talking to these teenage boys about the "proper" attitude to take towards "the enemy". Compare it with *Children of War,* for a different view of soldiers and soldiering. Is it important to hear from the civilians affected? Why?

4

Singly or in groups, come up with a definition of heroism. Compare the excerpt from *The Kid Who Couldn't Miss* (in *Docudrama: Fact and Fiction,* THE POLITICS OF TRUTH, video location 25) and *Children of War* in terms of your definition.

5

Screen a newscast. How many items deal with events in countries outside North America? Are the people of these countries represented? Do they speak for themselves? If not, who speaks for them? Is there a difference between what they say and the information offered by the foreign commentator?

6

Monitor an evening's television programs. What programs are on what channels? Who's represented and who's not, in terms of race, class, gender, age, ability, sexual orientation? Who are the "good guys", who are the villains, who are the victims? Who are the experts and who are the witnesses?

FURTHER RESOURCES

film/video

Return to Dresden records, among other things, a moving encounter between a former RCAF pilot and some of the civilians he had firebombed 40 years before, as an 18-year-old "following orders". Available from the NFB.

The World Is Watching examines the way in which North American and British print and broadcast journalists report on the situation in Nicaragua. The people who live there almost never get to speak for themselves; when they do, it's in 10-second sound bites. The film is available from the NFB.

black mother, black daughter

VIDEO LOCATION 26 IN *VOICES OF EXPERIENCE,*
VOICES FOR CHANGE, PART 2

30 MINUTES

1989

DIRECTORS: *SYLVIA HAMILTON, CLAIRE PRIETO*

PRODUCER: *SHELAGH MACKENZIE, NFB*

DISTRIBUTOR: *NFB*

SUGGESTIONS *for* USE

- *Students' comments have been included to initiate discussion.*

- *Ask students to share their responses to the film and brainstorm any questions they might have about it, before giving them copies of the Sylvia Hamilton interview.*

Journalist/researcher/filmmaker Sylvia Hamilton focusses on the power of film — particularly documentary film — to encourage social and political change. She wants the people of her community to create and control images of themselves, to construct a body of historical knowledge and testimony from which they can draw strength. She has set out to document (and thereby preserve) the contributions of Black women in Nova Scotia to the maintenance and growth of their community; by doing so, she honors their role in the struggle for justice and equality in their province.

Black Mother, Black Daughter is, very consciously, a collection of stories and images "from the inside", with Hamilton acting as personal guide and commentator. *Black Mother* is the polar opposite of the "anthropological eye" or travelogue, narrated by a supposedly knowledgeable outsider, as satirized in *The Spaghetti Story* (in THE POLITICS OF TRUTH, video location 00).

In its aims and its liberal use of techniques of oral history and of the personal interview, *Black Mother, Black Daughter* recalls the pioneering work of feminist documentarians during the 1970s. They, too, sought to give voice to experiences and history that had for too long been silent and hidden.

students' comments

I didn't know that there was so much Black history and Black culture. I also had no idea that there was slavery in Canada. I personally thought that this kind of thing happened only in the southern U.S.
18-YEAR-OLD VIEWER

The most interesting part was the characters in the film. They know what it was like to be discriminated against.
19-YEAR-OLD VIEWER

The scenes I liked best were where the old Black people were interviewed about their life because it felt very touching to see how they survived and told their story.
17-YEAR-OLD VIEWER

I especially enjoyed the sense of tradition and family, of history and the women's issues raised.
30-YEAR-OLD VIEWER

I don't think they should have shown the Black singing group so much. Is it a video or a documentary?
19-YEAR-OLD VIEWER

The film was interesting because it had a lot of personal viewpoints and it made you see just how much society has changed.
16-YEAR-OLD VIEWER

interview with Sylvia Hamilton,
co-director

how they had hardly ever been given the recognition that was their due. I published some articles and gave talks about this topic. I also began looking for a new medium in which to disseminate these stories because we were starting to lose the older women in the community and I wanted them to be preserved through images as well as through oral history. I wanted to do this both for the younger generation and for the women too, so they could really see themselves. These groups were my core audience. *Black Mother, Black Daughter* wasn't made to educate white people about the Black community although, if that happened, it was marvellous. Many of the women in the film I'd known all my life. It was complicated to choose just a few of them to represent so many more. I wanted women who had something to say but also women who had never had their initial moment in the sun.

To find others I went to a lot of different functions, especially to women's groups in the African Baptist Association. During my visits, I did some photography and tape recording to acclimatize them to being filmed.

I knew I wanted the film to have certain key elements. I wanted to highlight the stories and oral traditions that get passed on from one generation to the next. The family in the Black community is

What is the story behind the making of *Black Mother, Black Daughter?*

In the early 1970s, I was doing research on Black Nova Scotia and a lot of information and stories about different Black women kept popping up. I saw how integral they had been to the community's development over the last few hundred years but an extended family, both formally and informally, so I thought that including material about fostering children might be the way to get at that aspect. Also, I wanted to concentrate on the specific transfer of skills. Basket weaving, for instance, was prevalent among the first group of settlers who arrived in 1812. Now it's dying out, and I wanted to be part of spurring on its revival. Finally, I chose Daurene Lewis because her family had been part of the Loyalist connection, and I wanted to show what these families were doing in the contemporary situation.

Though I had done radio work and journalism before, I had never directed a film, so I wanted to find a Black woman filmmaker to work with me on the project and I settled on Claire Prieto. Claire had grown up in Trinidad but she had made Home to Buxton about a Black community reunion in Ontario, so I was sure she'd be sympathetic to the material in Nova Scotia.

Initially, I wasn't present in the film but, as the research continued, it made sense to include myself because it seemed to be the best way to tell the story. At a certain point, the film became the record of how I was seeing these particular women, and I wanted to make it clear that this wasn't the only perspective on Black women in Nova Scotia.

Since I had a personal connection with all these women, I felt it wouldn't have been honest to pretend otherwise.

What about your new film?

The new film's title is *Speak It! From the Heart of Black Nova Scotia* and its themes are knowing about your history and your culture, and how that knowledge shapes your identity and self-esteem and gives you a strong base from which to deal with racism. I'm doing it with a group of young Black students in a high school in Halifax who are part of the Cultural Awareness Youth Group of Nova Scotia.

The young people speak very directly about themselves. They talk about the shock of still having to deal with racism in 1992, without being able to learn about Black history and culture in the curriculum. They do the talking in the film, rather than adults, which isn't that common but I wanted to challenge the notion that all youth are disaffected.

The choice of what I shot for that film was made in consultation with them. One of the young people in the film writes music and we'll work on the narration together. For instance, there's a historical context for young people being active in our community which they don't necessarily know about, and that's part of what I have to contribute.

Why do you choose to work in documentary rather than drama?

Right now there are a number of concrete things I want to explore with real-life people who have something to say and have never yet had a chance to say it. I want to give people a chance to tell their own stories, stories which other people can relate to in a different way than they could relate to fiction. I think we, as Black people, need a body of work that can document our stories, be the background we need. It's shameful that we don't have that yet. I came into film through my work in the community, not through art school, so I didn't begin by seeing film mainly as a form of artistic expression. I think of film as playing an important role in social change, as a way of giving voice to people.

After screenings of *Black Mother, Black Daughter*, so many people would comment on how grateful they were to have been given images of themselves, and so many white people were amazed to learn about this history they had known nothing about. So I've seen how film can open doors, point out to people things they never thought of before.

For me, film can be both a mirror and a hammer: it can show us what is as well as a vision of what can be. So I ask myself: Do I have the luxury right now of experimenting with an obscure subject in film for my own personal satisfaction? Or, given the intensity of the process and the costs involved in filmmaking, should I use it — dare I say this? — for a grander purpose?

—HALIFAX, 1992

some considerations regarding oral history

Oral history, like most documentary film, uses the experiences and memories of "real-life" people as its subject matter. As the people involved are not actors (nor are they being paid for their participation), ethical and moral questions are vital to these activities.

Before beginning an oral history project, it is important to generate guidelines for how to proceed. Some of the following were suggested by Sylvia Hamilton:

- Respect people's sense of privacy, what they want to talk about.

- Establish some ground rules about how the material will be used. Will it be shared or published?

- Can the encounter be envisioned in the form of an exchange rather than a one-way gathering of information? For instance, will the people interviewed ever get to see or hear this material? Can they receive a copy of the transcript or tape? Is it possible to donate copies of the material collected to a local archive?

- Have a series of questions prepared in advance so there is some structure to the encounter, but also try to give yourself the freedom to follow any interesting turn of conversation.

- Consider inviting members of the local historical society to talk about their projects and the guidelines they have evolved.

IDEAS *for* DISCUSSION

1

Was there anything about this film that surprised you? Have you heard stories like these before?

2

From whose point of view is the film presented? Do you think the film might have been different if it had been made by a filmmaker who was not part of the community? Why?

3

What role do you think this film might play for a Black audience? For an audience composed of other racial and ethnic groups?

4

In what ways are you aware of the impact of history — family, community, country, global — in your own lives? What documents (photo albums, passports, letters, etc.) do you have that chronicle personal histories? Is anyone "keeper of the stories"?

5

In her interview, Sylvia Hamilton states that people relate to personal "real-life" stories in a different way than they relate to fiction. Do you agree or disagree? Give reasons and examples.

6

Sylvia Hamilton talks about the power of film to play a role in social change. Can you think of any film/video you have seen that opened your eyes to a subject that you had never thought of before, or caused you to think differently about some person or situation?

ACTIVITIES

1

Chart who is seen on TV, in terms of race, class, gender, age, ability, sexual orientation, etc., in an evening's viewing. Who's there? Who isn't there? Are all people presented in the same way? Is the presentation stereotyped or complex?

2

This film deals with oral history — the personal, subjective telling of a past. Screen *Our Marilyn* (WAYS OF STORYTELLING, video location 85), which tries to do something similar, though that film uses a fictional narrator.

3

Screen *The Ballad of Crowfoot* (VOICES OF EXPERIENCE, VOICES FOR CHANGE PART 1, video location 00), which is also an "inside story" about the history of a people. Compare it with *Black Mother, Black Daughter* in tone and manner of presentation. Do you react more strongly to one than to the other? Why?

4

Screen *The Spaghetti Story* (THE POLITICS OF TRUTH, video location 00). Now view the basket-making sequence in *Black Mother* again. Imagine how it might have been presented, had it been made by a crew doing a "quickie" travelogue. Who might be doing the speaking? Rewrite the narration to reflect that narrator's point of view.

5

Work out a treatment for a film or video that you would like to make about your family or aspects of your own particular community. Who and what would you include? Why? Would you use still photos? How? Music? What kind? (For a definition of a treatment, see the FILM AND VIDEO TERMS: AN INTRODUCTION, p. 260.)

6

If it is possible, interview someone in your family or community who knows about its history. (Photos are often a great stimulus to memory: bring along family albums or find pictures in the local archives.) Make an audio or video recording of your interview. Review the material to decide what you want to keep and what you want to share with the subject(s) you have interviewed. Justify your decisions.

FURTHER RESOURCES

film/video

For further material about advocacy in filmmaking, see the *Interview with Alanis Obomsawin* (VOICES OF EXPERIENCE, VOICES FOR CHANGE, PART 1, video location 41).

Sylvia Hamilton's film *Speak It! From the Heart of Black Nova Scotia* is available from the NFB.

Fresh Looks is a three-tape compilation of anti-racist films and videos produced in Canada. The 15-title collection comes with a study guide for teachers and educators. Available from V-Tape, 183 Bathurst St., Toronto, Ont., M5T 2R7. Tel: (416) 863-9897. Fax: (416) 360-0781.

print

The catalogue *Colour Positive: Films and Videos on Race and Immigrant Experience* contains some very useful guidelines for using films and videos for anti-racist work. Available from Full Frame Film and Video, 394 Euclid Ave., Toronto, Ont., M6G 2S9. Tel: (416) 925-9338.

Black on Screen: Images of Black Canadians, 1950s-1990s is a catalogue available from Studio D of the National Film Board, P.O. Box 6100, Station A, Montreal, Quebec, H3C 3H5.

The *Foxfire* books use the principles of oral history to disseminate the recollections, lore and skills of people in Appalachia.

The best-known practitioner of oral history in Canada is probably Barry Broadfoot (*Ten Lost Years 1929-1939: Memories of Canadians Who Survived*). Studs Terkel in the U.S. has been working in this genre for decades. One recent book is *Race: How Blacks and Whites Think and Feel About the American Obsession*.

the poetry of motion

For many people, documentaries and social issues seem indissolubly wedded. Yet, as the two productions included in this section so ably show, there is another tradition in this genre, one that honors the vitality and exuberance of the actual, and seeks through the poetry of film to pay homage to that which surrounds us.

The Academy Award-winning documentary *Flamenco at 5:15* is the record of one such moment, an evocation of the music, motion, energy and light that animate a group of young dancers and their dedicated teachers who offer more than technical instruction. Director Cynthia Scott has crafted a hybrid, an aesthetically satisfying combination of documentary content and carefully pre-scripted camera moves.

Sandspit to Dildo offers a delightful cross-country glimpse of Canada through encounters with some of its inhabitants — a dazzling, playful blend of documentary and music video which gives new meaning to the re-presentation of recorded memory.

flamenco at 5:15

VIDEO LOCATION 56 IN *THE POETRY OF MOTION*

29 MINUTES

1983

DIRECTOR: *CYNTHIA SCOTT*

PRODUCERS: *CYNTHIA SCOTT, ADAM SYMANSKY,*

    KATHLEEN SHANNON, NFB

DISTRIBUTOR: *NFB*

Must documentaries always be about serious social issues? Is it enough to capture moments of beauty, to be a source of profound aesthetic pleasure? Does every film have to have a clear-cut "story" that culminates in a climax? Screening *Flamenco at 5:15,* an impressionistic record of a dance class for senior students at the National Ballet School in Toronto, raises these sorts of questions, and more. A celebration of creative expression, energy and life, *Flamenco* is a poetic, lyrical film about a process. It is, moreover, part of a long tradition of non-fiction films about the fine arts — painting, sculpture, theatre and dance.

Flamenco at 5:15 won the Academy Award for Best Short Documentary in 1984.

SUGGESTIONS *for* USE

- *Some pre-screening discussion is needed to establish a context for this film. See "Ideas for Discussion", p. 249.*

- *This film was actually shot in 35mm, so seeing it on video is another viewing experience altogether. (The video has been "letterboxed", so viewers can see the entire original image.) If you have good projection facilities (large screen, dark room, good sound), try screening the film in 16mm as well so students can talk about how differences in image size, quality and colour affect their reactions to the film.*

- *Students' comments have been included to spark discussion.*

- *Give students copies of the interview with Cynthia Scott after they've had a chance to share their own responses to the film, and explore any questions the interview may raise for them.*

THE POETRY *of* MOTION

students' comments

"This isn't really a film about dance. I mean, it is about dance but what it's really about is energy."
16-YEAR-OLD STUDENT/HOCKEY PLAYER

"Why would anybody make a dance film without putting in a final performance?"
17-YEAR-OLD STUDENT

"A film about a controversial subject would be better. At least, that way we would learn something moral and concrete."
17-YEAR-OLD STUDENT

"This documentary isn't really true because they didn't film it all in one class."
16-YEAR-OLD STUDENT

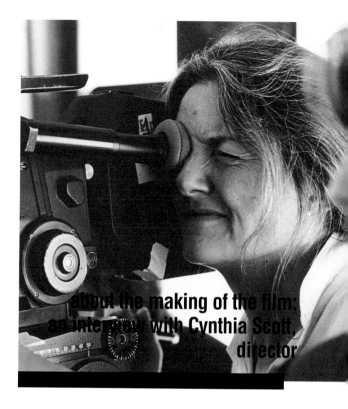

about the making of the film: an interview with Cynthia Scott, director

In this interview, Cynthia Scott talks about, among other things, the rhythms of flamenco and the rhythms and styles of different ways of working.

genesis

I had decided I wanted to do a film about how you become a dancer. So I went down to the National Ballet School in Toronto and spent a week looking at all the kids, from the babies coming in, to the senior class. The minute I walked in the door, everyone said, "You have to go and see Susana. She's here doing her flamenco class." And I kept saying, "No, no, thank you very much. I don't want to see flamenco. I'm here to look at ballet."

By the fourth day everything had become a blur. I was overwhelmed and exhausted. Finally, I decided to relax and go watch the flamenco class, which was the last one of the day. When I walked in, some kids were sitting on the floor, others were fooling around, doing steps. I could see that they were really tired but there was a special anticipation in the air. Then Antonio arrived, and the students gathered around him at the piano to try out various "palmas". About ten minutes later, Susana came in and within moments she had them beating out impossible rhythms with their feet. I was enchanted.

The kids were enchanted, too, because everything else they were doing had to be perfect, everything else had to be just the way the school wanted it — whereas, with flamenco, once they learned their steps it was much more free-wheeling and it energized them. I was really intrigued with the energy.

The rhythms were irresistible, the music was wonderful, and what Susana and Antonio were as people seemed as important as what they taught. They seemed to me to be talking about a way of living that is both disciplined and exuberant. I'd never seen anybody like Susana before — just the way she stood, she gave life to those kids. So even though what she was doing was teaching them a

dance, I felt she was giving them — and anyone who happened to be in the room with her — something special. The class lasted probably an hour and fifteen minutes, and I was completely exhilarated; I felt I had been in a perfect moment. But I could not get the sounds out of my head.

The next day I carried on with my research, but I went back again, as an indulgence, to see the class on a Friday. And I came home to Montreal with those sounds still in my consciousness. I remember very clearly, about four days later I woke up in the middle of the night thinking to myself, "Well, if you loved it that much, why don't you propose a film?"

I tore in the next day to Adam [Symansky, the producer] and said "Adam, I want to do a film about this class." "What do you mean a film about a class? What's the story in the class?" "It's just a class," I said.

I knew it would sound weird. It's certainly not a traditional documentary idea, but I became obsessed with it. I wrote a proposal very quickly, raced down to Toronto and asked Susana and Antonio if they'd be willing to be filmed. They agreed. Adam came and looked at a class and then he understood why I wanted to make the film.

shooting the film

My goal in making *Flamenco at 5:15* was to try and recapture what I had experienced the first time I saw Susana and Antonio with their students in a way that would work filmically. First, I had to learn some very basic palmas so I could understand what they were doing. Also, Susana was adamant that the film had to feel like it was spontaneous because flamenco is spontaneous. So we had to figure out steps that she might teach her students on the spot but we still had to have some idea of what they were beforehand so Paul Cowan, the cinematographer, would know how to film them.

We were shooting in 35mm, like a feature. That's very expensive film racing through the camera, and when you're doing documentary shooting, it can be pretty terrifying. Every shot had to be measured [i.e., the distance between the camera lens and the subjects] before we did anything, to make sure that the image would stay in focus. For Susana, the whole process of filmmaking went against the tradition of flamenco because we had to try and control things.

I asked Paul if we could film without any lights or cables in the rehearsal space. I had discovered from a previous documentary I had made, *For The Love of Dance,* that if there was any way of keeping the lights away from the dancers, it made everything easier for everybody. Instead, we built a scaffolding right around the building and put giant lights outside the windows. The idea was that the sun would be going down as the class was proceeding. In fact, our light was actually more beautiful than real sunlight. It also had a fabulous effect on Susana. She just loved that glowing late-afternoon sun.

The crew started Friday night and lit all day Saturday; and by about 7 p.m. all the lights were up. We turned them on and the room looked exquisite. Then Paul said, "We're going to have to boost this light, it's going to have to go up" [because the 16mm film stock they were originally working with was not sensitive enough to handle low light levels]. I said to them, "If there's any way that I could find the money for us to shoot this film in 35mm instead of 16mm, would you guys be willing to go through all the work and changeover that would be required?" (It would mean they would have to go find the film stock, which was out at the Kodak plant. They'd have to go get the 35mm cameras, which was a huge amount of work, well above and beyond the call of duty. Director changing her mind at the last minute.) And then, because they were all thrilled by the look of this room, they said "Absolutely!" Film crews like working in 35mm.

So I got on the phone. I called everybody at the Film Board and said, "I want to shoot this movie in 35. Can you find me some money?" Finally, we did get the money — from an anonymous benefactor of the ballet school. And that's why the movie looks so gorgeous, because it was shot in 35.

editing the film

We had shot for four days, afternoons and evenings. David Wilson was going to edit the footage. I thought it was a half-hour film but David felt it would probably be 10 minutes. David likes to work very fast and very precisely: he looks at the material, makes a decision and then just goes. He did an edit which didn't feel right to me. He didn't like it much either.

So we started over from scratch and did a much longer assembly with some help from John Smith and from Paul Demers, who finally cut the film with me. I'm more comfortable starting with something big and then just whittling away until I get what I want. Now that it's finished, it seems quite simple but the editing was very complicated musically. Antonio said that it was very flamenco, the way that we kept the rhythms. [For more information about the steps involved in the editing process, see p. 55 in SHAPING REALITY.]

I'm slow. It took me a year to get *Flamenco* finished — that's a long time for a half-hour film — but it was an act of love. I wanted it to be as lovely as I could make it. That's certainly one of the privileges of the Film Board, to have been given that time. In the end, the film did capture my experience, although it wasn't as great as being there in the class.

art and documentary

Art is a difficult word to use in relation to documentary. But from the time I first started seeing films as a kid, one of the things that could really thrill me was getting very close to some kind of aesthetic or artistic experience. So I loved film because I thought that it was sometimes incredibly beautiful.

I don't make films about controversial or difficult social issues. That's what I think of as being the traditional documentary—on abortion, pornography, violence in society. They're incredibly important but that's not something that I can do comfortably.

Paul Cowan would never have done *Flamenco* the way I did it. He would have had it filled with bullfighters and matadors, and he kept asking me to please consider doing that — because he needs more. I guess I'm willing to do something quite simply, to make films that give you that gasp of recognition, where you suddenly feel life and are very moved by it.

Celebratory things are what I love to do — to capture some expression of life or energy, to honor excellence or beauty. Almost everything I've made has been an act of homage or sharing.

—Montreal, 1991

comment by Paul Cowan, cinematographer on *flamenco at 5:15*

When you are making a documentary, you are mostly interested in content. When you are making a drama, you are mostly interested in form. *Flamenco at 5:15* is a kind of hybrid; it contains elements of a scripted-type film with a documentary subject. Scripted in the sense that several of the camera moves were very carefully rehearsed and we knew exactly what they were going to say or do and we'd get them them to do it several times, so we could get different angles and the proper coverage for it. At the same time, we didn't tell them what to do or say. We'd just ask, "What would you do in this situation?" They'd tell us and then we'd say, "Fine, do that. And now we're going to ask you to do it ten times."

IDEAS *for* DISCUSSION

Before Viewing

1

As Flamenco *is more about process than product — capturing a moment or mood — we found it helpful to ask students the following questions before showing the film: Is there anything you do just for the sheer pleasure of doing it, rather than for any tangible goal or reward? Can you think of an incident or a moment that you wished would never end, perhaps dancing with someone you like — a moment you would like to recreate?*

2

In which films, videos, or TV broadcasts have you been particularly conscious of movement or rhythm, either of objects or people on the screen or of the camera itself?

After Viewing

1

Share responses to the film. Were there any specific images, moments, or sequences that stood out for you? (It is an enlightening exercise to see how varied reactions to a film can be, and to learn about some of the factors influencing those reactions.) Do you have to like dance to respond to this film?

2

Read Cynthia Scott's interview about why and how she made Flamenco. *She talks about the creative process involved in making the film — the changes, surprises, trial-and-error efforts and decisions made along the way, the differences in style and approach of the people working with her. Was there anything that surprised you when you read the interview?*

3

Cynthia Scott mentions that Flamenco *is "not a traditional documentary idea". What might such traditional ideas be? If you were going to make a documentary, what would your subject be?*

4

Flamenco at 5:15 *lies somewhere between cinéma vérité and staged recreation, as some of the dance sequences had to be filmed several times from different angles. (For a fuller discussion of cinéma vérité and direct cinema, see* THE CANDID EYE, *p. 144, and the chapter on* Lonely Boy, *p. 146.) Do these re-creations make the film seem less "true" to you? Why or why not? What does the editing process imply about the notion of documentary film capturing life "just like it is"? (For more information and activities related to editing, see* SHAPING REALITY, *p. 55.)*

5

How does this film compare to other films you might have seen about dancing, especially features like **Fame, Dirty Dancing, The Mambo Kings, The Tuning Point** *and* **Strictly Ballroom?** *What "story" has the director Cynthia Scott chosen to tell? Why might she have decided not to put in a final performance, in a film about dance? Can you think of a situation in your own life where the process of doing something is more important than the ultimate goal?*

ACTIVITIES

Before Viewing

Working in pairs or in small groups, quickly brainstorm the following: You have been asked to make a film that conveys a sense of rhythm and movement. What would you choose as your subject? How would you shoot it? What would you have on the soundtrack?

After Viewing

1

Pick out a sequence from the film that you find particularly effective (the hand-clapping around the piano and the skirt sequence at the end are frequently mentioned) and chart how the sense of rhythm has been created by the editing. How many shots are there? When do the shots change? What connection is there between the changes in the visuals and what is happening on the soundtrack? How do the shots vary — in what they show and in the camera's distance from what is being filmed?

2

As a class presentation, some students might want to screen a scene from *Flamenco* and a scene from a feature film about dancers and dancing, and analyze the differences between them. Or they might choose to compare the representation of bodies in motion in *Flamenco* with the coverage of certain kinds of athletic endeavours.

3

Screen Norman McLaren's film *Pas de deux,* which focusses on the movement of a pair of dancers. Could this also be considered a "creative treatment of actuality"?

4

Flamenco at 5:15 and *Anybody's Son Will Do* (THE CANDID EYE?, video location 52) consider, among other things, teaching and learning. Screen a scene from each film that seems to show this clearly. What are the differences and similarities in the teaching/learning philosophies and styles being presented in the two films?

5

Capture an event or a moment in an impressionistic style, using slides and a taped soundtrack or a camcorder.

6

Compare *Flamenco* with *Our Marilyn* (WAYS OF STORYTELLING, video location 85) and *Sandspit to Dildo* (THE POETRY OF MOTION, video location 86) which also attempt to capture the essence of the body in motion.

FURTHER RESOURCES

film/video

Like *Flamenco at 5:15, Nails* is a lyrical, poetic, process film; it has an evocative soundtrack but no commentary. Available from the NFB.

Pas de deux, by Norman McLaren, uses optical printing to create multiple images of a pair of ballet dancers whose movements coalesce and unfurl in a magical way. Available from the NFB.

Though its music track is somewhat dated, *Volleyball,* an encounter between the Russian and American teams, is interesting as an example of choreographic movement. Available from the NFB.

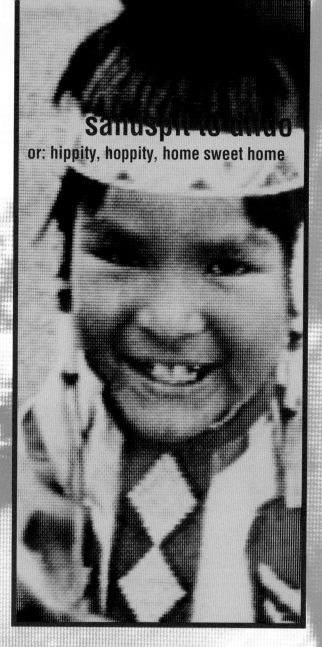

sandspit to dildo
or: hippity, hoppity, home sweet home

VIDEO LOCATION 86 IN *THE POETRY OF MOTION*

28 MINUTES

1989

DIRECTOR: *CHRIS MULLINGTON*

PRODUCER: *FAST FORWARD PRODUCTIONS*

DISTRIBUTOR: *FULL FRAME*

Sandspit to Dildo is a travelogue of sorts — an exhilarating, exuberant blend of documentary and music video which offers glimpses of Canada and Canadians far from the "official" versions. Director Chris Mullington, a video artist, gives new meaning to Grierson's definition of documentary as the "creative treatment of actuality". Sandspit is a personal record of a cross-country tour, graced with freshness, humor, imagination and an intoxication with the beauty of motion.

Like the Russian film *Man with a Movie Camera*, made in the late 1920s, *Sandspit* is the creation of someone exploring the potential of a new visual medium (in this case, Hi8 video), and taking delight in the potential of editing. While most films strive to look transparent and seamless (more like "real life" than movies), *Sandspit* makes it clear that its footage has been manipulated. This manipulation and self-conscious creating of effects become part of the delight of watching the video.

Sandspit to Dildo won a Golden Sheaf Award for best production in the Arts and Entertainment category at the Yorkton Film Festival; the Tuktoyaktuk segment was a winner at the International Video Shorts Festival held in Seattle.

SUGGESTIONS *for* USE

- *As the film is divided into very short segments, it is worth replaying some of the group's favourite sections to appreciate how they are constructed.*

- *Students' comments have been included to spur discussion.*

- *Students should receive copies of the interview with Chris Mullington after they have discussed their own responses and explored their own ideas.*

- *An excerpt from* Sandspit *also appears as part of the "Study Extracts" in* SHAPING REALITY, *video location 69. See p. 111 for further activities related to the editing, sound, and shooting elements of this production.*

interview with Chris Mullington, director

I work in video rather than film because film is just too damn expensive. It takes so much time to round up the funding before you can begin to do anything. With video, I find I can be much more productive. I own the means of production — I have my own video camcorder and my own editing equipment. Besides it gives me great flexibility: I can see what I've shot right away, I don't have to wait till it comes back from the lab. And if I don't like it, then I can try it again.

I usually have a working idea that I'm playing around with. In *Sandspit,* it was to take a cross-country look at Canada through some of its people. In the summer of 1989, I travelled across the

country for 2 1/2 months. I used every means of transportation possible, including a bicycle. Some places I chose beforehand, because I had to book my plane tickets in advance; but I also left myself free to go wherever the trail led. Tuktoyaktuk I picked because I liked the name, whereas Whitehorse I figured I should go to. The only province that's not represented in the tape is New Brunswick. I went there but I didn't get anything that I wanted to use.

The way I work is I put myself in situations and if something happens, great. If it doesn't, I move on. When I land in a city, I might go to a tavern, sit down and start talking to people. Or I'll position myself on a street corner that looks interesting. Or walk around. The guys in Whitehorse I found in a tavern — they're part of an all-male cancan troupe. They do their routines for charity and as a way of meeting women. The couple in Cornwall I heard about through a friend who is a make-up artist, so I just called them up from Ottawa and arranged to go out and videotape them.

I do think that if you respect people, in general you'll have no problems in getting them to talk to you on camera. You can't be pushy, you can't make judgments about them. You have to go into the situation with a very open mind, because if you don't, what happens is that people will then give you what they think you want.

I'm sure that people are less intimidated because I'm working in Hi8. The size of the camera doesn't say "TV news" or "big-time TV". It says "home video", and with home video people are much more relaxed. Besides, I can shoot two hours worth of tape for $20 and the batteries last for 40 minutes. So I can keep going and eventually they start to forget about the technology.

Sometimes you just have to roll until what you get is right. Generally, people are a little camera-shy so you have to keep going until they get used to you. And I make mistakes in my shots. I try out things and if they don't work, then I throw them away. I don't worry about it too much. I know that I'm the one who's going to be looking at the material, so I don't have to be concerned about some editor cackling over my shooting. I give myself a lot of freedom while I'm shooting, but when I go into editing I have to change into another person and be quite ruthless with the footage. With *Sandspit,* I shot 20 hours and I knew that I would cut that down to one half-hour in the end.

editing and sound

The clips I used in *Sandspit* were chosen for different reasons: because they had strong characters or good mood or because they flowed from one part of the country to the next. More than anything else, I went for soul — something evocative.

After I had made my initial selection of clips I sat down with my composer, Ed Eagan, and we looked at them together. I had a structure based on my shooting and my idea of what that segment should be, and then we shaped the sound to that structure.

I play a lot with repeating images or sounds because often there's something that sticks in my head about a place when I recall it later. For instance, the phrase about Jack London brought up all those associations with *Call of the Wild* and Jack London as an icon of the Yukon and Alaska. For me, it was a key to the feel up there.

As for Tuktoyaktuk, I just loved the sound of that word. I was personal about it. I felt that if it meant something to me, then maybe it meant something to some other part of the audience too. Maybe they had similar backgrounds, had read similar books when they were kids. I was trying to convey some of the essences of what I had experienced. I wanted to capture what was the truth, whether it was the real truth or whether it was my truth. Because it's partly about me and my impressions, as a Canadian, about my country.

Being of my generation, I felt that that I could use the language of music, the styles which Ed and I were into at the time. The tape evolved organically. It wasn't something that could have been storyboarded or scripted in advance. It was something that was shaped as we went along. We work in such an integrated way that the images and music are constructed together; one isn't used to prop up the other.

We did the editing, sound and on-line [final stage in the editing process, in which special effects and dissolves are added in] in two weeks. While Ed was doing sound, I was cutting picture. It was like jamming. His studio was right next door to mine, and we kept walking back and forth to see what the other was doing.

the poetry of images

I guess you could say that I work in a cross-over area and that what I produce is a hybrid between a music video and a documentary. I'm not that interested in conventional documentaries because I'm not particularly drawn to facts. There's something else I'm after — mood, gesture, the unspoken, something intangible or intuitive. Like music, really.

There are problems, though, with the music video because the form has been so bastardized and co-opted — by big business, the record companies, the television networks — that it's been turned into a cliché. It's no longer video music, free and spontaneous expression with a camera to make things sing. It's advertising.

At the same time, what I like about the form is that it allows you to get back into images, it lets pictures and feelings drive one another, rather than having the images be subservient to words or stories.

When sound film came in, I think we lost the poetry of motion that a camera can give you. The early films were so eloquent just by virtue of their pictures. And they were scored too by someone playing along with the images. Maybe it wasn't so precise but it was very evocative.

It's not that I'm railing against content — it's important in its place — but what I like to do is play pictures the way someone would play a musical instrument. That's where I feel that form has potential: to be music itself. Or maybe I can say that I aspire to create poetry with pictures.

—OTTAWA, 1992

students' comments

I found the marriage of visuals and music to be the most interesting aspect of the film.
21-YEAR-OLD VIEWER

This film was totally unlike other documentaries that I have seen. It gave a good feeling of the different cultures in Canada in an absorbing way.
17-YEAR-OLD VIEWER

I loved the way it was filmed. The visual imagery was incredible and just blew me away.
17-YEAR-OLD VIEWER

I liked the way it was filmed, the interesting ideas and seeing things I've never seen before.
18-YEAR-OLD VIEWER

IDEAS *for* DISCUSSION

1

What were your reactions to the video? What sequences, moments, images do you particularly remember? How does this video fit with your notion of what constitutes a documentary? How does it compare with other films you may have seen about Canada?

2

Grierson described documentary as the "creative treatment of actuality". In what ways does Sandspit *fit that definition? Were there particular things that Chris Mullington did that struck you as especially imaginative ways to present material about "real life"?*

ACTIVITIES

1

Re-read what Chris Mullington has to say about how he gets people to speak on camera. Choose a topic you're interested in and then find a person you would like to interview. How will you make the initial contact? Will you have prepared questions? What will they be? Try using an audio recorder or a camcorder or even a pen and notebook. Find out about the possibility of donating your interview to an archive or organization that might be interested in your material.

2

Compare *Sandspit to Dildo* with *Helicopter Canada*, a classic NFB documentary that presents images of the country in a very different way. What effects are achieved by each of these two approaches?

3

Look at *The Spaghetti Story* (in THE POLITICS OF TRUTH, video location 00), which is a parody of a conventional travelogue. How does it differ from *Sandspit* in terms of the presentation of the people, and the audience's awareness of the manipulation achieved by editing? How is voice used in these two productions? Who speaks? Who doesn't?

4

Screen *Our Marilyn* (in WAYS OF STORYTELLING, video location 85), which also manipulates actuality-based images to suggest something of the unspoken, intuitive world that exists below or outside the realm of words.

5

Sandspit is partly Chris Mullington's document of his trip, a moving photo album/memory bank. Produce your own "poetry with pictures". With slides and a taped soundtrack or a camcorder to evoke a mood or capture an emotion, use material from a real-life experience or event as your starting point.

6

Screen a classic silent film (perhaps von Stroheim's *Greed* or some of Chaplin's early productions such as *Gold Rush*). Do you agree with Mullington's comment about the eloquence they achieved by virtue of their pictures alone, or with music but no dialogue?

7

Chris Mullington makes a distinction between his documentary and most music videos, which he characterizes as "advertising". Do you agree with his comments? Screen a music video and compare it with *Sandspit to Dildo*.

FURTHER RESOURCES

For those interested in viewing other films or
videos in which manipulation of the image is an
integral part of the production, see Norman
McLaren's haunting dance film *Pas de deux*
(available from NFB) and David Rimmer's
mesmerizing *Variations on a Cellophane Wrapper.*
Variations is available from Canadian Filmmakers
Distribution Centre, 67A Portland St., Toronto,
Ont., M5V 2M9, tel.: (416) 593-1808 and
Canadian Filmmakers Distribution West, 1131
Howe St., Suite 100, Vancouver, B.C., V6Z 2L7,
tel.: (604) 684-3014.

film and video terms: an introduction

One source of apprehension for teachers preparing to teach media may be the prospect of learning the technical jargon of film and video. What is a "shot"? How many "frames" are there per second? What's the difference between a "dolly shot" and a "zoom"?

We feel that knowing the ins and outs of film jargon is much less important to teaching media than one might suppose. Just as it is possible to appreciate literature without first developing expertise in the finer points of grammar, so one can talk about the mass media and their impact without memorizing pages of technical terms. We have therefore used as few technical words as possible in discussing the issues raised by the films in this collection.

Nevertheless, some basic film and video terms can be useful in providing a common vocabulary with which to discuss and analyze the media and the processes involved in media construction. A number of terms referred to in this Resource Book are explained below.

mini index

Framing, Camera Angle, Camera Movement

Framing, camera angle, and camera movement are important means by which a filmmaker determines how a scene, event, or character is presented on the screen. How the camera photographs the subject can strongly influence the way we, the audience, relate to the subject on an emotional or psychological level.

FRAME

A single, still image from a film or video.

The illusion of movement in film is created by projecting a series of still pictures, or frames, in rapid succession. If the rate of projection is fast enough, the human eye cannot make out the separateness of each image, and the picture appears to represent smooth continuous motion. You can see a series of frames by looking at a strip of 16mm film. A single frame of video can be frozen with the "pause" button on a VCR.

The edges of the frame form the boundary between what the camera sees and records, and what it doesn't see and record. People and objects within the picture are said to be "ON SCREEN" or "IN

FRAME". Objects that are not in the picture are said to be "OFF SCREEN" or "OUT OF FRAME". Characters can move in or out of frame, depending on the action within the scene.

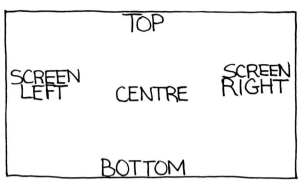

Basic SCREEN geography: *Left* and *right* are determined from the point of view of the audience facing the screen.

FOREGROUND and BACKGROUND: Character "A" is in the foreground. Character "B" is in the background.

A series of FRAMES: The illusion of motion in film is created by projecting a series of still pictures in rapid succession.

FRAMES PER SECOND

The speed at which a camera or projection device runs.

Today most film is shot and projected at the rate of 24 frames per second, i.e., one second of action is broken down into 24 separate photographic images. Video images are recorded and run at 30 frames per second.

ASPECT RATIO

The ratio of the width to the height of the film or television image.

The original standard aspect ratio (still used by television) is 1.33:1. Present-day widescreen movie ratios vary. In North America 1.85:1 is most common (see *Flamenco at 5:15*, THE POETRY OF MOTION, video location 56). Panavision and Cinemascope processes give an even wider image.

CAMERA ANGLE

The position or vantage point — e.g., HIGH ANGLE, LOW ANGLE — from which the camera frames the subject.

HIGH ANGLE SHOT

A shot in which the camera looks down upon the subject from a higher vantage point.

LOW ANGLE SHOT

A shot in which the camera looks up at the subject from a lower vantage point.

CLOSEUP (CU)

An emphasis shot in which an important detail, object or facial expression fills the entire screen.

EXTREME CLOSEUP (ECU)

An exaggerated CLOSEUP in which a small detail, such as an eye or mouth, fills the entire screen.

MEDIUM SHOT (MS)

A medium-close shot, in which the subject's head, shoulders, and chest are normally included in the frame.

LONG SHOT (LS)

A wide shot or a scene, which relates the subject to the background or setting.

EXTREME LONG SHOT (ELS)

A very wide shot - often a panoramic view of an exterior location photographed from a considerable distance.

ESTABLISHING SHOT (ES)

Generally a LONG SHOT or EXTREME LONG SHOT used to show the setting in which a scene is about to take place.

POINT OF VIEW SHOT (POV)

A subjective shot that shows the scene from the point of view of a particular character. A POV is almost always preceded by a shot of a character "looking." The POV then shows what that character is "looking at."

AERIAL SHOT

A shot taken from a crane, plane or helicopter. Not necessarily a moving shot.

STATIC SHOT

Any shot in which the camera remains stationary, regardless of whether there is action or movement within the frame.

PAN

Short for "panoramic" shot. A horizontal movement in which the camera is turned from left to right or right to left to follow a moving subject or to give a sweeping view across a scene.

TILT

The vertical equivalent of a pan, in which the camera is tilted up or down.

The expressions PAN UP or PAN DOWN are also used.

TRACKING or DOLLY SHOT

A shot in which the camera, mounted on a wheeled platform or DOLLY, is moved along tracks on the floor or ground.

Used to create smooth, steady movements.

TRAVELLING SHOT

A shot taken from a moving vehicle.

HAND-HELD SHOT

A shot in which the camera is held by the cameraperson rather than mounted on a tripod.

CRANE SHOT

A shot in which the camera is mounted on a crane — often computer-controlled — which allows the camera to move in any direction.

ZOOM

Often confused with a tracking shot, a ZOOM shot creates the illusion of moving towards or away from a subject simply by changing the focal length of the lens. A ZOOM IN magnifies objects to make them appear to move closer; a ZOOM OUT widens the angle of view, making objects appear to move farther away.

Editing and Structure

EDITING is the process by which film or video footage is selected or rejected for inclusion in the final film or program. It is also the process by which meaning is created through the ordering and juxtaposition of sounds and images. Editing determines the final length of a film or program, its pacing, its emphasis, and its overall structure.

SHOT

A segment of footage without internal cuts or edits. Varying in length from one frame (a fraction of a second) to several minutes, a shot is the basic unit of film and video editing.

SEQUENCE

One or more SHOTS edited together to form a larger grammatical unit within a film.

A sequence can represent the equivalent of a scene in a play or novel, i.e., depict actions or events that take place in the same setting or time period. It can also be a grouping of shots whose relationship is didactic or thematic in nature. See MONTAGE, below.

CUT

The point at which two different SHOTS have been joined or edited together.

TAKE

A version of a SHOT, unedited, as it was originally recorded by the camera.

OUT-TAKES

Footage or SHOTS not used in the finished film or program.

CUTAWAY

A usually brief SHOT, inserted into a scene to show action happening elsewhere.

Cutaways are commonly used to disguise an edit made in a longer TAKE: for example, an edit in an interview can be hidden by a cutaway of the interviewer listening.

REACTION SHOT

A SHOT that cuts away from a scene in order to show a character's reaction to it (see CUTAWAY).

CROSS-CUTTING

Intermingling SHOTS of different events, used to suggest parallel action or to create suspense.

MONTAGE

A sequence of SHOTS cut together, often in a stylized way, to suggest a theme or idea rather than a continuous event.

CONTINUITY

The appearance created through editing of a seamless, uninterrupted flow of events within a scene.

In fact, the scene may have been shot as a series of separate SHOTS recorded from different camera positions at different times.

JUMP CUT

An edit that disrupts the continuity of a SHOT or scene.

A jump cut occurs when one or more frames of picture are removed from the middle of a shot, creating an unexpected discontinuity or "jump" in the image.

RUSHES (or DAILIES)

Film that is processed as soon as possible after shooting so that it can be viewed by the director and crew, preferably before the next day of shooting begins.

Once SYNCHRONIZED SOUND is added, the rushes become the raw material from which the film will be edited.

ROUGH CUT

The first assembly of a film or program, in which selected SHOTS are edited together in the order called for by the script or by the director.

Finer details of timing and editing are created at a later stage called the FINE CUT. (See below.)

FINE CUT

The final edited version of the film, in which all picture elements have been fine-tuned.

Sound elements (music, effects) will be conformed to the fine cut during the SOUND EDITING phase. (See section on sound, below.)

Transitions and Special Effects

In addition to cuts, filmmakers may use a variety of visual transitions and effects to punctuate and enliven their program. In film these effects involve special optical processes. In video they are created electronically.

FADE IN

Beginning a SHOT by fading up from black screen to full brightness; used to denote the start of a new scene or sequence.

FADE OUT

Ending a shot by fading out from full brightness to black screen; used to denote the end of a scene or SEQUENCE.

DISSOLVE

A scene transition in which a FADE OUT of one shot is superimposed upon the FADE IN of another. The two images appear to "dissolve" or blend together.

WIPE

A transition between SHOTS in which one image appears to push the other off the screen, in any one of dozens of patterns.

FREEZE FRAME

An effect in which a single FRAME of picture is held on the screen for an indefinite period of time.

SLOW MOTION

Action which appears to happen at slower than normal speed.

In film this is achieved by shooting a scene at greater than 24 frames per second, so that when the film is projected at normal speed the subject appears to be slowed down.

FAST MOTION or ACCELERATED MOTION

The opposite of SLOW MOTION: the subject is filmed at fewer than 24 frames per second so that normal projection causes it to be speeded up.

SPLIT SCREEN

An effect in which two or more SHOTS occupy different portions of the screen at the same time. (See *Track Stars* in SHAPING REALITY, video location 45.)

OPTICAL PRINTING

A film process, using an OPTICAL PRINTER, in which footage is re-shot frame by frame and manipulated to produce a variety of special effects. These include, among others, FREEZE FRAME, SUPERIMPOSITION, SPLIT SCREEN, and

MULTIPLE EXPOSURE. (See *Our Marilyn* in WAYS OF STORYTELLING, video location 42.)

ANIMATION

The process by which inanimate objects or drawings are made to appear to move on the screen. Techniques include drawing directly on film, photographing drawings or CELLS one at a time, or photographing real objects one frame at a time, and adjusting their positions between frames (PIXILLATION).

Sound

Sound adds the final creative touch to a film or program. Music and sound effects are usually edited to the picture after the FINE CUT of the picture is completed. The selection and placement of these elements can greatly enhance the realism of a film, and its emotional impact on the audience. For an explanation of the process, see "Constructing Sound: How Soundtracks Are Made", pp. 93.

SYNC or ACTUAL SOUND

Sound whose source is an object or person within the picture.

VOICE-OVER (V.O.)

Voices or commentary recorded for use on the film's soundtrack.

NARRATION

Scripted VOICE-OVER commentary, read by a narrator or participant in the film.

SOUND EFFECTS (SFX, FX)

Sound from any source other than voice-over narration, lip-sync dialogue, or music.

SYNCHRONIZATION

The exact matching of sound to the action on the screen: for example, the matching of speech to lip movements.
Sounds and actions that do not match are said to be "out of sync".

MOS

(pronounced "M - O - S")
From a Hollywood slang phrase, "mit out sound," referring to picture footage that has been shot "silent," i.e., without sound to accompany it.

SOUND EDITING

The stage after picture FINE CUTTING in which sound effects and music are added to the program. Sound elements are separated onto different TRACKS in preparation for the SOUND MIX.

SOUND MIX

The event at which separate sound tracks (music, dialogue, FX) are blended or "married" onto one finished soundtrack.

(See SOUND MIXER, below.)

Crew

Unlike dramatic films, which often require the labour of dozens, even hundreds, of people (actors, costume and set designers, lighting, sound and special effects crews, to name but a few), documentaries usually involve relatively small crews. The key people are listed below. For additional information see illustrations, pp. 60 -61.

DIRECTOR

The person responsible for the creative interpretation of the script, story, or issue, and the supervision of its filming and editing.

PRODUCER

The person who plans, coordinates, and supervises the overall production of a film, including personnel and budget.

EXECUTIVE PRODUCER

The person, usually in a film company or television corporation, who has ultimate budget and editorial responsibility for the film, program, or series.*

CINEMATOGRAPHER

The person responsible for photographing the film. In documentaries the cinematographer operates the camera. In dramas, the cinematographer — often called the Director of Photography (D.O.P.) — supervises the composition, camera movement, and lighting while a camera crew executes the shots.

SOUND RECORDIST

The person responsible for recording sound during shooting.

ASSISTANT CAMERAPERSON

The cinematographer's helper in handling camera equipment and lenses, loading film, and related duties.

PRODUCTION MANAGER

The person responsible for the shooting schedule, and for solving problems on location during filming.

GAFFER

The chief electrician responsible for lights. The gaffer supervises the setting up of lights according to the cinematographer's instructions. In documentaries, gaffers are only needed in situations which require extensive lighting. The gaffer's assistant is called the BEST BOY.

PICTURE EDITOR

The person responsible for cutting the picture in the editing room.

SOUND EDITOR

The person who edits the sound elements (dialogue, sound effects, music) onto separate tracks in preparation for the sound mix.

FOLEY ARTIST

A person who creates sound effects with props in a specially equipped studio, by acting out scenes in time to the picture.

(See *Track Stars* in SHAPING REALITY, video location 45.)

SOUND MIXER

The person responsible for the SOUND MIX.

Scriptwriting and Preproduction

The preproduction phase of film and video making comprises everything up until the actual shooting (or "production") begins: research, scripting, budgeting and fundraising, choosing subjects and locations, hiring crews, and planning shooting schedules.

PROPOSAL

For a documentary or factual film, a proposal is a brief statement — from a few sentences to several paragraphs long — describing the idea for the film, including its purpose, "target" audience, concept, and specifications (length, film or video, colour or black-and-white).

TREATMENT

A third-person, present-tense summary — from a few paragraphs to many pages long — of a proposed documentary or dramatic film.

The treatment should give the reader a visual sense of how the film will begin and end, what characters and scenes will be included, and how the story or argument of the film will be structured.

STORYBOARD

A series of sketches with commentary, rather like a cartoon strip, designed to present the film's story line in visual terms.

SCREENPLAY

A dramatic script for a film or television program that includes both dialogue and action descriptions; it may include some general descriptions of camera movements.

SHOOTING SCRIPT

A detailed script for a dramatic film or program in

which the film's action is broken down shot by shot. It serves as a blueprint for production (shooting).

ACCESS

Permission to film a particular person, place, or event.
Gaining access to a subject is crucial in determining whether a documentary film about that subject can be made.

CASTING

The selection of individuals who will appear in the film or program.
In documentary this almost always involves non-actors, who must be capable of articulating the issues or stories the filmmaker wishes to convey to the audience.

Miscellaneous

CINEMA VERITE

A style of documentary filmmaking involving lightweight portable equipment and very small crews (often only camera and sound), in which the filmmakers act as participants in the film's events.
The French filmmaker Jean Rouche was a seminal figure in cinéma vérité. (See THE CANDID EYE, p. 145.)

DIRECT CINEMA

A style of documentary similar to CINEMA VERITE in its use of lightweight portable equipment.
However in DIRECT CINEMA, the filmmakers remain strictly observers of the action. DIRECT CINEMA films are often noted for their avoidance of narration. (See THE CANDID EYE, p. 145.)

DOCUDRAMA

A semi-fictionalized film or program that mixes documentary footage with dramatic scenes or re-enactments.
(See "Docudrama: Fact and Fiction", p. 124.)

Hi8

A small videotape and camera format, sometimes used by TV professionals, which yields better picture quality than regular 8mm home video camcorders.
(See *Sandspit to Dildo*, in THE POETRY OF MOTION, video location 86.)

lists and indexes

list of background articles

list of interviews with filmmakers

index of themes

This index of additional themes suggests some of the multiple linkages between the film and video selections and encourages users to develop their own thematic juxtapositions.

MUSIC

THE BALLAD OF CROWFOOT

BLACK MOTHER, BLACK DAUGHTER

CITY OF GOLD

FLAMENCO AT 5:15

LONELY BOY

MEMORANDUM

OF LIVES UPROOTED

ONE MORE RIVER

OUR MARILYN

RICHARD CARDINAL: CRY FROM A DIARY OF A
    METIS CHILD

SANDSPIT TO DILDO

THE SPAGHETTI STORY

SPEAK WHITE

PEACE/WAR

ANYBODY'S SON WILL DO

CHILDREN OF WAR

DOCUDRAMA: FACT AND FICTION

HAS ANYBODY HERE SEEN CANADA?

MEMORANDUM

OF LIVES UPROOTED

PHOTOGRAPHY/STILLS

THE BALLAD OF CROWFOOT

CITY OF GOLD

SPEAK WHITE

POWER/AUTHORITY

ANYBODY'S SON WILL DO

THE BALLAD OF CROWFOOT

BLACK MOTHER, BLACK DAUGHTER

THE JOURNEY

MEMORANDUM

OF LIVES UPROOTED

ONE MORE RIVER

RICHARD CARDINAL: CRY FROM A DIARY OF A
    METIS CHILD

SPEAK WHITE

PROCESS FILM

ANYBODY'S SON WILL DO

THE EDIT

FLAMENCO AT 5:15

READY WHEN YOU ARE

THE SPAGHETTI STORY

"TECHNO-BABIES": THE MAKING OF A TELEVISION
    DOCUMENTARY

TRACK STARS

PROPAGANDA

ANYBODY'S SON WILL DO

DOCUDRAMA: FACT AND FICTION

THE EDIT

HAS ANYBODY HERE SEEN CANADA?

MEMORANDUM

index of films and topics

acknowledgments

photographs and illustrations

Lois Segal, p. 10

Merrill Fearon, p. 21; p. 49

Star photo by George Bryant, p. 42

Paul Till, p. 45

Tracy Lewis, pp. 60-61

David Adkin, p. 62; p. 79; pp. 83-86; p. 254

Rick McGinnis, p. 70

Paul Caulfield, p. 74; pp. 74-75

All other photos are production shots and video images from National Film Board productions.

articles

Page 127, "Enough with the shakycam in commercials, Howard Green says" by Howard Green. Originally published in the *Globe and Mail,* July 23, 1992. Reprinted by permission.

Page 129, "Valour and horror: not politically correct?" by Pierre Berton. Originally published in the Toronto *Star,* May 30, 1992, in longer form. Reprinted by permission.

Pages 139-140, "Jingoism: Mad Dogs and Englishmen". Originally published in the *Guardian,* 1991; reprinted in the *Globe and Mail.* Reprinted by permission.

Page 184, "A different perspective: Morris Wolfe argues for the voices of change", by Morris Wolfe. Originally published in the *Globe and Mail,* Nov. 12, 1991. Reprinted by permission.

how to obtain NFB films and videos

Quebec   1-800-363-0328
Ontario   1-800-267-7710
Western and Northern Canada   1-800-661-9867

buy your own NFB videos

All recent NFB films are available on video. Department heads and school librarians are encouraged to build up their own video collections. With the NFB's new VHS video prices, this is now possible. As of this book's printing, most videos are priced by length at:

15 min. or less	$21.95
15:01 to 60 min.	$26.95
over 60 min.	$34.95

rent NFB films and videos

You can reserve NFB videos and films by telephone, by mail, by fax or in person at NFB offices within 90 days prior to playdate. Videos are $3.00 per day or per weekend; films $5.00 for 5 days. If you cannot pick up your order at our library, we will mail it to you free of charge. All you pay is the return mailing cost.

If you live at a distance from the NFB library, call us toll free to purchase or rent videos and films:
Atlantic Canada   1-800-561-7104

NFB services are offered in both official languages. The hearing impaired may also contact us directly by dialling these numbers.

Prepay $100 or more and save 25% on rental rates. Valid for a period of 12 months from date of payment.

A special contract is available to public libraries, schools, media and cultural centres who acquire a minimum of 50 videos per year for 3 years. Under this agreement, the price per video is only $21.00.

obtain NFB films and videos from your media centre

Media resource centres often own the NFB films frequently used by teachers. Increasingly, media centres are also buying electronic reproduction rights for specific titles, allowing them to make as many video copies as they wish for use by teachers in their district. Consult your media centre staff for information on those NFB film and video titles they own and those for which they have electronic reproduction rights.

how to obtain NFB multimedia products

The NFB has produced hundreds of slide sets and sound filmstrips (many of which are now available) especially for the classroom. These are distributed, for sale only, by McIntyre Educational Media, 30 Kelfield Street, Rexdale, Ontario, M9W 5A2. Write for an NFB multimedia catalogue or call 1-800-268-1429 (Ontario), 1-800-268-1470 (outside Ontario) or 245-7800 (in Toronto).

For extra copies of this *Constructing Reality Resource Book,* write to:

Education Office,
Marketing, D-5,
National Film Board of Canada,
P.O. Box 6100
Station A,
Montreal, P.Q. H3C 3H5